ALGORITHMIC TRADING

Founded in 1807, John Wiley & Sons is the oldest independent publishing company in the United States. With offices in North America, Europe, Australia, and Asia, Wiley is globally committed to developing and marketing print and electronic products and services for our customers' professional and personal knowledge and understanding.

The Wiley Trading series features books by traders who have survived the market's ever changing temperament and have prospered—some by reinventing systems, others by getting back to basics. Whether a novice trader, professional, or somewhere in-between, these books will provide the advice and strategies needed to prosper today and well into the future.

For a list of available titles, visit our website at www.WileyFinance.com.

ALGORITHMIC TRADING

Winning Strategies and
Their Rationale

Ernest P. Chan

WILEY

Published by John Wiley & Sons, Inc., Hoboken, New Jersey.
Published simultaneously in Canada.

For general information on our other products and services or for technical support, please contact our
Customer Care Department within the United States at (800) 762-2974, outside the United States at
(317) 572-3993 or fax (317) 572-4002.

Wiley publishes in a variety of print and electronic formats and by print-on-demand. Some material
included with standard print versions of this book may not be included in e-books or in print-on-demand.
If this book refers to media such as a CD or DVD that is not included in the version you purchased,
you may download this material at http://booksupport.wiley.com. For more information about Wiley
products, visit www.wiley.com.

Library of Congress Cataloging-in-Publication Data:

Chan, Ernest P., 1966–
   Algorithmic trading : winning strategies and their rationale / Ernest P. Chan.
      pages cm. — (Wiley trading series)
   Includes bibliographical references and index.
   ISBN 978-1-118-46014-6 (cloth)
   1. Investment analysis.   2. Stocks.   3. Exchange traded funds.   4. Algorithms.
   5. Program trading (Securities)   I. Title.
   HG4529.C443   2013
   332.63'2042—dc23

                                                           2013008380

Printed in the United States of America.
V10008484_022619

To my parents, Hung Yip and Ching, and my partner, Ben

CONTENTS

Contents

This book is a practical guide to algorithmic trading strategies that can be readily implemented by both retail and institutional traders. It is not an academic treatise on financial theory. Rather, I hope to make accessible to the reader some of the most useful financial research done in the past few decades, mixing them with insights I gained from actually exploiting some of those theories in live trading.

Because strategies take a central place in this book, we will cover a wide array of them, broadly divided into the mean-reverting and momentum camps, and we will lay out standard techniques for trading each category of strategies, and equally important, the fundamental reasons why a strategy should work. The emphasis throughout is on simple and linear strategies, as an antidote to the overfitting and data-snooping biases that often plague complex strategies.

In the mean-reverting camp, we will discuss the multiple statistical techniques (augmented Dickey-Fuller [ADF] test, Hurst exponent, Variance Ratio test, half-life) for detecting "time series" mean reversion or stationarity, and for detecting cointegration of a portfolio of instruments (cointegrated augmented Dickey Fuller [CADF] test, Johansen test). Beyond the mechanical application of these statistical tests to time series, we strive to convey an intuitive understanding of what they are really testing and the simple mathematical equations behind them.

We will explain the simplest techniques and strategies for trading mean-reverting portfolios (linear, Bollinger band, Kalman filter), and whether using raw prices, log prices, or ratios make the most sense as inputs to these tests and strategies. In particular, we show that the Kalman filter is useful to traders in multiple ways and in multiple strategies. Distinction between time series versus cross-sectional mean reversion will be made. We will debate the pros and cons of "scaling-in" and highlight the danger of data errors in mean-reverting strategies, especially those that deal with spreads.

Examples of mean-reverting strategies will be drawn from interday and intraday stocks models, exchange-traded fund (ETF) pairs and triplets, ETFs versus their component stocks, currency pairs, and futures calendar and intermarket spreads. We will explain what makes trading some of these strategies quite challenging in recent years due to the rise of dark pools and high-frequency trading. We will also illustrate how certain fundamental considerations can explain the temporary unhinging of a hitherto very profitable ETF pair and how the same considerations can lead one to construct an improved version of the strategy. When discussing currency trading, we take care to explain why even the calculation of returns may seem foreign to an equity trader, and where such concepts as rollover interest may sometimes be important. Much emphasis will be devoted to the study of spot returns versus roll returns in futures, and several futures trading strategies can be derived or understood from a simple mathematical model of futures prices. The concepts of backwardation and contango will be illustrated graphically as well as mathematically. The chapter on mean reversion of currencies and futures cumulates in the study of a very special future: the volatility (VX) future, and how it can form the basis of some quite lucrative strategies.

In the momentum camp, we start by explaining a few statistical tests for times series momentum. The main theme, though, is to explore the four main drivers of momentum in stocks and futures and to propose strategies that can extract time series and cross-sectional momentum. Roll returns in futures is one of those drivers, but it turns out that forced asset sales and purchases is the main driver of stock and ETF momentum in many diverse circumstances. Some of the newer momentum strategies based on news events, news sentiment, leveraged ETFs, order flow, and high-frequency trading will be covered. Finally, we will look at the pros and cons of momentum versus mean-reverting strategies and discover their diametrically different risk-return characteristics under different market regimes in recent financial history.

I have always maintained that it is easy to find published, supposedly profitable, strategies in the many books, magazines, or blogs out there, but much harder to see why they may be flawed and perhaps ultimately doomed. So, despite the emphasis on suggesting prototype strategies, we will also discuss many common pitfalls of algorithmic trading strategies, which may be almost as valuable to the reader as the description of the strategies themselves. These pitfalls can cause live trading results to diverge significantly from their backtests. As veterans of algorithmic trading will also agree, the same theoretical strategy can result in spectacular profits and abysmal losses, depending on the details of implementation. Hence, in this book I have lavished attention on the nitty-gritties of backtesting and sometimes live implementation of these strategies, with discussions of concepts such as data-snooping bias, survivorship bias, primary versus consolidated quotes, the venue dependence of currency quotes, the nuances of short-sale constraints, the construction of futures continuous contracts, and the use of futures closing versus settlement prices in backtests. We also highlight some instances of "regime shift" historically when even the most correct backtest will fail to predict the future returns of a strategy.

I have also paid attention to choosing the right software platform for backtesting and automated execution, given that MATLAB©, my favorite language, is no longer the only contender in this department. I will survey the state of the art in technology, for every level of programming skills, and for many different budgets. In particular, we draw attention to the "integrated development environment" for traders, ranging from the industrial-strength platforms such as Deltix to the myriad open-source versions such as TradeLink. As we will explain, the ease of switching from backtesting to live trading mode is the most important virtue of such platforms. The fashionable concept of "complex event processing" will also be introduced in this context.

I covered risk and money management in my previous book, which was built on the Kelly formula—a formula that determines the optimal leverage and capital allocation while balancing returns versus risks. I once again cover risk and money management here, still based on the Kelly formula, but tempered with my practical experience in risk management involving black swans, constant proportion portfolio insurance, and stop losses. (U.S. Supreme Court Justice Robert H. Jackson could have been talking about the application of the Kelly formula when he said we should "*temper* its doctrinaire logic with a little practical wisdom.") We especially focus on finding the optimal leverage in realistic situations when we can no longer assume Gaussian distribution of returns. Also, we consider whether "risk indicators" might be a useful component of a comprehensive risk management scheme.

One general technique that I have overlooked previously is the use of Monte Carlo simulations. Here, we demonstrate using simulated, as opposed to historical, data to test the statistical significance of a backtest as well as to assess the tail risk of a strategy.

This book is meant as a follow-up to my previous book, *Quantitative Trading*. There, I focused on basic techniques for an algorithmic trader, such as how to find ideas for new strategies, how to backtest a strategy, basic considerations in automating your executions, and, finally, risk management via the Kelly formula. Yes, a few useful example strategies were sprinkled throughout, but those were not the emphasis. If you are completely new to trading algorithmically, that is a good book to read. *Algorithmic Trading*, however, is all about strategies.

All of the examples in this book are built around MATLAB codes, and they are all available for download from www.wiley.com/go/algotrading or my website at www.epchan.com/book2. Readers will find the password embedded in the first example. Readers unfamiliar with MATLAB may want to study the tutorial in *Quantitative Trading*, or watch the free webinars on mathworks.com. Furthermore, the MATLAB Statistics Toolbox was occasionally used. (All MATLAB products are available as free trials from MathWorks.)

Software and mathematics are the twin languages of algorithmic trading. Readers will find this book involves somewhat more mathematics than my previous one. This is because of my desire to inject more precision in discussing the concepts involved in financial markets, and also because I believe using simple mathematical models for trading can be more advantageous than using the usual "data-mining" approach. That is to say, instead of throwing as many technical trading indicators or rules at a price series to see which indicator or rule is profitable—a practice that invites data-snooping bias—we try to distill the fundamental property of that price series using a simple mathematical model. We can then exploit that model to our financial benefit. Nevertheless, the level of mathematics needed in the trading of stocks, futures, and currencies is far lower than that needed in derivatives trading, and anyone familiar with freshman calculus, linear algebra, and statistics should be able to follow my discussions without problems. If you find the equations too confusing, you can just go straight to the examples and see their concrete implementations as software codes.

When I wrote my first book, I was an independent trader, though one who had worked in the institutional investment management industry for many years. In the subsequent years, I have started and managed two hedge funds, either with a partner or by myself. I have survived the 2007 summer quant funds meltdown, the 2008 financial crisis, the 2010 flash crash, the

2011 U.S. federal debt downgrade, and the 2011–2012 European debt crisis. Therefore, I am more confident than before that my initial approach to algorithmic trading is sound, though I have certainly learned much more in the interim. For instance, I have found that it is seldom a good idea to manually override a model no matter how treacherous the market is looking; that it is always better to be underleveraged than overleveraged, especially when managing other people's money; that strategy performance often mean-reverts; and that overconfidence in a strategy is the greatest danger to us all. One learns much more from mistakes and near-catastrophes than from successes. I strove to record much of what I have learned in the past four years in this book.

My fund management experience has not changed my focus on the serious retail trader in this book. With sufficient determination, and with some adaptations and refinements, all the strategies here can be implemented by an independent trader, and they do not require a seven-figure brokerage account, nor do they require five-figure technology expenditure. My message to these traders is still the same: An individual with limited resources and computing power can still challenge powerful industry insiders at their own game.

■ The Motive

Books written by traders for other traders need to answer one basic question: Why are they doing it? More specifically, if the strategies described are any good, why would the trader publicize them, which would surely render them less profitable in the future?

To answer the second question first: Many of the strategies I will describe are quite well known to professional traders, so I am hardly throwing away any family jewels. Others have such high capacities that their profitability will not be seriously affected by a few additional traders running them. Yet others have the opposite properties: They are of such low capacity, or have other unappealing limitations that I no longer find them attractive for inclusion in my own fund's portfolio, but they may still be suitable for an individual trader's account. Finally, I will often be depicting strategies that at first sight are very promising, but may contain various pitfalls that I have not fully researched and eliminated. For example, I have not included transaction costs in my example backtest codes, which are crucial for a meaningful backtest. I often use in-sample data to both optimize parameters and measure performance, which would surely inflate results. I am committing all these pitfalls in my examples because the simplified version is more illustrative and readable. These may be called "prototype strategies." They are not meant to be traded "as-is," but they are useful as illustrations of common algorithmic trading techniques, and as inspirations for the reader to further refine and improve them.

What about the basic motive question? It comes down to this: Crowdsourcing knowledge is often more efficient than any other method for gathering information. And so—as with my first book—I welcome your feedback on the strategies discussed in this book.

■ A Note about Sources and Acknowledgments

Naturally, I did not invent most of the materials presented here. Besides the traditional and commonly accessible sources of books, academic journals, magazines, blogs, and online trader forums (such as elitetrader.com and nuclearphynance.com), there are now new online expert networks such as Hightable.com and Quora.com where specific questions can be posted and often answered by true industry experts. I have personally benefited from all these sources and am grateful to the various online experts who have answered my questions with unexpected depth and details.

By virtue of my previous book and my blog (http://epchan.blogspot .com), I am also fortunate to have heard from a great many insightful readers, many of whom have contributed to my knowledge base.

I have also taught regular workshops in London and Singapore on various topics in algorithmic trading that were attended by many institutional analysts and traders. They have contributed valuable insights to me that may not be easily accessible in any public forums. Special workshops held for clients in Canada, China, Hong Kong, India, South Africa, and the United States have also exposed me to broad international perspectives and concerns.

I am also privileged to have collaborated with many knowledgeable finance professionals even as an independent trader and fund manager. Some of these collaborations are short-term and informal, while others lead to the formal formation of fund management companies. In particular, I thank Steve Halpern and Roger Hunter for their extensive discussions and countless joint projects and ventures.

I am indebted to Bryan Downing for introducing me to some of the trading technologies mentioned in Chapter 1, and to Rosario Ingargiola for showcasing his FXOne platform to me.

Finally, many thanks to my editor Bill Falloon at John Wiley & Sons for being always enthusiastic and supportive of my book ideas, to development editor Meg Freeborn for her unfailingly valuable suggestions, and to production editor Steven Kyritz for shepherding this book to its final form.

Backtesting and Automated Execution

While the focus of this book is on specific categories of strategies and not on general techniques of backtesting, there are a number of important considerations and common pitfalls to all strategies that need to be addressed first. If one blithely goes ahead and backtests a strategy without taking care to avoid these pitfalls, the backtesting will be useless. Or worse—it will be misleading and may cause significant financial losses.

Since backtesting typically involves the computation of an expected return and other statistical measures of the performance of a strategy, it is reasonable to question the statistical significance of these numbers. We will discuss various ways of estimating statistical significance using the methodologies of hypothesis testing and Monte Carlo simulations. In general, the more round trip trades there are in the backtest, the higher will be the statistical significance. But even if a backtest is done correctly without pitfalls and with high statistical significance, it doesn't necessarily mean that it is predictive of future returns. Regime shifts can spoil everything, and a few important historical examples will be highlighted.

The choice of a software platform for backtesting is also an important consideration and needs to be tackled early on. A good choice not only will vastly increase your productivity, it will also allow you to backtest the broadest possible spectrum of strategies in the broadest variety of asset classes.

And it will reduce or eliminate the chances of committing the aforementioned pitfalls. We will also explain why the choice of a good backtesting platform is often tied to the choice of a good automated execution platform: often, the best platform combines both functions.

■ The Importance of Backtesting

Backtesting is the process of feeding historical data to your trading strategy to see how it would have performed. The hope is that its historical performance tells us what to expect for its future performance. The importance of this process is obvious if you have developed a strategy from scratch, since you would certainly want to know how it has performed. But even if you read about a strategy from a publication, and you trust that the author did not lie about its stated performance, it is still imperative that you independently backtest the strategy. There are several reasons for this.

Often, the profitability of a strategy depends sensitively on the details of implementation. For example, are the stock orders supposed to be sent as market-on-open orders or as market orders just after the open? Are we supposed to send in an order for the E-mini Standard & Poor's (S&P) 500 future just before the 4:00 P.M. stock market closing time, or just before the 4:15 P.M. futures market closing time? Are we supposed to use the bid or ask price to trigger a trade, or are we supposed to use the last price? All these details tend to be glossed over in a published article, often justifiably so lest they distract from the main idea, but they can affect the profitability of a live-traded strategy significantly. The only way to pin down these details exactly, so as to implement them in our own automated execution system, is to backtest the strategy ourselves. In fact, ideally, our backtesting program can be transformed into an automated execution program by the push of a button to ensure the exact implementation of details.

Once we have implemented every detail of a strategy as a backtest program, we can then put them under the microscope and look for pitfalls in the backtesting process or in the strategy itself. For example, in backtesting a stock portfolio strategy with both long and short positions, have we taken into account the fact that some stocks were hard to borrow and cannot easily be shorted at any reasonable size? In backtesting an intermarket pair-trading strategy in futures, have we made sure that the closing prices of the two markets occur at the same time? The full list of pitfalls is long and tedious, but I will highlight a few common ones in the section "Common Pitfalls of

Backtesting." Often, each market and each strategy presents its own very specific set of pitfalls. Usually, a pitfall tends to inflate the backtest performance of a strategy relative to its actual performance in the past, which is particularly dangerous.

Even if we have satisfied ourselves that we have understood and implemented every detail of a strategy in a backtesting program, and that there is no pitfall that we can discover, backtesting a published strategy can still yield important benefits.

Backtesting a published strategy allows you to conduct true out-of-sample testing in the period following publication. If that out-of-sample performance proves poor, then one has to be concerned that the strategy may have worked only on a limited data set. This is actually a more important point than people realize. Many authors will claim in their articles that the backtest results were "verified with out-of-sample data." But, actually, if the out-of-sample testing results were poor, the authors could have just changed some parameters, or they could have tweaked the model substantially so that the results look good with the "out-of-sample" data. Hence, true out-of-sample testing cannot really begin until a strategy is published and cast in stone.

Finally, by backtesting a strategy ourselves, we often can find ways to refine and improve the strategy to make it more profitable or less risky. The backtesting process in trading should follow the "scientific method." We should start with a hypothesis about an arbitrage opportunity, maybe based on our own intuition about the market or from some published research. We then confirm or refute this hypothesis by a backtest. If the results of the backtest aren't good enough, we can modify our hypothesis and repeat the process.

As I emphasized earlier, performance of a strategy is often very sensitive to details, and small changes in these details can bring about substantial improvements. These changes can be as simple as changing the look-back time period for determining the moving average, or entering orders at the open rather than at the close. Backtesting a strategy allows us to experiment with every detail.

■ Common Pitfalls of Backtesting

Although almost every strategy allows for unique opportunities in committing errors in backtesting, there are a number of common themes, some generally applicable to all markets, others pertain to specific ones.

Look-ahead Bias

As its name implies, look-ahead bias means that your backtest program is using tomorrow's prices to determine today's trading signals. Or, more generally, it is using future information to make a "prediction" at the current time. A common example of look-ahead bias is to use a day's high or low price to determine the entry signal during the same day during backtesting. (Before the close of a trading day, we can't know what the high and low price of the day are.) Look-ahead bias is essentially a programming error and can infect only a backtest program but not a live trading program because there is no way a live trading program can obtain future information. This difference between backtesting and a live trading program also points to an obvious way to avoid look-ahead bias. If your backtesting and live trading programs are one and the same, and the only difference between backtesting versus live trading is what kind of data you are feeding into the program (historical data in the former, and live market data in the latter), then there can be no look-ahead bias in the program. Later on in this chapter, we will see which platforms allow the same source code to be used for both backtest and live execution.

Data-Snooping Bias and the Beauty of Linearity

Data-snooping bias is caused by having too many free parameters that are fitted to random ethereal market patterns in the past to make historical performance look good. These random market patterns are unlikely to recur in the future, so a model fitted to these patterns is unlikely to have much predictive power.

The way to detect data-snooping bias is well known: We should test the model on out-of-sample data and reject a model that doesn't pass the out-of-sample test. But this is easier said than done. Are we really willing to give up on possibly weeks of work and toss out the model completely? Few of us are blessed with such decisiveness. Many of us will instead tweak the model this way or that so that it finally performs reasonably well on both the in-sample and the out-of-sample result. But voilà! By doing this we have just turned the out-of-sample data into in-sample data.

If you are unwilling to toss out a model because of its performance on a fixed out-of-sample data set (after all, poor performance on this out-of-sample data may just be due to bad luck), or if you have a small data set to start with and really need to tweak the model using most of this data, you should consider the idea of cross-validation. That is, you should select a number of different subsets of the data for training and tweaking your model and, more important, making sure that the model performs well on these different subsets. One reason why we prefer models with a high Sharpe ratio and short maximum drawdown duration is that this almost automatically ensures that the model will pass the cross-validation test: the only subsets where the model will fail the test are those rare drawdown periods.

There is a general approach to trading strategy construction that can minimize data-snooping bias: make the model as simple as possible, with as few parameters as possible. Many traders appreciate the second edict, but fail to realize that a model with few parameters but lots of complicated trading rules are just as susceptible to data-snooping bias. Both edicts lead to the conclusion that nonlinear models are more susceptible to data-snooping bias than linear models because nonlinear models not only are more complicated but they usually have more free parameters than linear models.

Suppose we attempt to predict price by simple extrapolation of the historical price series. A nonlinear model would certainly fit the historical data better, but that's no guarantee that it can predict a future value better. But even if we fix the number of parameters to be the same for a nonlinear model versus its linear contender, one has to remember that we can usually approximate a nonlinear model by Taylor-series expansion familiar from calculus. That means that there is usually a simpler, linear approximation corresponding to every nonlinear model, and a good reason has to be given why this linear model cannot be used. (The exceptions are those singular cases where the lower-order terms vanish. But such cases seldom describe realistic financial time series.)

An equivalent reasoning can be made in the context of what probability distributions we should assume for returns. We have heard often that the Gaussian distribution fails to capture extreme events in the financial market. But the problem with going beyond the Gaussian distribution is that we will be confronted with many choices of alternative distributions. Should it be a Student's t-distribution that allows us to capture the skew and kurtosis of the returns, or should it be a Pareto distribution that dispenses with a finite second moment completely? Any choice will have some element of arbitrariness, and the decision will be based on a finite number of observations. Hence, Occam's razor dictates that unless there are strong theoretical and empirical reasons to support a non-Gaussian distribution, a Gaussian form should be assumed.

Linear models imply not only a linear price prediction formula, but also a linear capital allocation formula. Let's say we are considering a mean-reverting model for a price series such that the change in the price dy in the next time period dt is proportional to the difference between the mean price and the current price: $dy(t) = (\lambda y(t-1) + \mu)dt + d\varepsilon$, the so-called "Ornstein-Uhlenbeck" formula, which is explained and examined in greater detail in Chapter 2. Often, a trader will use a Bollinger band model to capture profits from this mean-reverting price series, so that we sell (or buy) whenever the price exceeds (or falls below) a certain threshold. However, if we are forced to stick to linear models, we would be forced to sell (or buy) at every price increment, so that the total market value is approximately proportional to the negative deviation from the mean. In common traders' parlance, this may be called "averaging-in," or "scaling-in," a technique that is discussed in Chapter 3.

You will find several examples of linear trading models in this book because the simplicity of this technique lets us illustrate the point that profits are not derived from some subtle, complicated cleverness of the strategy but from an intrinsic inefficiency in the market that is hidden in plain sight. The impatient reader can look ahead to Example 4.2, which shows a linear mean-reverting strategy between an exchange-traded fund (ETF) and its component stocks, or Examples 4.3 and 4.4, showing two linear long-short statistical arbitrage strategies on stocks.

The most extreme form of linear predictive models is one in which all the coefficients are equal in magnitude (but not necessarily in sign). For example, suppose you have identified a number of factors (f's) that are useful in predicting whether tomorrow's return of a stock index is positive. One factor may be today's return, with a positive today's return predicting a positive future return. Another factor may be today's change in the volatility index (VIX), with a negative change predicting positive future return. You may have several such factors. If you normalize these factors by turning them first into Z-scores (using in-sample data!):

$$z(i) = (f(i) - mean(f))/std(f), \tag{1.1}$$

where $f(i)$ is the ith factor, you can then predict tomorrow's return R by

$$R = mean(R) + std(R)\sum_{i}^{n} sign(i)z(i)/n. \tag{1.2}$$

The quantities $mean(f)$ and $std(f)$ are the historical average and standard deviation of the various $f(i)$, $sign(i)$ is the sign of the historical correlation between $f(i)$ and R, and $mean(R)$ and $std(R)$ are the historical average and standard deviation of one-day returns, respectively. Daniel Kahneman, the Nobel Prize-winning economist, wrote in his bestseller *Thinking, Fast and Slow* that "formulas that assign equal weights to all the predictors are often superior, because they are not affected by accidents of sampling" (Kahneman, 2011). Equation 1.2 is a simplified version of the usual factor model used in stock return prediction. While its prediction of the *absolute* returns may or may not be very accurate, its prediction of *relative* returns between stocks is often good enough. This means that if we use it to rank stocks, and then form a long-short portfolio by buying the stocks in the top decile and shorting those in the bottom decile, the average return of the portfolio is often positive.

Actually, if your goal is just to rank stocks instead of coming up with an expected return, there is an even simpler way to combine the factors f's without using Equations 1.1 and 1.2. We can first compute the $rank_s(i)$ of a stock s based on a factor $f(i)$. Then we multiply these ranks by the sign of the correlation between $f(i)$ and the expected return of the stock. Finally, we sum all these signed ranks to form the rank of a stock:

$$rank_s = \sum_i^n sign(i)\, rank_s(i). \qquad (1.3)$$

As an example, Joel Greenblatt has famously used a two-factor model as a "magic formula" to rank stocks: $f(1) = $ return on capital and $f(2) = $ earnings yield (Greenblatt, 2006). We are supposed to buy the top 30 ranked stocks and hold them for a year. The annual percentage rate (APR) for this strategy was 30.8 percent from 1988 to 2004, compared with 12.4 percent for the S&P 500. Quite a triumph of linearity!

In the end, though, no matter how carefully you have tried to prevent data-snooping bias in your testing process, it will somehow creep into your model. So we must perform a walk-forward test as a final, true out-of-sample test. This walk-forward test can be conducted in the form of paper trading, but, even better, the model should be traded with real money (albeit with minimal leverage) so as to test those aspects of the strategy that eluded even paper trading. Most traders would be happy to find that live trading generates a Sharpe ratio better than half of its backtest value.

Stock Splits and Dividend Adjustments

Whenever a company's stock has an N-to-1 split, the stock price will be divided by N times. However, if you own a number of shares of that company's stock before the split, you will own N times as many shares after the split, so there is in fact no change in the total market value. But in a backtest, we typically are looking at just the price series to determine our trading signals, not the market-value series of some hypothetical account. So unless we back-adjust the prices before the ex-date of the split by dividing them by N, we will see a sudden drop in price on the ex-date, and that might trigger some erroneous trading signals. This is as true in live trading as in backtesting, so you would have to divide the historical prices by N just before the market opens on the ex-date during live trading, too. (If it is a reverse 1-to-N split, we would have to multiply the historical prices before the ex-date by N.)

Similarly, when a company pays a cash (or stock) dividend of $\$d$ per share, the stock price will also go down by $\$d$ (absent other market movements). That is because if you own that stock before the dividend ex-date, you will get cash (or stock) distributions in your brokerage account, so again there should be no change in the total market value. If you do not back-adjust the historical price series prior to the ex-date, the sudden drop in price may also trigger an erroneous trading signal. This adjustment, too, should be applied to any historical data used in the live trading model just before the market opens on an ex-date. (This discussion applies to ETFs as well. A slightly more complicated treatment needs to be applied to options prices.)

You can find historical split and dividend information on many websites, but I find that earnings.com is an excellent free resource. It not only records such historical numbers, but it shows the announced split and dividend amounts and ex-dates in the future as well, so we can anticipate such events in our automated trading software. If you are interested in historical stock data that are already adjusted for stock splits and dividends, and are easy to download, try csidata.com.

Survivorship Bias in Stock Database

If you are backtesting a stock-trading model, you will suffer from survivorship bias if your historical data do not include delisted stocks. Imagine an extreme case: suppose your model asks you to just buy the one stock that dropped the most in the previous day and hold it forever. In actuality, this strategy will most certainly perform poorly because in many cases the company whose stock dropped the most in the previous day will go on to bankruptcy, resulting in 100 percent loss of the stock position. But if your historical data do not include delisted stocks—that is, they contain only stocks that survive until today—then the backtest result may look excellent. This is because you would have bought a stock when it was beaten down badly but subsequently survived, though you could not have predicted its eventual survival if you were live-trading the strategy.

Survivorship bias is more dangerous to mean-reverting long-only stock strategies than to mean-reverting long-short or short-only strategies. This is because, as we saw earlier, this bias tends to inflate the backtest performance of a long-only strategy that first buys low and then sells high, whereas it will deflate the backtest performance of a short-only strategy that first sells high and then buys low. Those stocks that went to zero would have done very well with a short-only strategy, but they would not be present in backtest data with survivorship bias. For mean-reverting long-short strategies, the two effects are of opposite signs, but inflation of the long strategy return tends to outweigh the deflation of the short portfolio return, so the danger is reduced but not eliminated. Survivorship bias is less dangerous to momentum models. The profitable short momentum trade will tend to be omitted in data with survivorship bias, and thus the backtest return will be deflated.

You can buy reasonably priced historical data that are free of survivorship bias from csidata.com (which provides a list of delisted stocks). Other vendors include kibot.com, tickdata.com, and crsp.com. Or you can in fact collect your own survivorship bias–free data by saving the historical prices of all the stocks in an index every day. Finally, in the absence of such survivorship bias–free data, you can limit yourself to backtesting only the most recent, say, three years of historical data to reduce the damage.

Primary versus Consolidated Stock Prices

Many U.S. stocks are traded on multiple exchanges, electronic communication networks (ECNs), and dark pools: The New York Stock Exchange (NYSE), NYSE Arca, Nasdaq, Island, BATS, Instinet, Liquidnet, Bloomberg Tradebook, Goldman Sachs' Sigma X, and Credit Suisse's CrossFinder are just some of the example markets. When you look up the historical daily closing price of a stock, it reflects the last execution price on any one of these venues during regular trading hours. Similarly, a historical daily opening price reflects the first execution price on any one of these venues. But when you submit a market-on-close (MOC) or market-on-open (MOO) order, it will always be routed to the primary exchange only. For example, an MOC order on IBM will be routed to NYSE, an MOC order on SPY will be routed to NYSE Arca, and an MOC order on Microsoft (MSFT) will be routed to Nasdaq. Hence, if you have a strategy that relies on market-on-open or market-on-close orders, you need the historical prices from the primary exchange to accurately backtest your model. If you use the usual consolidated historical prices for backtesting, the results can be quite unrealistic. In particular, if you use consolidated historical prices to back-test a mean-reverting model, you are likely to generate inflated backtest performance because a small number of shares can be executed away from the primary exchange at a price quite different from the auction price on the primary exchange. The transaction prices on the next trading day will usually mean-revert from this hard-to-achieve outlier price. (The close and open prices on the U.S. primary exchanges are always determined by an auction, while a transaction at the close on a secondary exchange is not the result of an auction.)

A similar consideration applies to using high or low prices for your strategy. What were recorded in the historical data are usually the consolidated highs or lows, not that of the primary exchange. They are often unrepresentative, exaggerated numbers resulting from trades of small sizes on secondary exchanges. Backtest performance will also be inflated if these historical prices are used.

Where can we find historical prices from the primary exchanges? Bloomberg users have access to that as part of their subscription. Of course, just as in the case of storing and using survivorship bias–free data discussed earlier, we can also subscribe to direct live feeds from the (primary) exchanges and store those prices into our own databases in real time. We can then use these databases in the future as our source of primary exchange data. Subscribing to such feeds independently can be an expensive proposition, but if your broker has such subscriptions and it redistributes such data to its clients that colocate within its data center, the cost can be much lower. Unfortunately, most retail brokers do not redistribute direct feeds from the exchanges, but institutional brokers such as Lime Brokerage often do.

If we don't have access to such data, all we can do is to entertain a healthy skepticism of our backtest results.

Venue Dependence of Currency Quotes

Compared to the stock market, the currency markets are even more fragmented and there is no rule that says a trade executed at one venue has to be at the best bid or ask across all the different venues. Hence, a backtest will be realistic only if we use historical data extracted from the same venue(s) as the one(s) we expect to trade on.

There are quotes aggregators such as Streambase that consolidate data feeds from different venues into one order book. In this case, you may use the consolidated historical data for backtesting, as long as you can execute on the venue that formed part of the consolidated order book.

Another feature of currency live quotes and historical data is that trade prices and sizes, as opposed to bid and ask quotes, are not generally available, at least not without a small delay. This is because there is no regulation that says the dealer or ECN must report the trade price to all market participants. Indeed, many dealers view transaction information as proprietary and valuable information. (They might be smart to do that because there are high-frequency strategies that depend on order flow information and that require trade prices, as mentioned in Chapter 7. The banks' forex proprietary trading desks no doubt prefer to keep this information to themselves.) But using bid-ask quotes for backtesting forex strategies is recommended anyway, since the bid-ask spreads for the same currency pair can vary significantly between venues. As a result, the transaction costs are also highly venue dependent and need to be taken into account in a backtest.

Short-Sale Constraints

A stock-trading model that involves shorting stocks assumes that those stocks can be shorted, but often there are difficulties in shorting some stocks. To short a stock, your broker has to be able to "locate" a quantity of these stocks from other customers or other institutions (typically mutual funds or other asset managers that have large long positions in many stocks) and arrange a stock loan to you. If there is already a large short interest out there so that a lot of the shares of a company have already been borrowed, or if the float of the stock is limited, then your stock can be "hard to borrow." Hard to borrow may mean that you, as the short seller, will have to pay interest to the stock lender, instead of the other way around in a normal situation. In more extreme cases, hard to borrow may mean that you cannot borrow the stock in the quantity you desire or at all. After Lehman Brothers collapsed during the financial crisis of 2008–2009, the U.S. Securities and Exchange Commission (SEC) banned short sales in all the financial industry stocks for several months. So if your backtesting model shorts stocks that were hard or impossible to borrow, it may show a wonderful return because no one else was able to short the stock and depress its price when your model shorted it. But this return is completely unrealistic. This renders short-sale constraints dangerous to backtesting. It is not easy, though, to find a historically accurate list of hard-to-borrow stocks for your backtest, as this list depends on which broker you use. As a general rule, small-cap stocks are affected much more by short-sale constraint than are large-cap stocks, and so the returns of their short positions are much more suspect. Bear in mind also that sometimes ETFs are as hard to borrow as stocks. I have found, for example, that I could not even borrow SPY to short in the months after the Lehman Brothers' collapse!

An additional short-sale constraint is the so-called "uptick rule" imposed by the SEC. The original uptick rule was in effect from 1938 to 2007, where the short sale had to be executed at a price higher than the last traded price, or at the last traded price if that price was higher than the price of the trade prior to the last. (For Nasdaq stocks, the short sale price must be higher than the last bid rather than the last trade.) The Alternative Uptick Rule that took effect in 2010 also requires a short sale to have a trade price higher than the national best bid, but only when a circuit breaker has been triggered. A circuit breaker for a stock is triggered when that stock traded at 10 percent lower than its previous close. The circuit breaker is in effect for the following day after the initial trigger as well. This effectively prevents any short market orders from being filled. So, again, a really accurate backtest that involves short sales must take into account whether these constraints were in effect when the historical trade was supposed to occur. Otherwise, the backtest performance will be inflated.

Futures Continuous Contracts

Futures contracts have expiry dates, so a trading strategy on, say, crude oil futures, is really a trading strategy on many different contracts. Usually, the strategy applies to front-month contracts. Which contract is the "front month" depends on exactly when you plan to "roll over" to the next month; that is, when you plan to sell the current front contract and buy the contract with the next nearest expiration date (assuming you are long a contract to begin with). Some people may decide to roll over 10 days before the current front contract expires; others may decide to roll over when there is an "open interest crossover"; that is, when the open interest of the next contract exceeds that of the current front contract. No matter how you decide your rollover date, it is quite an extra bother to have to incorporate that in your trading strategy, as this buying and selling is independent of the strategy and should result in minimal additional return or profit and loss (P&L). (P&L, or return, is certainly affected by the so-called "roll return," but as we discuss extensively in Chapter 5, roll return is in effect every day on every contract and is not a consequence of rolling over.) Fortunately, most futures historical data vendors also recognize this, and they usually make available what is known as "continuous contract" data.

We won't discuss here how you can go about creating a continuous contract yourself because you can read about that on many futures historical data vendors' websites. But there is a nuance to this process that you need to be aware of. The first step in creating a continuous contract is to concatenate the prices of the front-month contract together, given a certain set of rollover dates. But this results in a price series that may have significant price gaps going from the last date before rollover to the rollover date, and it will create a false return or P&L on the rollover date in your backtest.

To see this, let's say the closing price of the front contract on date T is $p(T)$, and the closing price of this same contract on date $T + 1$ is $p(T + 1)$. Also, let's say the closing price of the next nearby contract (also called the "back" contract) on date $T + 1$ is $q(T + 1)$. Suppose $T + 1$ is the rollover date, so if we are long the front contract, we should sell this contract at the close at $p(T + 1)$, and then buy the next contract at $q(T + 1)$. What's the P&L (in points, not dollars) and return of this strategy on $T + 1$? The P&L is just $p(T + 1) - p(T)$, and the return is $(p(T + 1) - p(T))/p(T)$. But the unadjusted continuous price series will show a price of $p(T)$ at T, and $q(T + 1)$ at $T + 1$. If you calculate P&L and return the usual way, you would have calculated the erroneous values of $q(T + 1) - p(T)$ and $(q(T + 1) - p(T))/p(T)$, respectively. To prevent this error, the data vendor can typically back-adjust the data series to eliminate the price gap, so that the P&L on $T + 1$ is $p(T + 1) - p(T)$. This can be done by adding the number $(q(T + 1) - p(T + 1))$ to every price $p(t)$ on every date t on or before T, so that the price change and P&L from T to $T + 1$ is correctly calculated as $q(T + 1) - (p(T) + q(T + 1) - p(T + 1)) = p(T + 1) - p(T)$. (Of course, to take care of every rollover, you would have to apply this back adjustment multiple times, as you go back further in the data series.)

Is our problem solved? Not quite. Check out what the return is at $T + 1$ given this adjusted price series: $(p(T + 1) - p(T))/(p(T) + q(T + 1) - p(T + 1))$, not $(p(T + 1) - p(T))/p(T)$. If you back-adjust to make the P&L calculation correct, you will leave the return calculation incorrect. Conversely, you can back-adjust the price series to make the return calculation correct (by multiplying every price $p(t)$ on every date t on or before T by the number $q(T+1)/p(T+1)$), but then the P&L calculation will be incorrect. You really can't have both. As long as you want the convenience of using a continuous contract series, you have to choose one performance measurement only, P&L or return. (If you bother to backtest your strategy on the various individual contracts, taking care of the rollover buying and selling yourself, then both P&L and return can be correctly calculated simultaneously.)

An additional difficulty occurs when we choose the price back-adjustment instead of the return back-adjustment method: the prices may turn negative in the distant past. This may create problems for your trading strategy, and it will certainly create problems in calculating returns. A common method to deal with this is to add a constant to all the prices so that none will be negative.

This subtlety in picking the right back-adjustment method is more important when we have a strategy that involves trading spreads between different contracts. If your strategy generates trading signals based on the price difference between two contracts, then you must choose the price back-adjustment method; otherwise, the price difference may be wrong and generate a wrong trading signal. When a strategy involves calendar spreads (spreads on contracts with the same underlying but different expiration dates), this back adjustment is even more important. This is because the calendar spread is a small number compared to the price of one leg of the spread, so any error due to rollover will be a significant percentage of the spread and very likely to trigger a wrong signal both in backtest and in live trading. However, if your strategy generates trading signals based on the ratio of prices between two contracts, then you must choose the return back-adjustment method.

As you can see, when choosing a data vendor for historical futures prices, you must understand exactly how they have dealt with the back-adjustment issue, as it certainly impacts your backtest. For example, csidata.com uses only price back adjustment, but with an optional additive constant to prevent prices from going negative, while tickdata.com allows you the option of choosing price versus return back-adjustment, but there is no option for adding a constant to prevent negative prices.

Futures Close versus Settlement Prices

The daily closing price of a futures contract provided by a data vendor is usually the settlement price, not the last traded price of the contract during that day. Note that a futures contract will have a settlement price each day (determined by the exchange), even if the contract has not traded at all that day. And if the contract has traded, the settlement price is in general different from the last traded price. Most historical data vendors provide the settlement price as the daily closing price. But some, such as vendors that provide tick-by-tick data, may provide actual transaction price only, and therefore the close price will be the last traded price, if there has been a transaction on that day. Which price should we use to backtest our strategies?

In most cases, we should use the settlement price, because if you had traded live near the close, that would have been closest to the price of your transaction. The last recorded trade price might have occurred several hours earlier and bear little relation to your transaction price near the close. This is especially important if we are constructing a pairs-trading strategy on futures. If you use the settlement prices to determine the futures spreads, you are guaranteed to be using two contemporaneous prices. (This is true as long as the two futures contracts have the same underlying and therefore have the same closing time. If you are trading intermarket spreads, see the discussion at the end of this section.) However, if you use the last traded prices to determine the spread, you may be using prices generated at two very different times and therefore incorrect. This incorrectness may mean that your backtest program will be generating erroneous trades due to an unrealistically large spread, and these trades may be unrealistically profitable in backtest when the spreads return to a correct, smaller value in the future, maybe when near-simultaneous transactions occur. As usual, an inflated backtest result is dangerous.

If you have an intraday spread strategy or are otherwise using intraday futures prices for backtesting a spread strategy, you will need either historical data with bid and ask prices of both contracts or the intraday data on the spread itself when it is native to the exchange. This is necessary because many futures contracts are not very liquid. So if we use the last price of every bar to form the spread, we may find that the last prices of contract A and contract B of the same bar may actually refer to transactions that are quite far apart in time. A spread formed by asynchronous last prices could not in reality be bought or sold at those prices. Backtests of intraday spread strategies using the last price of each leg of the spread instead of the last price of the spread itself will again inflate the resulting returns. One vendor that sells intraday historical calendar spread data (both quote and trade prices) is cqgdatafactory.com.

There is one general detail in backtesting intermarket spreads that should not be overlooked. If the contracts are traded on different exchanges, they are likely to have different closing times. So it would be wrong to form an intermarket spread using their closing prices. This is true also if we try to form a spread between a future and an ETF. The obvious remedy of this is to obtain intraday bid-ask data so that synchronicity is assured. The other possibility is to trade an ETF that holds a future instead of the future itself. For example, instead of trading the gold future GC (settlement price set at 1:30 P.M. ET) against the gold-miners ETF GDX, we can trade the gold trust GLD against GDX instead. Because both trade on Arca, their closing prices are set at the same 4:00 P.M. ET.

■ Statistical Significance of Backtesting: Hypothesis Testing

In any backtest, we face the problem of finite sample size: Whatever statistical measures we compute, such as average returns or maximum drawdowns, are subject to randomness. In other words, we may just be lucky that our strategy happened to be profitable in a small data sample. Statisticians have developed a general methodology called *hypothesis testing* to address this issue.

The general framework of hypothesis testing as applied to backtesting follows these steps:

1. Based on a backtest on some finite sample of data, we compute a certain statistical measure called the *test statistic*. For concreteness, let's say the test statistic is the average daily return of a trading strategy in that period.
2. We suppose that the true average daily return based on an infinite data set is actually zero. This supposition is called the *null hypothesis*.
3. We suppose that the probability distribution of daily returns is known. This probability distribution has a zero mean, based on the null hypothesis. We describe later how we determine this probability distribution.
4. Based on this null hypothesis probability distribution, we compute the probability p that the average daily returns will be at least as large as the observed value in the backtest (or, for a general test statistic, as extreme, allowing for the possibility of a negative test statistic). This probability p is called the *p-value*, and if it is very small (let's say smaller

than 0.01), that means we can "reject the null hypothesis," and conclude that the backtested average daily return is statistically significant.

The step in this procedure that requires most thought is step 3. How do we determine the probability distribution under the null hypothesis? Perhaps we can suppose that the daily returns follow a standard parametric probability distribution such as the Gaussian distribution, with a mean of zero and a standard deviation given by the sample standard deviation of the daily returns. If we do this, it is clear that if the backtest has a high Sharpe ratio, it would be very easy for us to reject the null hypothesis. This is because the standard test statistic for a Gaussian distribution is none other than the average divided by the standard deviation and multiplied by the square root of the number of data points (Berntson, 2002). The p-values for various critical values are listed in Table 1.1. For example, if the daily Sharpe ratio multiplied by the square root of the number days ($\sqrt{n}$) in the backtest is greater than or equal to the critical value 2.326, then the p-value is smaller than or equal to 0.01.

This method of hypothesis testing is consistent with our belief that high-Sharpe-ratio strategies are more statistically significant.

Another way to estimate the probability distribution of the null hypothesis is to use Monte Carlo methods to generate simulated historical price data and feed these simulated data into our strategy to determine the empirical probability distribution of profits. Our belief is that the profitability of the trading strategy captured some subtle patterns or correlations of the price series, and not just because of the first few moments of the price distributions. So if we generate many simulated price series with the same first moments and the same length as the actual price data, and run the trading strategy over all these simulated price series, we can find out in what fraction p of these price series are the average returns greater than or equal to the backtest return.

TABLE 1.1	Critical Values for $\sqrt{n}$ × Daily Sharpe Ratio
p-value	Critical values
0.10	1.282
0.05	1.645
0.01	2.326
0.001	3.091

Source: Berntson (2002).

Ideally, p will be small, which allows us to reject the null hypothesis. Otherwise, the average return of the strategy may just be due to the market returns.

A third way to estimate the probability distribution of the null hypothesis is suggested by Andrew Lo and his collaborators (Lo, Mamaysky, and Wang, 2000). In this method, instead of generating simulated price data, we generate sets of simulated trades, with the constraint that the number of long and short *entry* trades is the same as in the backtest, and with the same average holding period for the trades. These trades are distributed randomly over the actual historical price series. We then measure what fraction of such sets of trades has average return greater than or equal to the backtest average return.

In Example 1.1, I compare these three ways of testing the statistical significance of a backtest on a strategy. We should not be surprised that they give us different answers, since the probability distribution is different in each case, and each assumed distribution compares our strategy against a different benchmark of randomness.

Example 1.1: Hypothesis Testing on a Futures Momentum Strategy

We apply the three versions of hypothesis testing, each with a different probability distribution for the null hypothesis, on the backtest results of the TU momentum strategy described in Chapter 6. That strategy buys (sells) the TU future if it has a positive (negative) 12-month return, and holds the position for 1 month. We pick this strategy not only because of its simplicity, but because it has a fixed holding period. So for version 3 of the hypothesis testing, we need to randomize only the starting days of the long and short trades, with no need to randomize the holding periods.

The first hypothesis test is very easy. We assume the probability distribution of the daily returns is Gaussian, with mean zero as befitting a null hypothesis, and with the standard deviation given by the standard deviation of the daily returns given by our backtest. So if *ret* is the Tx1 MATLAB© array containing the daily returns of the strategy, the test statistic is just

```
mean(ret)/std(ret)*sqrt(length(ret))
```

Example 1.1 (*Continued*)

which turns out to be 2.93 for our data set. Comparing this test statistic with the critical values in Table 1.1 tells us that we can reject the null hypothesis with better than 99 percent probability.

The second hypothesis test involves generating a set of random, simulated daily returns data for the TU future (not the daily returns of the *strategy*) for the same number of days as our backtest. These random daily returns data will have the same mean, standard deviation, skewness, and kurtosis as the observed futures returns, but, of course, they won't have the same correlations embedded in them. If we find there is a good probability that the strategy can generate an as good as or better return on this random returns series as the observed returns series, it would mean that the momentum strategy is not really capturing any momentum or serial correlations in the returns at all and is profitable only because we were lucky that the observed returns' probability distribution has a certain mean and a certain shape. To generate these simulated random returns with the prescribed moments, we use the *pearsrnd* function from the MATLAB Statistics Toolbox. After the simulated returns *marketRet_sim* are generated, we then go on to construct a simulated price series *cl_sim* using those returns. Finally, we run the strategy on these simulated prices and calculate the average return of the strategy. We repeat this 10,000 times and count how many times the strategy produces an average return greater than or equal to that produced on the observed data set.

Assuming that *marketRet* is the Tx1 array containing the observed daily returns of TU, the program fragment is displayed below. (The source codes for these tests can be downloaded as *TU_mom_hypothesisTest.m* from www.wiley.com/go/algotrading.)

```
moments={mean(marketRet), std(marketRet), ...
  skewness(marketRet), kurtosis(marketRet)};
numSampleAvgretBetterOrEqualObserved=0;

for sample=1:10000
    marketRet_sim=pearsrnd(moments{:}, length(marketRet), 1);
    cl_sim=cumprod(1+marketRet_sim)-1;

    longs_sim=cl_sim > backshift(lookback, cl_sim) ;
    shorts_sim=cl_sim < backshift(lookback, cl_sim) ;
```

(Continued)

Example 1.1 (*Continued*)

```
        pos_sim=zeros(length(cl_sim), 1);

    for h=0:holddays-1
        long_sim_lag=backshift(h, longs_sim);
        long_sim_lag(isnan(long_sim_lag))=false;
        long_sim_lag=logical(long_sim_lag);

        short_sim_lag=backshift(h, shorts_sim);
        short_sim_lag(isnan(short_sim_lag))=false;
        short_sim_lag=logical(short_sim_lag);

        pos_sim(long_sim_lag)=pos_sim(long_sim_lag)+1;
        pos_sim(short_sim_lag)=pos_sim(short_sim_lag)-1;

    end

    ret_sim=backshift(1, pos_sim).*marketRet_sim/holddays;
    ret_sim(~isfinite(ret_sim))=0;

    if (mean(ret_sim) >= mean(ret))
        numSampleAvgretBetterOrEqualObserved=numSampleAvgret
        BetterOrEqualObserved+1;
    end
end
```

We found that out of 10,000 random returns sets, 1,166 have average strategy return greater than or equal to the observed average return. So the null hypothesis can be rejected with only 88 percent probability. Clearly, the shape of the returns distribution curve has something to do with the success of the strategy. (It is less likely that the success is due to the mean of the distribution since the position can be long or short at different times.)

The third hypothesis test involves randomizing the long and short entry dates, while keeping the same number of long trades and short trades as the ones in the backtest, respectively. We can accomplish this quite easily by the MATLAB function *randperm*:

```
numSampleAvgretBetterOrEqualObserved=0;
for sample=1:100000
    P=randperm(length(longs));
```

Example 1.1 (*Continued*)

```
longs_sim=longs(P);
shorts_sim=shorts(P);

pos_sim=zeros(length(cl), 1);

for h=0:holddays-1
    long_sim_lag=backshift(h, longs_sim);
    long_sim_lag(isnan(long_sim_lag))=false;
    long_sim_lag=logical(long_sim_lag);

    short_sim_lag=backshift(h, shorts_sim);
    short_sim_lag(isnan(short_sim_lag))=false;
    short_sim_lag=logical(short_sim_lag);

    pos(long_sim_lag)=pos(long_sim_lag)+1;
    pos(short_sim_lag)=pos(short_sim_lag)-1;
end

ret_sim=backshift(1, pos_sim).*marketRet/holddays;

ret_sim(isnan(ret_sim))=0;

if (mean(ret_sim)>= mean(ret))
numSampleAvgretBetterOrEqualObserved=...
   numSampleAvgretBetterOrEqualObserved+1;
end

end
```

There is not a single sample out of 100,000 where the average strategy return is greater than or equal to the observed return. Clearly, the third test is much weaker for this strategy.

The fact that a null hypothesis is not unique and different null hypotheses can give rise to different estimates of statistical significance is one reason why many critics believe that hypothesis testing is a flawed methodology (Gill, 1999). The other reason is that we actually want to know the conditional probability that the null hypothesis is true given that we have observed the test statistic R: $P(H_0 \mid R)$. But the procedure we outlined previously actually just computed the conditional probability of obtaining a test statistic R given that the null hypothesis is true: $P(R \mid H_0)$. Rarely is $P(R \mid H_0) = P(H_0 \mid R)$.

Even though hypothesis testing and the rejection of a null hypothesis may not be a very satisfactory way to estimate statistical significance, the *failure* to reject a null hypothesis can inspire very interesting insights. Our Example 1.1 shows that any random returns distribution with high kurtosis can be favorable to momentum strategies.

■ When Not to Backtest a Strategy

We have spent much effort earlier convincing you that you should backtest every strategy that comes your way before trading it. Why would we recommend against backtesting some strategies? The fact is that there are some published strategies that are so obviously flawed it would be a waste of time to even consider them. Given what you know now about common pitfalls of backtesting, you are in a good position to judge whether you would want to backtest a strategy without even knowing the details. We will look at a few examples here.

Example 1: A strategy that has a backtest annualized return of 30 percent and a Sharpe ratio of 0.3, and a maximum drawdown duration of two years.

Very few traders (as opposed to "investors") have the stomach for a strategy that remains "under water" for two years. The low Sharpe ratio coupled with the long drawdown duration indicates that the strategy is not consistent. The high average return may be just a fluke, and it is not likely to repeat itself when we start to trade the strategy live. Another way to say this is that the high return is likely the result of data-snooping bias, and the long drawdown duration will make it unlikely that the strategy will pass a cross-validation test. Do not bother to backtest high return but low Sharpe ratio strategies. Also, do not bother to backtest strategies with a maximum drawdown duration longer than what you or your investors can possibly endure.

Example 2: A long-only crude oil futures strategy returned 20 percent in 2007, with a Sharpe ratio of 1.5.

A quick check of the total return of holding the front-month crude oil futures in 2007 reveals that it was 47 percent, with a Sharpe ratio of 1.7. Hence, this trading strategy is not in any way superior to a simple buy-and-hold strategy! Moral of the story: We must always choose the appropriate benchmark to measure a trading strategy against. The appropriate benchmark of a long-only strategy is the return of a buy-and-hold position—the information ratio rather than the Sharpe ratio.

Example 3: A simple "buy-low-sell-high" strategy picks the 10 lowest-priced stocks at the beginning of the year and holds them for a year. The backtest return in 2001 is 388 percent.

The first question that should come to mind upon reading this strategy is: Was the strategy backtested using a survivorship-bias-free stock database? In other words, does the stock database include those stocks that have since been delisted? If the database includes only stocks that have survived until today, then the strategy will most likely pick those lucky survivors that happened to be very cheap at the beginning of 2001. With the benefit of hindsight, the backtest can, of course, achieve a 388 percent return. In contrast, if the database includes delisted stocks, then the strategy will most likely pick those stocks to form the portfolio, resulting in almost 100 percent loss. This 100 percent loss would be the realized return if we had traded the strategy back in 2001, and the 388 percent return is an inflated backtest return that can never be realized. If the author did not specifically mention that the data used include delisted stocks, then we can assume the backtest suffers from survivorship bias and the return is likely to be inflated.

Example 4: A neural net trading model that has about 100 nodes generates a backtest Sharpe ratio of 6.

My alarms always go off whenever I hear the term *neural net trading model,* not to mention one that has 100 nodes. All you need to know about the nodes in a neural net is that the number of parameters to be fitted with in-sample training data is proportional to the number of nodes. With at least 100 parameters, we can certainly fit the model to any time series we want and obtain a fantastic Sharpe ratio. Needless to say, it will have little or no predictive power going forward due to data-snooping bias.

Example 5: A high-frequency E-mini S&P 500 futures trading strategy has a backtest annual average return of 200 percent and a Sharpe ratio of 6. Its average holding period is 50 seconds.

Can we really backtest a high-frequency trading strategy? The performance of a high-frequency trading strategy depends on the order types used and the execution method in general. Furthermore, it depends crucially on the market microstructure. Even if we have historical data of the entire order book, the profit from a high-frequency strategy is still very dependent on the reactions of other market participants. One has to question whether there is a "Heisenberg uncertainty principle" at work: The act of placing or executing an order might alter the behavior of the other market participants. So be very skeptical of a so-called backtest of a high-frequency strategy.

Life is too short to backtest every single strategy that we read about, so we hope awareness of the common pitfalls of backtesting will help you select what strategies to backtest.

■ Will a Backtest Be Predictive of Future Returns?

Even if we manage to avoid all the common pitfalls outlined earlier and there are enough trades to ensure statistical significance of the backtest, the predictive power of any backtest rests on the central assumption that the statistical properties of the price series are unchanging, so that the trading rules that were profitable in the past will be profitable in the future. This assumption is, of course, invalidated often in varying degrees: A country's economic prospect changes, a company's management changes, and a financial market's structure changes. In the past decade in the United States, we have witnessed numerous instances of the last category of changes. Among them:

■ Decimalization of U.S. stock quotes on April 9, 2001. (Prior to this date, U.S. stocks were quoted in one-eighth or one-sixteenth of a penny.) This caused bid-ask spreads to decrease, but also caused the "displayed liquidity" at the best bid and ask prices to decrease (Arnuk and Saluzzi, 2012). This in turn caused profitability of many statistical arbitrage strategies to decrease while increasing the profitability of many high-frequency strategies.

■ The 2008 financial crisis that induced a subsequent 50 percent collapse of average daily trading volumes (Durden, 2012). Retail trading and ownership of common stock is particularly reduced. This has led to decreasing average volatility of the markets, but with increasing frequency of sudden outbursts such as that which occurred during the flash crash in May 2010 and the U.S. federal debt credit rating downgrade in August 2011. The overall effect has been a general decrease in profits for mean-reverting strategies, which thrive on a high but constant level of volatility.

■ The same 2008 financial crisis, which also initiated a multiyear bear market in momentum strategies, as discussed in Chapter 6.

- The SEC's Regulation NMS implemented in July 2007, which also contributed to the drastic decrease in the average trade sizes and the obsolescence of the NYSE block trade (Arnuk and Saluzzi, 2012).

- The removal of the old uptick rule for short sales in June 2007 and the reinstatement of the new Alternative Uptick Rule in 2010.

Strategies that performed superbly prior to each of these "regime shifts" may stop performing and vice versa. Backtests done using data prior to such regime shifts may be quite worthless, while backtests done using recent data may be no more indicative of future profits if and when a future regime shift is to occur. The general point of this is that algorithmic trading is not just about algorithms, programming, and mathematics: An awareness of such fundamental market and economic issues is also needed to inform us on whether a backtest is predictive and will continue to be predictive.

◼ Choosing a Backtesting and Automated Execution Platform

Software companies have worked very hard to provide traders with a wide variety of backtesting and automated execution platforms that cater to every possible level of programming skills. We are faced with two basic choices when it comes to deciding on a trading platform:

1. Buying a special-purpose backtesting and execution platform, and implementing your strategy using that platform's special-purpose graphical user interface (GUI) or programming language.
2. Writing your own backtest and execution program in a generic programming language such as C++, either in a completely standalone manner with piecemeal purchases of software libraries to make the task easier or within an integrated development environment (IDE) that comes with a comprehensive library catering to algorithmic trading.

We consider some criteria for making this choice next.

How Good Is Your Programming Skill?

If you have little skill in programming, then the only choice is to pick a special-purpose trading platform. These platforms unburden the user from having to learn a programming language by presenting a graphical "drag-and-drop" user interface for building a trading strategy. Examples of these products are Deltix and Progress Apama. However, I have found that these GUIs can be quite limiting in the variety of strategies that you can build, and in the long run, it is far more efficient to become adept in a programming language in order to express your strategy. (Note that Deltix and Progress Apama also allow other ways to specify a strategy, as explained below.)

Traders possessing the next level of programming skill should consider implementing both backtesting and automated execution using one of the scripting languages. These languages do not require compilation, and you can instantly see the results the moment you finish typing in the mathematical or logical expressions. Many traders' favorite backtesting platform, Microsoft Excel, perhaps used in conjunction with Visual Basic (VB) macros, belongs to this category. But it is actually quite hard to build a reasonably complicated strategy in Excel, and even harder to debug it. Excel also is not a particularly high-performance language, so if your strategy is very computationally intensive, it is not going to work. If you use Excel for automated executions, you may find that you have to use DDE links provided by your brokerage for market data updates, and you will likely need to add Visual Basic macros to handle more complicated trading logic, which is quite inefficient. (However, see Box 1.1 for an Excel-like trading platform that is supercharged for efficiency.)

BOX 1.1

Excel on Steroids—The FXone Automated Execution Platform

There is a currency trading platform called FXone that looks like Excel, but the underlying computational engine is written in a high-performance language like C++ instead of relying on VB macros. It is a true tick-driven application: Every tick (in the FX case, a tick is a new quote) triggers a recalculation of all the values in all of the cells of the spreadsheet. Furthermore, it has an internal cache for real-time data so that different cells that require the same data to compute can simply retrieve it from the cache, instead of duplicating subscriptions of the same data. It is also a true multithreaded platform at two different levels. First, different strategies written on different Excel workbooks can get market data updates and submit orders simultaneously. Second, different cells within the same workbook can also get updates and act on new data simultaneously. That is to say, even if the calculation in one cell happens to take very long to complete, it will not prevent other cells from responding to a new tick by, say, submitting an order. A screenshot of FXone is shown in Figure 1.1.

BOX 1.1 (Continued)

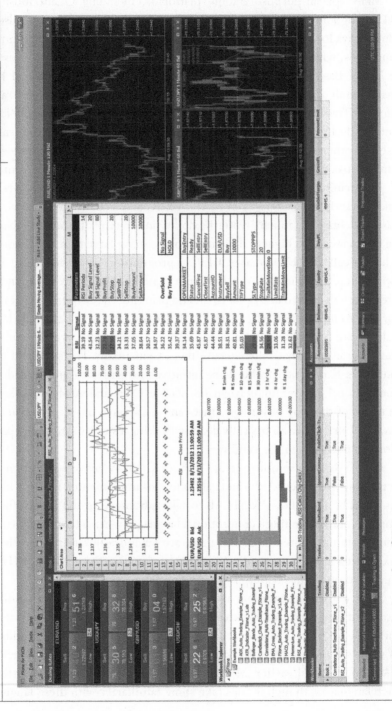

FIGURE 1.1 Screenshot of FXone.

27

BACKTESTING AND AUTOMATED EXECUTION

Many special-purpose trading platforms, including QuantHouse and RTD Tango and the aforementioned Deltix and Progress Apama, also include ways for coding a strategy with their own proprietary programming languages, which are usually quite simple and easy to learn, maybe as easy as Visual Basic. Aside from the institutional platforms mentioned here, many retail traders are familiar with MetaTrader, NinjaTrader, Trading Blox, or TradeStation Easy Language. I have not tried all of these platforms personally, but I have a lingering suspicion that despite the apparent ease of use and other advantages I mention later, they all in some way place some limitations on the type of strategies that can be backtested and executed.

Requiring just slightly more skills than programming in VB, traders will find the scripting languages of MATLAB, R, and Python offer vastly more ease of debugging, much greater flexibility in the type of strategies that can be backtested, and higher efficiency in backtesting large data sets. These are what we call "REPL" languages. REPL is programmer-speak for "Read-Eval-Print-Loop." That is, you can type in a mathematical expression, and the program will immediately evaluate it and print out the answer, and get ready for you to input the next expression. It works exactly like a handheld calculator, but better: You can also save all these expressions in a file, and have the program automatically execute them sequentially. The syntax of these languages is designed to be more intuitive and easier to understand than conventional programming languages such as C++ and much more flexible in terms of the type of variables that can be used in a program. Scalars, arrays, and strings are all basically dealt with using a similar syntax and passed along to functions in the same way.

MATLAB can also utilize Java, C++, or C# libraries or application programming interfaces (APIs) and call functions implemented in those libraries or APIs. This allows MATLAB to take advantage of the more efficient implementations in those conventional languages when a task is particularly computationally intensive. Also, there are far more libraries and APIs that are written in those conventional languages than those written in MATLAB, R, or Python, so this feature is often essential.

Many algorithmic traders are aware that MATLAB, R, and Python are excellent languages for backtesting. But less well known is the fact that they can be turned into execution platforms as well with the addition of some toolboxes. Most brokerages have APIs written in Java, C++, or C#; and, as I said earlier, MATLAB can call functions in APIs written in such languages, though it does take some familiarity with these languages to know how to call these functions. If you would prefer a solution that obviates making "foreign-language" API calls in MATLAB, there are a number of commercial products available. MATLAB's own Datafeed Toolbox can send orders to Trading Technologies' X_TRADER. To connect MATLAB to Interactive Brokers, undocumentedmatlab.com has developed an API called IB-Matlab. Another vendor, www.exchangeapi.com, has a similar API called quant2ib, as well as one called quant2tt for connecting MATLAB to Trading Technologies. For other brokerages, www.pracplay.com offers a bridge from MATLAB or R to 15 or more brokers for a monthly fee. A free, open-source MATLAB API for connecting to Interactive Brokers was developed by Jev Kuznetsov and is available for download from MATLAB Central's File Exchange. Meanwhile, the MATFIX software from agoratron.com lets your MATLAB program send orders using the Financial Information eXchange (FIX) protocol to brokers or exchanges. You can also use MATLAB to call the Java or .NET functions in QuickFIX, an open source FIX engine (Kozola, 2012). For Python users, the free, open-source software IbPy will connect your Python trading program to Interactive Brokers. While these add-ons to MATLAB and Python make it possible to connect to a broker, they nevertheless do not shield you from all the complexity of such connections. And, more important, it is cumbersome to use the same program for both backtesting and execution.

If you are a hard-core programmer, you will, of course, have no problem backtesting and automating execution directly in the most flexible, most efficient, and most robust of programming languages, such as aforementioned trio of Java, C++, or C#. As I said earlier, all brokerages or exchanges that cater to algorithmic traders provide APIs in one or more of these languages, or they allow you to submit orders using the FIX messages, which in turn can be created and transmitted using a program written in one of these languages. (For example, QuickFIX, mentioned previously, is available in C++, C#, VB, Python, and Ruby.) But even here the software industry has come to make our strategy implementation easier and more robust by providing IDEs designed just for backtesting. In fact, many of the special-purpose trading platforms (Deltix, Progress Apama, QuantHouse, RTD Tango, etc.) include ways for coding strategies using general-purpose, advanced programming languages that make them resemble IDEs. There are also free, open-source class libraries or IDEs that I describe in the next section.

Can Backtesting and Execution Use the Same Program?

Special-purpose *execution* platforms typically hide the complexity of connecting to a brokerage or exchange, receiving live market data, sending orders and receiving order confirmations, updating portfolio positions etc. from the programmer. Meanwhile, special-purpose *backtesting* platforms typically come integrated with historical data. So for many special-purpose trading platforms, the backtest program can be made the same as the live execution program by factoring out the pure trading logic into a function, unencumbered with details of how to retrieve data or where to submit orders, and switching between backtesting mode and live execution mode can be done by pushing a button to switch between feeding in historical data versus live market data.

This ease of switching between backtesting and live execution is more than just convenience: It eliminates any possibility of discrepancies or errors in transcribing a backtest strategy into a live strategy, discrepancies that often plague strategies written in a general programming language whether it is C++ or MATLAB. Just as importantly, it eliminates the possibility of look-ahead bias. As explained before, look-ahead bias means mistakenly incorporating future, unknowable information as part of the historical data input to the backtest engine. Special-purpose platforms feed in historical market data into the trade generating engine one tick or one bar at a time, just as it would feeding in live market data. So there is no possibility that future information can be used as input. This is one major advantage of using a special-purpose trading platform.

There is one more advantage in using a platform where the backtesting and live execution programs are one and the same—it enables true tick-based high-frequency trading strategies backtesting. This is because most industrial-strength live execution programs are "event-driven"; that is, a trade is triggered by the arrival of a new tick, not the end of an arbitrary time bar. So if the input historical data is also tick-based, we can also backtest a high-frequency strategy that depends on the change of every tick or even every change in the order book. (I said "in theory" assuming that your hardware is powerful enough. Otherwise, see the discussion later in this chapter in the section "What Type of Asset Classes or Strategies Does the Platform Support?") Of course, we can backtest tick-based strategies in MATLAB by feeding every tick into the program as well, though that is quite a cumbersome procedure.

		Asset		Tick	CEP
IDE	Language(s)	class(es)	Broker(s)	based?	enabled?
ActiveQuant	Java, MATLAB, R	Various	CTS, FIX, Trading Technologies-supported brokers	Yes	No
Algo-Trader	Java	Various	Interactive Brokers, FIX	Yes	Yes
Marketcetera	Java, Python, Ruby	Various	Various, FIX	Yes	Yes
OpenQuant	.NET (C#, VB)	Various	Various, FIX	?	No
TradeLink	.NET (C#, C++, VB), Java, Pascal, Python	Various	Various, FIX	Yes	No

TABLE 1.2 Comparisons of Open-Source Integrated Development Environments (IDEs) for Backtesting and Automated Execution

If you are a competent programmer who prefers the flexibility of a general purpose programming language, yet you want to use the same program for both backtesting and live trading because of the preceding considerations, you can still use the institutional-grade special-purpose platforms as IDEs, or you can use the many open-source IDEs available: Marketcetera, Trade-Link, Algo-Trader, ActiveQuant. I call them IDEs, but they are more than just a trading strategy development environment: They come with libraries that deal with the nuts and bolts of connecting to and exchanging data with your broker, much like a special-purpose platform does. Many of them are also integrated with historical data, which is an important time saver. As an added bonus, these open-source IDEs are either free or quite low-cost compared to special-purpose platforms. I display in Table 1.2 the languages, markets, and brokers that they support. (FIX as a broker means that the system can directly access any execution venues via the FIX protocol, regardless of clearing broker.) I also indicate whether the IDE is tick based (sometimes called *event driven* or *stream based*).

One should note that Table 1.2 only compares features of open-source IDEs. The institutional-grade special-purpose platforms typically have all of these features.

What Type of Asset Classes or Strategies Does the Platform Support?

While using a special-purpose platform for trading strategies has several important advantages described earlier, few but the most high end of these platforms support all possible asset classes, including stocks, futures, currencies, and options. For example, the popular MetaTrader is for currencies trading only. It is especially difficult for these platforms to trade strategies that involve arbitrage between different asset classes, such as between futures and stocks or currencies and futures. The open-source IDEs are better able to handle these situations. As Table 1.2 indicates, most IDEs can trade a variety of asset classes. But, as usual, the most flexible solution in this respect is a stand-alone program written outside of any IDE.

Beyond asset classes, many special-purpose platforms also place restrictions on the type of strategies that they support even within one asset class. Often, simple pairs trading strategies require special modules to handle. Most lower-end platforms cannot handle common statistical arbitrage or portfolio trading strategies that involve many symbols. Open-source IDEs do not have such restrictions, and, of course, neither do stand-alone programs.

What about high(er)-frequency trading? What kind of platforms can support this demanding trading strategy? The surprising answer is that most platforms can handle the execution part of high-frequency trading without too much latency (as long as your strategy can tolerate latencies in the 1- to 10-millisecond range), and since special-purpose platforms as well as IDEs typically use the same program for both backtesting and execution, backtesting shouldn't in theory be a problem either.

To understand why most platforms have no trouble handling high-frequency executions, we have to realize that most of the latency that needs to be overcome in high-frequency trading is due to live market data latency, or brokerage order confirmation latency.

1. Live market data latency:
   For your program to receive a new quote or trade price within 1 to 10 milliseconds (ms), you have to colocate your program at the exchange or in your broker's data center (see Box 1.2); furthermore, you have to receive a direct data feed from the exchanges involved, not from a consolidated data feed such as SIAC's Consolidated Tape System (CTS). (For example, Interactive Brokers' data feed only offers snapshots of market data every 250 ms.)
2. Brokerage order confirmation latency:
   If a strategy submits limit orders, it will depend on a timely order status confirmation before it can decide what to do next. For some retail brokerages, it can take up to six seconds between the execution of an order and your program receiving the execution confirmation, virtually

BOX 1.2

Colocation of Trading Programs

The general term *colocation* can mean several ways of physically locating your trading program outside of your desktop computer. Stretching the definition a bit, it can mean installing your trading program in a cloud server or VPS (virtual private server) such as Amazon's EC2, slicehost.com, or gogrid. com. The advantage of doing so is to prevent power or Internet outages that are more likely to strike a private home or office than a commercial data center, with its backup power supply and redundant network connectivity. Colocating in a cloud server does not necessarily shorten the time data take to travel between your brokerage or an exchange to your trading program, since many homes or offices are now equipped with a fiber optics connection to their Internet service provider (e.g., Verizon's FiOS in the United States, and Bell's Fibe Internet in Canada). To verify whether colocating in a virtual private server (VPS) actually reduces this latency, you would need to conduct a test yourself by "pinging" your broker's server to see what the average round trip time is. Certainly, if your VPS happens to be located physically close to your broker or exchange, and if they are directly connected to an Internet backbone, this latency will be smaller. (For example, pinging the Interactive Brokers' quote server from my home desktop computer produces an average round trip time of about 55 ms, pinging the same server from Amazon's EC2 takes about 25 ms, and pinging it from various VPSs located near Interactive Brokers takes about 16 to 34 ms.)

I mention VPS only because many trading programs are not so computationally intensive as to require their own dedicated servers. But if they are, you can certainly upgrade to such services at many of the hosting companies familiar with the requirements of the financial trading industry such as Equinix and Telx, both of whom operate data centers in close proximity to the various exchanges.

If your server is already in a secure location (whether that is your office or a data center) and is immune to power outage, then all you need is a fast connection to your broker or the exchange. You can consider using an "extranet," which is like the Internet but operated by a private company, which will guarantee a minimum communication speed. BT Radianz, Savvis, and TNS are examples of such companies. If you have a large budget, you can also ask these companies to build a dedicated communication line from your server to your broker or exchange as well.

The next step up in the colocation hierarchy is colocating inside your brokerage's data center, so that quotes or orders confirmation generated by your broker are transmitted to your program via an internal network, unmolested by the noise and vagaries of the public Internet. Various brokers that cater to professional traders have made available colocation service: examples are Lime Brokerage and FXCM. (Because of colocation, clients of Lime Brokerage can even receive direct data feeds from the NYSE at a
(Continued)

BOX 1.2 (Continued)

relatively low rate, which, as I mentioned before, is faster than the consolidated SIAC CTS data feed.)

The ultimate colocation is, of course, situating your trading server at the exchange or ECN itself. This is likely to be an expensive proposition (except for forex ECNs), and useful only if you have a prime broker relationship, which allows you to have "sponsored access" to connect to the exchange without going through the broker's infrastructure (Johnson, 2010). Such prime broker relationships can typically be established only if you can generate institutional-level commissions or have multimillion-dollar account. The requirements as well as expenses to establish colocation are lower for forex prime brokers and ECNs. Most forex ECNs including Currenex, EBS, FXall, and Hotspot operate within large commercial data centers such as Equinix's NY4 facility, and it is not too expensive to colocate at that facility or sign up with a VPS that does.

Some traders have expressed concern that colocating their trading programs on a remote server exposes them to possible theft of their intellectual property. The simplest way is eliminate this risk is to just store "executables" (binary computer codes that look like gibberish to humans) on these remote servers, and not the source code of your trading algorithm. (Even with a MATLAB program, you can convert all the .m files to .p files before loading them to the remote server.) Without source codes, no one can know the operating instructions of running the trading program, and no one will be foolish enough to risk capital on trading a black-box strategy of which they know little about. For the truly paranoid, you can also require an ever-changing password that depends on the current time to start a program.

ensuring that no high-frequency trading can be done. Even if your brokerage has order confirmation latency below 10 ms, or if they allow you to have direct market access to the exchanges so you get your order status confirmation directly from the exchanges, you would still need to colocate your program with either your broker in the former case, or with the exchange in the latter case.

Practically any software program (other than Excel running with a VB macro) takes less than 10 ms to submit a new order after receiving the latest market data and order status updates, so software or hardware latency is usually not the bottleneck for high-frequency trading, unless you are using one program to monitor thousands of symbols. (Concerning this last point, see Box 1.3 for issues related to multithreading.) But backtesting a high-frequency strategy is entirely a different matter. To do this, you will be required to input many months of tick data (trades and quotes), maybe on many symbols, into the backtesting platform. Worse, sometimes you have to input level 2 quotes, too. Just the quantity of

BOX 1.3

Multithreading and High-Frequency Trading of Multiple Symbols

Multithreading for a trading platform means that it can respond to multiple events (usually the arrival of a new tick) simultaneously. This is particularly important if the program trades multiple symbols simultaneously, which is often the case for a stock-trading program. You certainly don't want your buy order for AAPL to be delayed just because the program is deciding whether to sell BBRY! If you write your own stand-alone trading program using a modern programming language such as Java or Python, you won't have any problem with multithreading because this ability is native to such languages. However, if you use MATLAB, you will need to purchase the Parallel Computing Toolbox as well; otherwise, there is no multithreading. (Even if you purchase that Toolbox, you are limited to 12 independent threads, hardly enough to trade 500 stocks simultaneously!) But do not confuse the lack of multithreading in MATLAB with the "loss of ticks." If you write two "listeners," A and B, in MATLAB to receive tick data from two separate symbols, because the fact that listener A is busy processing a tick-triggered event doesn't mean that listener B is "deaf." Once listener A has finished processing, listener B will start to process those tick events that it has received while A was busy, with no lost ticks (Kuznetsov, 2010).

data will overwhelm the memory of most machines, if they are not handled in special ways (such as using parallel computing algorithms). Most special-purpose backtesting platforms are not designed to be especially intelligent when handling this quantity of data, and most of them are not equipped at all to backtest data with all of bid/ask/last tick prices (and sizes) nor level 2 quotes either. So backtesting a high-frequency strategy usually requires that you write your own stand-alone program with special customization. Actually, backtesting a high-frequency strategy may not tell you much about its real-life profitability anyway because of the Heisenberg uncertainty principle that I mentioned before.

Besides high-frequency trading, news-driven trading often causes all but the top-end special-purpose platforms to stumble. News-driven trading by definition requires as input a machine-readable news feed. Most special-purpose platforms do not have this capability, and neither do most open-source IDEs. Exceptions include Progress Apama, which incorporates both Dow Jones and Reuters machine-readable news feed, and Deltix, which integrates Ravenpack's News Sentiment data feed. Among IDE's, Marketcetera offers a newsfeed from benzinga.com (which is unlikely to match the speed of delivery of Bloomberg, Dow Jones, and Reuters). If you are writing your own stand-alone trading program, you have the flexibility of connecting to these news feed either using the news provider's API (e.g., both Dow Jones and Thomson Reuters have made available their machine-readable news through an API) or simply read a news XML file ftp'ed to your hard-drive periodically by the news provider. If you are news trading at high frequency, the former expensive solution is an absolute necessity. Otherwise, there are much more affordable solutions from vendors such as Newsware. I will discuss more on the topic of event-driven trading in Chapter 7.

Does the Platform Have Complex Event Processing?

Complex event processing (CEP) is a fashionable term to describe a program responding to an event instantaneously and taking appropriate action. The events that concern us are usually the arrival of a new tick, or the delivery of a news item. For an algorithmic trader, one important point is that the program is event driven, and not bar driven. That is, the program does not go poll prices or news items at the end of each bar and then decide what to do. Because CEP is event driven, there is no delay between the occurrence of an event and the response to it.

If instantaneity is the only strength of CEP, then we can just use the so-called callback functions that almost every brokerage API provides. A callback function is also triggered whenever a new tick or news item arrives, and based on this new data we can perform all kinds of computations and determine whether to submit an order. This is easy when the rule required is simply "moving average of the price over the last hour."

But what if the rules are "complex," such as "sell when the order flow in the last half hour is positive, the price is above the moving average, the volatility is low, and an important news item just arrived"?

What if the rule involves many clauses like during, between, afterwards, in parallel when applied to the sequence of events? According to CEP aficionados, it is much more succinct to express these complicated rules using a CEP language than a traditional programming language. But what about the argument that trading rules should be simple to avoid data-snooping bias? Their answer is that they are not data mining the data to find arbitrary rules, but simply implementing rules that seasoned traders already know are profitable. I am not entirely convinced by their arguments, but if you are, you should know that Progress Apama mentioned above is distinguished by their CEP technology. Certain free, open-source IDEs have CEP, too, as you can see from Table 1.2.

- Backtesting is useless if it is not predictive of future performance of a strategy, but pitfalls in backtesting will decrease its predictive power.
- Eliminating pitfalls:
  - A platform that uses the same program for both backtesting and live executions can eliminate look-ahead bias.
  - Out-of-sample testing, cross-validation, and high Sharpe ratios are all good practices for reducing data-snooping bias, but none is more definitive than walk-forward testing.
  - Simple models are a simple cure for data-snooping bias.
  - "Why did my model generate a 'short' signal for THQI on 2012/7/9? Oh, that's because I forgot to adjust its historical prices for a 1:10 reverse stock split!"
  - "Did your model just buy the stock CMC? Are you sure it didn't forget to adjust its historical prices because today is its ex-date for dividends?"
  - "I see that your model is long only. Did you make sure your data don't have survivorship bias?"
  - "The backtest of your mean-reverting stock-trading model using closing prices is excellent, but expect a deflation of the results if you test it again using primary exchange data."
  - "Your model performed brilliantly during November 2008. But did it short a lot of financial stocks back then? Don't forget that short sales of those stocks were banned."
  - "This high-frequency stock-trading model looks good on backtest, but I wonder if it incorporated uptick rules for their short trades."
  - "Your futures calendar spread model uses the differences in price to form the spread. Why are you back-adjusting your prices using returns gap?"
  - "Why is it that my mean-reverting intraday futures spread performed so well in backtest but so poorly in live trading? Oh, I should have used tick-based instead of bar-based data for my backtest."
  - "Your backtest of this momentum strategy seems to be without any pitfalls. But just because it performed well before 2008 doesn't mean it will perform well afterward."
- Statistical significance of backtests:
  - "What do you mean by saying that the expected APR of this strategy is 10 percent and is statistically significant to within 1 percent?" Answer: "It means by running the strategy on 10,000 simulated price series with the same length and the same first three moments as the historical price series, there are only 100 sample series where the APR is equal to or greater than 10 percent."

(Continued)

- "What do you mean by saying that the expected APR of this strategy is 10 percent and is statistically significant to within 1 percent?" Alternative answer: "It means by randomizing the entry dates of my trades, there is only 1 in 100 random permutations where the APR is equal to or greater than 10 percent."
- Which backtest platform to pick?
  - "I am a brilliant mathematician starting a fund with $50 million to invest, but I don't know how to program. What trading platform should I use?" Pick an institutional special-purpose platform like Deltix, QuantHouse, Progress Apama, or RTD Tango.
  - "I am an experienced, discretionary, independent trader, and I want to automate my strategies. What trading platform should I use?" Pick a retail special-purpose platform like MetaTrader, NinjaTrader, Trading Blox, or TradeStation.
  - "I am a quant who is great with strategy research using MATLAB. But how should I implement these strategies and go 'live'?" Try exchangeapi.com's quant2ib API for Interactive Brokers, quant2tt for Trading Technologies, www.pracplay.com for other brokers, or MATFIX for FIX connections.
  - "I am a good C++, C#, and Java programmer, but I hate dealing with low-level connections to the brokerage, and I hate having to rewrite my connections every time I change brokers." Try one of the IDEs such as Marketcetera, TradeLink, AlgoTrader, or ActiveQuant.
- Automating executions:
  - "I want to colocate my trading program at a data center to reduce my order confirmation latency below 10 ms." Are you sure your broker has an order confirmation latency shorter than 10 ms?
  - "I am colocated at Amazon's EC2. Market data fed to my trading programs should be much more up-to-date than getting them at my desktop PC." Not necessarily: EC2's server may be farther away (in Internet distance) from your broker's data server than your desktop PC.
  - "I am using MATLAB's Parallel Computing Toolbox, and I run my program on a GPU. Therefore, I can trade all 500 stocks in the SPX simultaneously." Even with MATLAB's Parallel Computing Toolbox, you are limited to handling 12 stocks simultaneously. Writing your own Java or Python program will allow true multithreading on a graphics processing unit (GPU).
  - "My IDE isn't CEP enabled. I can't really run a tick-based trading strategy." Even platforms that are not CEP enabled often have callback functions that enable your program to be triggered by ticks.

CHAPTER 2

The Basics of Mean Reversion

Whether we realize it or not, nature is filled with examples of mean reversion. Figure 2.1 shows the water level of the Nile from 622 AD to 1284 AD, clearly a mean-reverting time series. Mean reversion is equally prevalent in the social sciences. Daniel Kahneman cited a famous example: the "*Sports Illustrated* jinx," which is the claim that "an athlete whose picture appears on the cover of the magazine is doomed to perform poorly the following season" (Kahneman, 2011). The scientific reason is that an athlete's performance can be thought of as randomly distributed around a mean, so an exceptionally good performance one year (which puts the athlete on the cover of *Sports Illustrated*) is very likely to be followed by performances that are closer to the average.

Is mean reversion also prevalent in financial price series? If so, our lives as traders would be very simple and profitable! All we need to do is to buy low (when the price is below the mean), wait for reversion to the mean price, and then sell at this higher price, all day long. Alas, most price series are not mean reverting, but are geometric random walks. The *returns*, not the prices, are the ones that usually randomly distribute around a mean of zero. Unfortunately, we cannot trade on the mean reversion of returns. (One should not confuse mean reversion of returns with anti-serial-correlation of returns, which we can definitely trade on. But anti-serial-correlation of returns is the same as the mean reversion of prices.) Those few price series that are found to be mean reverting are called *stationary*, and in this chapter we will describe the statistical tests (ADF test and the Hurst exponent and Variance Ratio test) for stationarity. There are not too many prefabricated

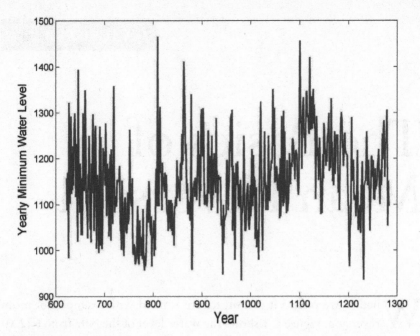

FIGURE 2.1 Minimum Water Levels of the Nile River, 622–1284 AD

prices series that are stationary. By *prefabricated* I meant those price series that represent assets traded in the public exchanges or markets.

Fortunately, we can manufacture many more mean-reverting price series than there are traded assets because we can often combine two or more individual price series that are not mean reverting into a portfolio whose net market value (i.e., price) is mean reverting. Those price series that can be combined this way are called cointegrating, and we will describe the statistical tests (CADF test and Johansen test) for cointegration, too. Also, as a by-product of the Johansen test, we can determine the exact weightings of each asset in order to create a mean reverting portfolio. Because of this possibility of artificially creating stationary portfolios, there are numerous opportunities available for mean reversion traders.

As an illustration of how easy it is to profit from mean-reverting price series, I will also describe a simple linear trading strategy, a strategy that is truly "parameterless."

One clarification: The type of mean reversion we will look at in this chapter may be called *time series* mean reversion because the prices are supposed to be reverting to a mean determined by its own historical prices. The tests and trading strategies that I depict in this chapter are all tailored to time series mean reversion. There is another kind of mean reversion, called "cross-sectional" mean reversion. Cross-sectional mean reversion means that the cumulative returns of the instruments in a basket will revert to the cumulative return of the basket. This also implies that the short-term *relative* returns of the instruments are serially anticorrelated. (Relative return of an instrument is the return of that instrument minus the return of the basket.) Since this phenomenon occurs most often for stock baskets, we will discuss how to take advantage of it in Chapter 4 when we discuss mean-reverting strategies for stocks and ETFs.

■ Mean Reversion and Stationarity

Mean reversion and stationarity are two equivalent ways of looking at the same type of price series, but these two ways give rise to two different statistical tests for such series.

The mathematical description of a mean-reverting price series is that the change of the price series in the next period is proportional to the difference between the mean price and the current price. This gives rise to the ADF test, which tests whether we can reject the null hypothesis that the proportionality constant is zero.

However, the mathematical description of a stationary price series is that the variance of the log of the prices increases slower than that of a geometric random walk. That is, their variance is a sublinear function of time, rather than a linear function, as in the case of a geometric random walk. This sublinear function is usually approximated by τ^{2H}, where τ is the time separating two price measurements, and H is the so-called Hurst exponent, which is less than 0.5 if the price series is indeed stationary (and equal to 0.5 if the price series is a geometric random walk). The Variance Ratio test can be used to see whether we can reject the null hypothesis that the Hurst exponent is actually 0.5.

Note that stationarity is somewhat of a misnomer: It doesn't mean that the prices are necessarily range bound, with a variance that is independent of time and thus a Hurst exponent of zero. It merely means that the variance increases slower than normal diffusion.

A clear mathematical exposition of the ADF and Variance Ratio tests can be found in Walter Beckert's course notes (Beckert, 2011). Here, we are interested only in their applications to practical trading strategies.

Augmented Dickey-Fuller Test

If a price series is mean reverting, then the current price level will tell us something about what the price's next move will be: If the price level is higher than the mean, the next move will be a downward move; if the price level is lower than the mean, the next move will be an upward move. The ADF test is based on just this observation.

We can describe the price changes using a linear model:

$$\Delta y(t) = \lambda y(t-1) + \mu + \beta t + \alpha_1 \Delta y(t-1) + \cdots + \alpha_k \Delta y(t-k) + \epsilon_t \quad (2.1)$$

where $\Delta y(t) \equiv y(t) - y(t-1)$, $\Delta y(t-1) \equiv y(t-1) - y(t-2)$, and so on. The ADF test will find out if $\lambda = 0$. If the hypothesis $\lambda = 0$ can be rejected, that means the next move $\Delta y(t)$ depends on the current level $y(t-1)$, and therefore it is not a random walk. The test statistic is the regression coefficient λ (with $y(t-1)$ as the independent variable and $\Delta y(t)$ as the dependent variable) divided by the standard error of the regression fit: $\lambda/SE(\lambda)$. The statisticians Dickey and Fuller have kindly found out for us the distribution of this test statistic and tabulated the critical values for us, so we can look up for any value of $\lambda/SE(\lambda)$ whether the hypothesis can be rejected at, say, the 95 percent probability level.

Notice that since we expect mean regression, $\lambda/SE(\lambda)$ has to be negative, and it has to be more negative than the critical value for the hypothesis to be rejected. The critical values themselves depend on the sample size and whether we assume that the price series has a non-zero mean $-\mu/\lambda$ or a steady drift $-\beta t/\lambda$. In practical trading, the constant drift in price, if any, tends to be of a much smaller magnitude than the daily fluctuations in price. So for simplicity we will assume this drift term to be zero ($\beta = 0$).

In Example 2.1, we apply the ADF test to a currency rate series USD.CAD.

Example 2.1: Using ADF Test for Mean Reversion

The ADF test is available as a MATLAB Econometrics function *adftest*, or from the open-source MATLAB package spatial-econometrics.com's *adf* function. We will use *adf* below, and my code is available for download as *stationarityTests.m* from http://epchan.com/book2.

(After you have downloaded the spatial-econometrics.com's jplv7 folder to your computer, remember to add all the subfolders of this package to your MATLAB path before using it.)

Example 2.1 (*Continued*)

The *adf* function has three inputs. The first is the price series in ascending order of time (chronological order is important). The second is a parameter indicating whether we should assume the offset μ and whether the drift β in Equation 2.1 should be zero. We should assume the offset is nonzero, since the mean price toward which the prices revert is seldom zero. We should, however, assume the drift is zero, because the constant drift in price tends to be of a much smaller magnitude than the daily fluctuations in price. These considerations mean that the second parameter should be 0 (by the package designer's convention). The third input is the lag k. You can start by trying $k = 0$, but often only by setting $k = 1$ can we reject the null hypothesis, meaning that the change in prices often does have serial correlations. We will try the test on the exchange rate USD.CAD (how many Canadian dollars in exchange for one U.S. dollar). We assume that the daily prices at 17:00 ET are stored in a MATLAB array γ. The data file is that of one-minute bars, but we will just extract the end-of-day prices at 17:00 ET. Sampling the data at intraday frequency will not increase the statistical significance of the ADF test. We can see from Figure 2.2 that it does not look very stationary.

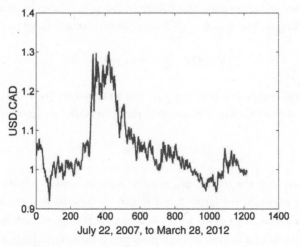

July 22, 2007, to March 28, 2012

FIGURE 2.2   USD.CAD Price Series

(*Continued*)

Example 2.1 (*Continued*)

And indeed, you should find that the ADF test statistic is about −1.84, but the critical value at the 90 percent level is −2.594, so we can't reject the hypothesis that λ is zero. In other words, we can't show that USD.CAD is stationary, which perhaps is not surprising, given that the Canadian dollar is known as a commodity currency, while the U.S. dollar is not. But note that λ is negative, which indicates the price series is at least not trending.

```
results=adf(y, 0, 1);
prt(results);
% Augmented DF test for unit root variable:    variable 1
%  ADF t-statistic       # of lags   AR(1) estimate
%       -1.840744            1           0.994120
%
%    1% Crit Value   5% Crit Value   10% Crit Value
%         -3.458         -2.871          -2.594
```

Hurst Exponent and Variance Ratio Test

Intuitively speaking, a "stationary" price series means that the prices diffuse from its initial value more slowly than a geometric random walk would. Mathematically, we can determine the nature of the price series by measuring this speed of diffusion. The speed of diffusion can be characterized by the variance

$$\text{Var}(\tau) = \left\langle \left| z(t + \tau) - z(t) \right|^2 \right\rangle \tag{2.2}$$

where z is the log prices ($z = log(y)$), τ is an arbitrary time lag, and $\langle \cdots \rangle$ is an average over all t's. For a geometric random walk, we know that

$$\left\langle \left| z(t + \tau) - z(t) \right|^2 \right\rangle \sim \tau \tag{2.3}$$

The $\sim$ means that this relationship turns into an equality with some proportionality constant for large τ, but it may deviate from a straight line for small τ. But if the (log) price series is mean reverting or trending (i.e., has positive correlations between sequential price moves), Equation 2.3 won't hold. Instead, we can write:

$$\left\langle \left| z(t + \tau) - z(t) \right|^2 \right\rangle \sim \tau^{2H} \tag{2.4}$$

where we have defined the Hurst exponent H. For a price series exhibiting geometric random walk, $H = 0.5$. But for a mean-reverting series, $H < 0.5$, and for a trending series, $H > 0.5$. As H decreases toward zero, the price series is more mean reverting, and as H increases toward 1, the price series is increasingly trending; thus, H serves also as an indicator for the degree of mean reversion or trendiness.

In Example 2.2, we computed the Hurst exponent for the same currency rate series USD.CAD that we used in the previous section using the MATLAB code. It generates an H of 0.49, which suggests that the price series is weakly mean reverting.

Example 2.2: Computing the Hurst Exponent

Using the same USD.CAD price series in the previous example, we now compute the Hurst exponent using a function called *genhurst* we can download from MATLAB Central (www.mathworks.com /matlabcentral/fileexchange/30076-generalized-hurst-exponent). This function computes a generalized version of the Hurst exponent defined by $\langle |z(t+\tau) - z(t)|^{2q} \rangle \sim \tau^{2H(q)}$, where q is an arbitrary number. But here we are only interested in $q = 2$, which we specify as the second input parameter to *genhurst*.

```
H=genhurst(log(y), 2);
```

If we apply this function to USD.CAD, we get $H = 0.49$, indicating that it may be weakly mean reverting.

Because of finite sample size, we need to know the statistical significance and MacKinlay of an estimated value of H to be sure whether we can reject the null hypothesis that H is really 0.5. This hypothesis test is provided by the Variance Ratio test (Lo, 2001).

The Variance Ratio Test simply tests whether

$$\frac{Var(z(t) - z(t - \tau))}{\tau Var(z(t) - z(t - 1))}$$

is equal to 1. There is another ready-made MATLAB Econometrics Toolbox function *vratiotest* for this, whose usage I demonstrate in Example 2.3.

The *vratiotest* from MATALB Econometric Toolbox is applied to the same USD.CAD price series y that have been used in the previous examples in this chapter. The outputs are h and $pValue$: $h = 1$ means rejection of the random walk hypothesis at the 90 percent confidence level, $h = 0$ means it may be a random walk. $pValue$ gives the probability that the null (random walk) hypothesis is true.

```
[h,pValue]=vratiotest(log(y));
```

We find that $h = 0$ and $pValue = 0.367281$ for USD.CAD, indicating that there is a 37 percent chance that it is a random walk, so we cannot reject this hypothesis.

Half-Life of Mean Reversion

The statistical tests I described for mean reversion or stationarity are very demanding, with their requirements of at least 90 percent certainty. But in practical trading, we can often be profitable with much less certainty. In this section, we shall find another way to interpret the λ coefficient in Equation 2.1 so that we know whether it is negative enough to make a trading strategy practical, even if we cannot reject the null hypothesis that its actual value is zero with 90 percent certainty in an ADF test. We shall find that λ is a measure of how long it takes for a price to mean revert.

To reveal this new interpretation, it is only necessary to transform the discrete time series Equation 2.1 to a differential form so that the changes in prices become infinitesimal quantities. Furthermore, if we ignore the drift (βt) and the lagged differences ($\Delta y(t - 1), \ldots, \Delta y(t - k)$) in Equation 2.1, then it becomes recognizable in stochastic calculus as the Ornstein-Uhlenbeck formula for mean-reverting process:

$$dy(t) = (\lambda y(t - 1) + \mu)dt + d\varepsilon \qquad (2.5)$$

where $d\varepsilon$ is some Gaussian noise. In the discrete form of 2.1, linear regression of $\Delta y(t)$ against $y(t - 1)$ gave us λ, and once determined, this value of λ carries over to the differential form of 2.5. But the advantage of writing the

ALGORITHMIC TRADING

equation in the differential form is that it allows for an analytical solution for the expected value of $y(t)$:

$$E(y(t)) = y_0 exp(\lambda t) - \mu/\lambda(1 - exp(\lambda t)) \qquad (2.6)$$

Remembering that λ is negative for a mean-reverting process, this tells us that the expected value of the price decays exponentially to the value $-\mu/\lambda$ with the half-life of decay equals to $-log(2)/\lambda$. This connection between a regression coefficient λ and the half-life of mean reversion is very useful to traders. First, if we find that λ is positive, this means the price series is not at all mean reverting, and we shouldn't even attempt to write a mean-reverting strategy to trade it. Second, if λ is very close to zero, this means the half-life will be very long, and a mean-reverting trading strategy will not be very profitable because we won't be able to complete many round-trip trades in a given time period. Third, this λ also determines a natural time scale for many parameters in our strategy. For example, if the half life is 20 days, we shouldn't use a look-back of 5 days to compute a moving average or standard deviation for a mean-reversion strategy. Often, setting the look-back to equal a small multiple of the half-life is close to optimal, and doing so will allow us to avoid brute-force optimization of a free parameter based on the performance of a trading strategy. We will demonstrate how to compute half-life in Example 2.4.

Example 2.4: Computing Half-Life for Mean Reversion

We concluded in the previous example that the price series USD.CAD is not stationary with at least 90 percent probability. But that doesn't necessarily mean we should give up trading this price series using a mean reversion model because most profitable trading strategies do not require such a high level of certainty. To determine whether USD.CAD is a good candidate for mean reversion trading, we will now determine its half-life of mean reversion.

To determine λ in Equations 2.1 and 2.5, we can run a regression fit with $y(t) - y(t-1)$ as the dependent variable and $y(t-1)$ as the independent variable. The regression function *ols* as well as the function *lag* are both part of the jplv7 package. (You can also use the

(Continued)

Example 2.4 (*Continued*)

MATLAB Statistics Toolbox *regress* function for this as well.) This code fragment is part of *stationaryTests.m*.

```
ylag=lag(y, 1);  % lag is a function in the jplv7
  % (spatial-econometrics.com) package.
deltaY=y-ylag;
deltaY(1)=[]; % Regression functions cannot handle the NaN
  in the first bar of the time series.
ylag(1)=[];
regress_results=ols(deltaY, [ylag ones(size(ylag))]);
halflife=-log(2)/regress_results.beta(1);
```

The result is about 115 days. Depending on your trading horizon, this may or may not be too long. But at least we know what look-back to use and what holding period to expect.

A Linear Mean-Reverting Trading Strategy

Once we determine that a price series is mean reverting, and that the half-life of mean reversion for a price series short enough for our trading horizon, we can easily trade this price series profitably using a simple linear strategy: determine the normalized deviation of the price (moving standard deviation divided by the moving standard deviation of the price) from its moving average, and maintain the number of units in this asset negatively proportional to this normalized deviation. The look-back for the moving average and standard deviation can be set to equal the half-life. We see in Example 2.5 how this linear mean reversion works for USD.CAD.

You might wonder why it is necessary to use a moving average or standard deviation for a mean-reverting strategy at all. If a price series is stationary, shouldn't its mean and standard deviation be fixed forever? Though we usually assume the mean of a price series to be fixed, in practice it may change slowly due to changes in the economy or corporate management. As for the standard deviation, recall that Equation 2.4 implies even a "stationary" price series with $0 < H < 0.5$ has a variance that increases with time, though not as rapidly as a geometric random walk. So it is appropriate to use moving average and standard deviation to allow ourselves to adapt to an ever-evolving mean and standard deviation, and also to capture profit more quickly. This point will be explored more thoroughly in Chapter 3, particularly in the context of "scaling-in."

Example 2.5: Backtesting a Linear Mean-Reverting Trading Strategy

In this simple strategy, we seek to own a number of units of USD.CAD equal to the negative normalized deviation from its moving average. The market value (in USD) of one unit of a currency pair USD.X is nothing but the quote USD.X, so in this case the linear mean reversion is equivalent to setting the market value of the portfolio to be the negative of the Z-Score of USD.CAD. The functions *movingAvg* and *movingStd* can be downloaded from my website. (This code fragment is part of *stationaryTests.m*.)

```
lookback=round(halflife); % setting lookback to the halflife
  % found above
mktVal=-(y-movingAvg(y, lookback))./movingStd(y, lookback);
pnl=lag(mktVal, 1).*(y-lag(y, 1))./lag(y, 1); % daily P&L of
  % the strategy
```

The cumulative P&L of this strategy is plotted in Figure 2.3.

Despite the long half-life, the total profit and loss (P&L) manages to be positive, albeit with a large drawdown. As with most example strategies in this book, we do not include transaction costs. Also, there is a look-ahead bias involved in this particular example due to

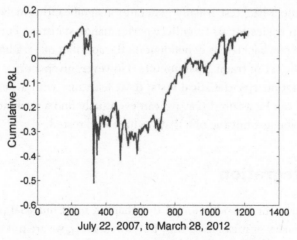

July 22, 2007, to March 28, 2012

FIGURE 2.3 Equity Curve of Linear Trading Strategy on AUDCAD.

(*Continued*)

Example 2.5 (Continued)

the use of in-sample data to find the half-life and therefore the look-back. Furthermore, an unlimited amount of capital may be needed to generate the P&L because there was no maximum imposed on the market value of the portfolio. So I certainly don't recommend it as a practical trading strategy. (There is a more practical version of this mean-reverting strategy in Chapter 5.) But it does illustrate that a nonstationary price series need not discourage us from trading a mean reversion strategy, and that we don't need very complicated strategies or technical indicators to extract profits from a mean-reverting series.

Since the goal for traders is ultimately to determine whether the expected return or Sharpe ratio of a mean-reverting trading strategy is good enough, why do we bother to go through the stationarity tests (ADF or Variance Ratio) and the calculation of half-life at all? Can't we just run a backtest on the trading strategy directly and be done with it? The reason why we went through all these preliminary tests is that their statistical significance is usually higher than a direct backtest of a trading strategy. These preliminary tests make use of every day's (or, more generally, every bar's) price data for the test, while a backtest usually generates a significantly smaller number of round trip trades for us to collect performance statistics. Furthermore, the outcome of a backtest is dependent on the specifics of a trading strategy, with a specific set of trading parameters. However, given a price series that passed the stationarity statistical tests, or at least one with a short enough half-life, we can be assured that we can eventually find a profitable trading strategy, maybe just not the one that we have backtested.

■ Cointegration

As we stated in the introduction of this chapter, most financial price series are not stationary or mean reverting. But, fortunately, we are not confined to trading those "prefabricated" financial price series: We can proactively create a portfolio of individual price series so that the market value (or price) series of this portfolio is stationary. This is the notion of cointegration: If we can find a stationary linear combination of several nonstationary price series, then these price series are called *cointegrated*. The most common combination is that of two price series: We long one asset and simultaneously short another asset, with an appropriate allocation of capital to each asset. This is the familiar "pairs trading" strategy. But the concept of cointegration easily extends to three or more assets. And in this section, we will look at two common cointegration tests: the CADF and the Johansen test. The former is suitable only for a pair of price series, while the latter is applicable to any number of series.

Cointegrated Augmented Dickey-Fuller Test

An inquisitive reader may ask: Why do we need any new tests for the stationarity of the portfolio price series, when we already have the trusty ADF and Variance Ratio tests for stationarity? The answer is that given a number of price series, we do not know *a priori* what hedge ratios we should use to combine them to form a stationary portfolio. (The hedge ratio of a particular asset is the number of units of that asset we should be long or short in a portfolio. If the asset is a stock, then the number of units corresponds to the number of shares. A negative hedge ratio indicates we should be short that asset.) Just because a set of price series is cointegrating does not mean that *any* random linear combination of them will form a stationary portfolio. But pursuing this line of thought further, what if we first determine the optimal hedge ratio by running a linear regression fit between two price series, use this hedge ratio to form a portfolio, and then finally run a stationarity test on this portfolio price series? This is essentially what Engle and Granger (1987) did. For our convenience, the spatial-econometrics.com jplv7 package has provided a *cadf* function that performs all these steps. Example 2.6 demonstrates how to use this function by applying it to the two exchange-traded funds (ETFs) EWA and EWC.

| | Example 2.6: Using the CADF Test for Cointegration | |

ETFs provide a fertile ground for finding cointegrating price series—and thus good candidates for pair trading. For example, both Canadian and Australian economies are commodity based, so they seem likely to cointegrate. The program *cointegrationTest.m* can be downloaded from my website. We assume the price series of EWA is

(Continued)

Example 2.6 (*Continued*)

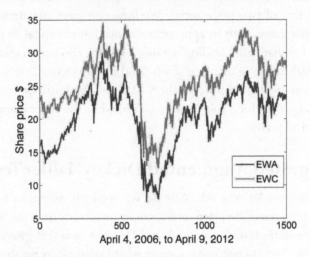

FIGURE 2.4 Share Prices of EWA versus EWC

contained in the array *x*, and that of EWC is contained in the array *y*. From Figure 2.4, we can see that they do look quite cointegrating.

A scatter plot of EWA versus EWC in Figure 2.5 is even more convincing, as the price pairs fall on a straight line.

We can use the *ols* function found in the jplv7 package to find the optimal hedge ratio.

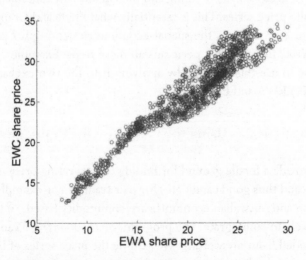

FIGURE 2.5 Scatter Plot of EWA versus EWC

Example 2.6 (*Continued*)

```
regression_result=ols(y, [x ones(size(x))]);
hedgeRatio=regression_result.beta(1);
```

As expected, the plot of the residual EWC-hedgeRatio*EWA in Figure 2.6 does look very stationary.

We use the *cadf* function of the jplv7 package for our test. Other than an extra input for the second price series, the inputs are the same as the *adf* function. We again assume that there can be a nonzero offset of the pair portfolio's price series, but the drift is zero. Note that in both the regression and the CADF test we have chosen EWA to be the independent variable *x*, and EWC to be the dependent variable *y*. If we switch the roles of EWA and EWC, will the result for the CADF test differ? Unfortunately, the answer is "yes." The hedge ratio derived from picking EWC as the independent variable will not be the exact reciprocal of the one derived from picking EWA as the independent variable. In many cases (though not for EWA-EWC, as we shall confirm later with Johansen test), only one of those hedge ratios is "correct," in the sense that only one hedge ratio will lead to a stationary portfolio. If you use the CADF test, you would have to try each variable as independent and see which order gives the best (most negative) *t*-statistic, and use that order to obtain the

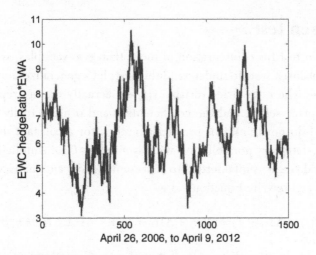

FIGURE 2.6 Stationarity of Residuals of Linear Regression between EWA versus EWC

(*Continued*)

Example 2.6 (*Continued*)

hedge ratio. For brevity, we will just assume EWA to be independent, and run the CADF test.

```
results=cadf(y, x, 0, 1);
% Print out results
prt(results);

% Output:
% Augmented DF test for co-integration variables:
    % variable   1,variable   2
% CADF t-statistic        # of lags   AR(1) estimate
%     -3.64346635                 1        -0.020411
%
%    1% Crit Value   5% Crit Value   10% Crit Value
%          -3.880          -3.359          -3.038
%          -3.880          -3.359          -3.038
```

We find that the ADF test statistic is about -3.64, certainly more negative than the critical value at the 95 percent level of -3.359. So we can reject the null hypothesis that λ is zero. In other words, EWA and EWC are cointegrating with 95 percent certainty.

ALGORITHMIC TRADING

Johansen Test

In order to test for cointegration of more than two variables, we need to use the Johansen test. To understand this test, let's generalize Equation 2.1 to the case where the price variable $y(t)$ are actually vectors representing multiple price series, and the coefficients λ and α are actually matrices. (Because I do not think it is practical to allow for a constant drift in the price of a stationary portfolio, we will assume $\beta t = 0$ for simplicity.) Using English and Greek capital letters to represent vectors and matrices respectively, we can rewrite Equation 2.1 as

$$\Delta Y(t) = \Lambda Y(t-1) + M + A_1 \Delta Y(t-1) + \cdots + A_k \Delta Y(t-k) + \epsilon_t \quad (2.7)$$

Just as in the univariate case, if $\Lambda = 0$, we do not have cointegration. (Recall that if the next move of Y doesn't depend on the current price level, there can be no mean reversion.) Let's denote the rank (remember this quaint linear algebraic term?) of Λ as r, and the number of price series n. The number of independent portfolios that can be formed by various linear combinations of the cointegrating price series is equal to r. The Johansen test will calculate r for us in two different ways, both based on eigenvector decomposition of Λ. One test produces the so-called trace statistic, and other produces the eigen statistic. (A good exposition can be found in Sorensen, 2005.) We need not worry what they are exactly, since the jplv7 package will provide critical values for each statistic to allow us to test whether we can reject the null hypotheses that $r = 0$ (no cointegrating relationship), $r \leq 1, \ldots$, up to $r \leq n - 1$. If all these hypotheses are rejected, then clearly we have $r = n$. As a useful by-product, the eigenvectors found can be used as our hedge ratios for the individual price series to form a stationary portfolio. We show how to run this test on the EWA-EWC pair in Example 2.7, where we find that the Johansen test confirms the CADF test's conclusion that this pair is cointegrating. But, more interestingly, we add another ETF to the mix: IGE, an ETF consisting of natural resource stocks. We will see how many cointegrating relations can be found from these three price series. We also use the eigenvectors to form a stationary portfolio, and find out its half-life for mean reversion.

| Example 2.7: Using the Johansen Test for Cointegration |

We take the EWA and EWC price series that we used in Example 2.6 and apply the Johansen test to them. There are three inputs to the *johansen* function of the jplv7 package: y, p, and k. y is the input matrix, with each column vector representing one price series. As in the ADF and CADF tests, we set $p = 0$ to allow the Equation 2.7 to have a constant offset ($M \neq 0$), but not a constant drift term ($\beta = 0$). The input k is the number of lags, which we again set to 1. (This code fragment is part of *cointegrationTests.m*.)

```
% Combine the two time series into a matrix y2 for input
  % into Johansen test
y2=[y, x];
results=johansen(y2, 0, 1);
% Print out results
prt(results);
```

(*Continued*)

Example 2.7 (*Continued*)

```
% Output:
Johansen MLE estimates
NULL:           Trace Statistic   Crit 90%   Crit 95%   Crit 99%
r <= 0  variable 1     19.983     13.429     15.494     19.935
r <= 1  variable 2      3.983      2.705      3.841      6.635


NULL:           Eigen Statistic   Crit 90%   Crit 95%   Crit 99%
r <= 0  variable 1     16.000     12.297     14.264     18.520
r <= 1  variable 2      3.983      2.705      3.841      6.635
```

We see that for the Trace Statistic test, the hypothesis $r = 0$ is rejected at the 99% level, and $r \leq 1$ is rejected at the 95 percent level. The Eigen Statistic test concludes that hypothesis $r = 0$ is rejected at the 95 percent level, and $r \leq 1$ is rejected at the 95 percent as well. This means that from both tests, we conclude that there are two cointegrating relationships between EWA and EWC.

What does it mean to have two cointegrating relations when we have only two price series? Isn't there just one hedge ratio that will allocate capital between EWA and EWC to form a stationary portfolio? Actually, no. Remember when we discussed the CADF test, we pointed out that it is order dependent. If we switched the role of the EWA from the independent to dependent variable, we may get a different conclusion. Similarly, when we use EWA as the dependent variable in a regression against EWC, we will get a different hedge ratio than when we use EWA as the independent variable. These two different hedge ratios, which are not necessarily reciprocal of each other, allow us to form two independent stationary portfolios. With the Johansen test, we do not need to run the regression two times to get those portfolios: Running it once will generate all the independent cointegrating relations that exist. The Johansen test, in other words, is independent of the order of the price series.

Now let us introduce another ETF to the portfolio: IGE, which consists of natural resource stocks. Assuming that its price series is contained in an array z, we will run the Johansen test on all three price series to find out how many cointegrating relationships we can get out of this trio.

Example 2.7 (*Continued*)

```
y3=[y2, z];
results=johansen(y3, 0, 1);
% Print out results
prt(results);

% Output:
%   Johansen MLE estimates
% NULL:          Trace Statistic   Crit 90%   Crit 95%   Crit 99%
% r <= 0   variable 1     34.429     27.067     29.796     35.463
% r <= 1   variable 2     17.532     13.429     15.494     19.935
% r <= 2   variable 3      4.471      2.705      3.841      6.635
%
% NULL:          Eigen Statistic   Crit 90%   Crit 95%   Crit 99%
% r <= 0   variable 1     16.897     18.893     21.131     25.865
% r <= 1   variable 2     13.061     12.297     14.264     18.520
% r <= 2   variable 3      4.471      2.705      3.841      6.635
```

Both Trace statistic and Eigen statistic tests conclude that we should have three cointegrating relations with 95 percent certainty.

The eigenvalues and eigenvectors are contained in the arrays *results.eig* and *results.evec*, respectively.

```
results.eig % Display the eigenvalues

% ans =
%
%        0.0112
%        0.0087
%        0.0030

results.evec % Display the eigenvectors

% ans =
%
%       -1.0460    -0.5797    -0.2647
%        0.7600    -0.1120    -0.0790
%        0.2233     0.5316     0.0952
```

Notice that the eigenvectors (represented as column vectors in *results.evec*) are ordered in decreasing order of their corresponding eigenvalues. So we should expect the first cointegrating relation to be

(*Continued*)

Example 2.7 (*Continued*)

the "strongest"; that is, have the shortest half-life for mean reversion. Naturally, we pick this eigenvector to form our stationary portfolio (the eigenvector determines the shares of each ETF), and we can find its half-life by the same method as before when we were dealing with a stationary price series. The only difference is that we now have to compute the $T \times 1$ array *yport,* which represents the net market value (price) of the portfolio, which is equal to the number of shares of each ETF multiplied by the share price of each ETF, then summed over all ETFs. *yport* takes the role of *y* in Example 2.4.

```
yport=smartsum(repmat(results.evec(:, 1)', [size(y3, 1) ...
   1]).*y3, 2);
```

```
% Find value of lambda and thus the half-life of mean
  % reversion by linear regression fit
ylag=lag(yport, 1);  % lag is a function in the jplv7
   % (spatial-econometrics.com) package.
deltaY=yport-ylag;
deltaY(1)=[];  % Regression functions cannot handle the NaN
   % in the first bar of the time series.
ylag(1)=[];
regress_results=ols(deltaY, [ylag ones(size(ylag))]);
halflife=-log(2)/regress_results.beta(1);
```

The half-life of 23 days is considerably shorter than the 115 days for USD.CAD, so we expect a mean reversion trading strategy to work better for this triplet.

Linear Mean-Reverting Trading on a Portfolio

In Example 2.7 we determined that the EWA-EWC-IGE portfolio formed with the "best" eigenvector from the Johansen test has a short half-life. We can now confidently proceed to backtest our simple linear mean-reverting strategy on this portfolio. The idea is the same as before when we own a number of units in USD.CAD proportional to their negative normalized deviation from its moving average (i.e., its Z-Score). Here, we also accumulate units of the portfolio proportional to the negative Z-Score of the "unit" portfolio's price. A unit portfolio is one with shares determined by the Johansen eigenvector. The share price of a unit portfolio is like the share price of a mutual fund or ETF: it is the same as its market value. When a unit portfolio has only a long and a short position in two instruments, it is usually called a *spread*. (We express this in more mathematical form in Chapter 3.)

Note that by a "linear" strategy we mean only that the number of units invested is proportional to the Z-Score, not that the market value of our investment is proportional.

This linear mean-reverting strategy is obviously not a practical strategy, at least in its simplest version, as we do not know the maximum capital required

---

Example 2.8: Backtesting a Linear Mean-Reverting Strategy on a Portfolio

The *yport* is a Tx1 array representing the net market value of the "unit" portfolio calculated in the preceding code fragment. *numUnits* is a Tx1 array representing the multiples of this unit portfolio we wish to purchase. (The multiple is a negative number if we wish to short the unit portfolio.) All other variables are as previously calculated. The *positions* is a Tx3 array representing the position (market value) of each ETF in the portfolio we have invested in. (This code fragment is part of *cointegrationTests.m*.)

```
% Apply a simple linear mean reversion strategy to EWA-EWC-
% IGE
lookback=round(halflife); % setting lookback to the halflife
% found above
numUnits =-(yport-movingAvg(yport, lookback))...
./movingStd(yport, lookback); % multiples of unit
% portfolio .  movingAvg and movingStd are functions from
% epchan.com/book2
positions=repmat(numUnits, [1 size(y3, 2)]).*repmat(results....
evec(:, 1)', [size(y3, 1) 1]).*y3;
% results.evec(:, 1)' is the shares allocation, while
% positions is the capital (dollar)
% allocation in each ETF.
pnl=sum(lag(positions, 1).*(y3-lag(y3, 1))./lag(y3, 1), 2);
% daily P&L of the strategy
ret=pnl./sum(abs(lag(positions, 1)), 2); % return is P&L
% divided by gross market value of portfolio
```

Figure 2.7 displays the cumulative returns curve of this linear mean-reverting strategy for a stationary portfolio of EWA, EWC, and IGE.

(Continued)

Example 2.8 (*Continued*)

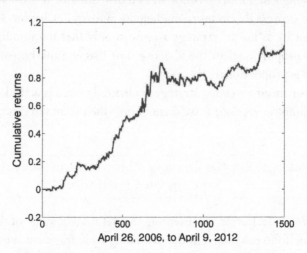

April 26, 2006, to April 9, 2012

FIGURE 2.7 Cumulative Returns of a Linear Trading Strategy on EWA-EWC-IGE Stationary Portfolio

We find that APR = 12.6 percent with a Sharpe ratio of 1.4 for the strategy.

at the outset and we cannot really enter and exit an infinitesimal number of shares whenever the price moves by an infinitesimal amount. Despite such impracticalities, the importance of backtesting a mean-reverting price series with this simple linear strategy is that it shows we can extract profits without any data-snooping bias, as the strategy has no parameters to optimize. (Remember that even the look-back is set equal to the half-life, a quantity that depends on the properties of the price series itself, not our specific trading strategy.) Also, as the strategy continuously enters and exits positions, it is likely to have more statistical significance than any other trading strategies that have more complicated and selective entry and exit rules.

■ Pros and Cons of Mean-Reverting Strategies

It is often fairly easy to construct mean-reverting strategies because we are not limited to trading instruments that are intrinsically stationary. We can pick and choose from a great variety of cointegrating stocks and ETFs to create our own stationary, mean-reverting portofolio. The fact that every year there are new ETFs created that may be just marginally different from existing ones certainly helps our cause, too.

Besides the plethora of choices, there is often a good fundamental story behind a mean-reverting pair. Why does EWA cointegrate with EWC? That's because both the Canadian and the Australian economies are dominated by commodities. Why does GDX cointegrate with GLD? That's because the value of gold-mining companies is very much based on the value of gold. Even when a cointegrating pair falls apart (stops cointegrating), we can often still understand the reason. For example, as we explain in Chapter 4, the reason GDX and GLD fell apart around the early part of 2008 was high energy prices, which caused mining gold to be abnormally expensive. We hope that with understanding comes remedy. This availability of fundamental reasoning is in contrast to many momentum strategies whose only justification is that there are investors who are slower than we are in reacting to the news. More bluntly, we must believe there are greater fools out there. But those fools do eventually catch up to us, and the momentum strategy in question may just stop working without explanation one day.

Another advantage of mean-reverting strategies is that they span a great variety of time scales. At one extreme, market-making strategies rely on prices that mean-revert in a matter of seconds. At the other extreme, fundamental investors invest in undervalued stocks for years and patiently wait for their prices to revert to their "fair" value. The short end of the time scale is particularly beneficial to traders like ourselves, since a short time scale means a higher number of trades per year, which in turn translates to higher statistical confidence and higher Sharpe ratio for our backtest and live trading, and ultimately higher compounded return of our strategy.

Unfortunately, it is because of the seemingly high consistency of mean-reverting strategy that may lead to its eventual downfall. As Michael Dever pointed out, this high consistency often lulls traders into over-confidence and overleverage as a result (Dever, 2011). (Think Long Term Capital Management.) When a mean-reverting strategy suddenly breaks down, perhaps because of a fundamental reason that is discernible only in hindsight, it often occurs when we are trading it at maximum leverage after an unbroken string of successes. So the rare loss is often very painful and sometimes catastrophic. Hence, risk management for mean reverting is particularly important, and particularly difficult since the usual stop losses cannot be logically deployed. In Chapter 8, I discuss why this is the case, as well as techniques for risk management that are suitable for mean-reverting strategies.

- Mean reversion means that the change in price is proportional to the difference between the mean price and the current price.
- Stationarity means that prices diffuse slower than a geometric random walk.
- The ADF test is designed to test for mean reversion.
- The Hurst exponent and Variance Ratio tests are designed to test for stationarity.
- Half-life of mean reversion measures how quickly a price series reverts to its mean, and is a good predictor of the profitability or Sharpe ratio of a mean-reverting trading strategy when applied to this price series.
- A linear trading strategy here means the number of units or shares of a unit portfolio we own is proportional to the negative Z-Score of the price series of that portfolio.
- If we can combine two or more nonstationary price series to form a stationary portfolio, these price series are called cointegrating.
- Cointegration can be measured by either CADF test or Johansen test.
- The eigenvectors generated from the Johansen test can be used as hedge ratios to form a stationary portfolio out of the input price series, and the one with the largest eigenvalue is the one with the shortest half-life.

ALGORITHMIC TRADING

CHAPTER 3

Implementing Mean Reversion Strategies

In the previous chapter, we described the statistical tests for determining whether a price series is stationary and therefore suitable for mean reversion trading. This price series may be the market value of a single asset, though it is rare that such stationary assets exist, or it may be the market value of a portfolio of cointegrating assets, such as the familiar long-short stock pair.

In practice, though, we should remember that we don't necessarily need true stationarity or cointegration in order to implement a successful mean reversion strategy: If we are clever, we can capture short-term or seasonal mean reversion, and liquidate our positions before the prices go to their next equilibrium level. (Seasonal mean reversion means that a price series will mean-revert only during specific periods of the day or under specific conditions.) Conversely, not all stationary series will lead to great profits—not if their half-life for mean reversion is 10 years long.

We also described a simple linear mean reversion strategy that simply "scales" into an asset in proportion to its price's deviation from the mean. It is not a very practical strategy due to the constant infinitesimal rebalancing and the demand of unlimited buying power. In this chapter, we discuss a more practical, but still simple, mean reversion strategy—

the Bollinger bands. We describe variations of this technique, including the pros and cons of using multiple entry and exit levels ("scaling-in"), and the use of the Kalman filter to estimate the hedge ratio and mean price. Finally, we highlight the danger data errors pose to mean-reverting strategies.

In presenting the backtests of any strategy in this book, we do not include transaction costs. We sometimes even commit a more egregious error of introducing look-ahead bias by using the same data for parameter optimization (such as finding the best hedge ratio) and for backtest. These are all pitfalls that we warned about in Chapter 1. The only excuse for doing this is that it makes the presentation and source codes simpler to understand. I urge readers to undertake the arduous task of cleaning up such pitfalls when implementing their own backtests of these prototype strategies.

■ Trading Pairs Using Price Spreads, Log Price Spreads, or Ratios

In constructing a portfolio for mean reversion trading in Chapter 2, we simply used the market value of the "unit" portfolio as the trading signal. This market value or price is just the weighted sums of the constituent price series, where the weights are the hedge ratios we found from linear regression or from the eigenvectors of the Johansen test:

$$y = h_1 y_1 + h_2 y_2 + \cdots + h_n y_n \qquad (3.1)$$

y is, by construction, a stationary time series, and the h_i's tell us the number of shares of each constituent stock (assuming we are trading a stock portfolio). In the case of just two stocks, this reduces to a spread familiar to many pair traders:

$$y = y_1 - h y_2. \qquad (3.2)$$

(We inserted a minus sign in Equation 3.2 to anticipate the fact that we will usually be long one stock and short another, so that h as defined this way will be positive.) Suppose instead of price series, we find that the log of prices are cointegrating, such that

$$\log(q) = h_1 \log(y_1) + h_2 \log(y_2) + \cdots + h_n \log(y_n) \qquad (3.3)$$

is stationary for some set of h's derived from either a regression fit or Johansen's eigenvectors. How do we interpret this equation, since q (for "query") is just a name given to a stationary time series that may or may not be the market value of a portfolio? To find out its properties, let's take its first difference in time:

$$\Delta\log(q) = h_1\Delta\log(y_1) + h_2\Delta\log(y_2) + \cdots + h_n\Delta\log(y_n). \qquad (3.4)$$

Remembering that $\Delta \log(x) \equiv \log(x(t)) - \log(x(t-1)) = \log(x(t)/x(t-1))$ $\approx \Delta x/x$ for small changes in x, the right hand side of Equation 3.4 becomes $h_1\Delta y_1/y_1 + h_2\Delta y_2/y_2 + \cdots + h_n\Delta y_n/y_n$, which is none other than the returns of a portfolio consisting of the n assets with weights h's. But unlike the hedge ratio h's in Equation 3.1 where they referred to the number of shares of each asset, here we can set the market value of each asset to h. So we can interpret q as the market value of a portfolio of assets with prices $y_1, y_2, \ldots, y_n$ and with constant capital weights $h_1, h_2, \ldots, h_n$, together with a cash component implicitly included, and this market value will form a stationary time series. Note that a cash component must be implicitly included in the portfolio q because if the capital weights h's are kept constant, there is no other way that the market value of the portfolio can vary with time. This cash does not show up in Equation 3.4 because its market value, of course, doesn't change from $t - 1$ to t as a result of market movement, but its value will change at t when the trader rebalances the portfolio to maintain the constancy of the capital weights, realizing some of the gains or losses, and adding to or subtracting from the cash balance. So to keep the market value of this portfolio stationary (but not constant!) requires a lot of work for the traders, as they need to constantly rebalance the portfolio, which is necessitated by using the log of prices.

The upshot of all these is that mean reversion trading using price spreads is simpler than using log price spreads, but both can be theoretically justified if both price and log price series are cointegrating. But what about the ratio of prices y_1/y_2 that many traders favor as the signal for a pair? If we look at Equation 3.1 in the case of just two price series, we notice that if $h_1 = -h_2$, then indeed $\log(y_1/y_2)$ or y_1/y_2 is stationary. But this is a special case: We normally don't expect the hedge ratios to be equal in magnitude, or equal to -1 if we normalize them. So the ratio y_1/y_2 does not necessarily form a stationary series. But as one reader mentioned, using ratios may have an advantage when the underlying pair is not truly cointegrating (http://epchan.blogspot .com/2012/02/ideas-from-psychologist.html?showComment=132980 1874131#c32786778864367113894). Suppose price A = \$10 and price B = \$5 initially, so the ratio is 2. After some time, price A increases to \$100 and price B to \$50. The spread has gone from \$5 to \$50, and we will probably find that it is not stationary. But the ratio remains 2, and a mean-reverting strategy that trades based on ratio can be equally effective whether their prices are \$10 versus \$5 or \$100 versus \$50. In other words, if your two assets are not really cointegrating but you believe their spread is still mean reverting on a short time frame, then using ratio as an indicator may work better than either price spreads or log price spreads. (This is the same idea as using moving average and standard deviation in our linear mean-reverting strategy.)

There is another good reason to use ratio when a pair is not truly cointegrating. For such pairs, we often need to use a dynamically changing hedge ratio to construct the spread. But we can dispense with this trouble if we use the ratio as a signal in this situation. But does a ratio work better than an adaptive hedge ratio with price (or log price) spreads? I don't know a general answer to this, but we can look at Example 3.1, where we compare the use of price spreads, log price spreads, and ratios in the linear mean reversion strategy involving GLD and USO, the gold and the crude oil exchange-traded funds (ETFs). You will find, in that example at least, price spreads with an adaptive hedge ratio work much better than ratio.

An interesting special case is currency trading. If we trade the currency pair EUR.GBP, we are using ratio because this is exactly equal to trading EUR.USD/GBP.USD. We already demonstrated a simple mean-reverting strategy on trading such currency pairs in Example 2.5 for USD.CAD using ratio as the signal. But about those pairs that have no ready-made cross rates on many brokerages or exchanges, such as MXN.NOK? Should we use the ratio USD.NOK/USD.MXN as the signal, or the spread USD.NOK–USD .MXN instead? Again, because MXN.NOK is not truly stationary, using the ratio MXN.NOK may be more effective. This is true even though we can't directly trade MXN.NOK, and have to trade USD.NOK and USD.MXN instead. (Trading USD.NOK and USD.MXN will generate profit and loss [P&L] denominated in both NOK and MXN. Trading MXN.NOK would have generated P&L denominated only in NOK. So the two methods are not identical.)

Example 3.1: Trading Price Spread, Log Price Spread, and Ratio

We apply the linear mean-reverting strategy from Examples 2.5 and 2.8 to the ETFs GLD and USO. But we try this strategy on the price spread, log price spread, and ratio for comparison.

Some traders believe that when oil prices go up, so do gold prices. The logic is that high oil price drives up inflation, and gold prices are positively correlated with inflation. But you can verify using one of the cointegration tests we studied in Chapter 2 that gold (represented by the ETF GLD) and oil prices (represented by USO) are not, in fact, cointegrated. (We will gloss over the difference between spot oil prices versus oil futures, which actually constitute USO. We will come back to this difference in Chapter 5). Nevertheless, we will see if there is enough short-term mean reversion to make a mean-reverting strategy profitable.

We will first try the price spread as the signal. But we need to dynamically recalculate the hedge ratio every day using a short look-back period (set to near-optimal 20 trading days with the benefit of hindsight) in order to adapt to the changing levels of the ETFs over time. The method we used to calculate the hedge ratio is linear regression, using the *ols* function from the jplv7 package as before. You can, of course, use the first eigenvector from the Johansen test instead.

The MATLAB source code can be downloaded from my website as *PriceSpread.m*. We assume the price series of GLD is contained in the Tx1 array *x*, and that of USO is contained in the Tx1 array *y*. Note that what is usually referred to as the "spread" USO-hedgeRatio*GLD is equal to the price of the unit portfolio, which we denote as *yport* in the program.

```
% lookback period for calculating the dynamically changing
  % hedge ratio
lookback=20;
hedgeRatio=NaN(size(x, 1), 1);
for t=lookback:size(hedgeRatio, 1)
    regression_result=ols(y(t-lookback+1:t), ...
    [x(t-lookback+1:t) ones(lookback, 1)]);
    hedgeRatio(t)=regression_result.beta(1);
```

(Continued)

Example 3.1 (*Continued*)

```
end
y2=[x y];
yport=sum([-hedgeRatio ones(size(hedgeRatio))].*y2, 2);
```

Plotting this spread in Figure 3.1 shows that it looks very stationary. We will now see if we can create a profitable linear mean reversion strategy. Once again, the number of units (shares) of the unit portfolio we should own is set to be the negative Z-Score, and the Tx2 *positions* array represents the market value (in dollars) of each of the constituent ETFs we should be invested in.

```
numUnits=-(spread-movingAvg(spread, lookback)) ...
   ./movingStd(spread, lookback);
positions=repmat(numUnits, [1 size(y2, 2)]).*[hedgeRatio ...
   -ones(size(hedgeRatio))].*y2; pnl=sum(lag(positions, ...
   1).*(y2-lag(y2, 1))./lag(y2, 1), 2); % daily P&L of the
   % strategy
ret=pnl./sum(abs(lag(positions, 1)), 2); % return is P&L
   % divided by gross market value of portfolio
```

We obtain an annual percentage rate (APR) of about 10.9 percent and Sharpe ratio of about 0.59 using price spread with a dynamic hedge ratio, even though GLD and USO are by no means cointegrated.

Next, we will see if using log prices will make any difference. The source code for this is in *LogPriceSpread.m*, but we will display here the only two lines that are different from *PriceSpread.m*:

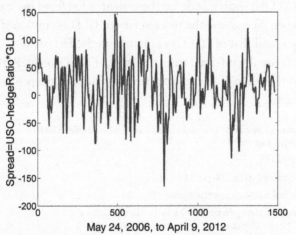

May 24, 2006, to April 9, 2012

FIGURE 3.1 Spread between USO and GLD Using a Changing Hedge Ratio

Example 3.1 (*Continued*)

```
regression_result=ols(log(y(t-lookback+1:t)), ...
    [log(x(t-lookback+1:t)) ones(lookback, 1)]);
```

and

```
yport=sum([-hedgeRatio ones(size(hedgeRatio))].*log(y2), ...
    2); % The net market value of the portfolio is same as
    % the "spread"
```

The APR of 9 percent and Sharpe ratio of 0.5 are actually lower than the ones using the price spread strategy, and this is before accounting for the extra transactions costs associated with rebalancing the portfolio every day to maintain the capital allocation to each ETF.

Next, we will try using ratio as the signal. In this case, we will also require the long and short side to have the same dollar capital. The source code is in *Ratio.m*. It is interesting to look at a plot of the ratio in Figure 3.2 first.

You can see that the ratio actually doesn't look very stationary at all, compared with either the price spread or adaptive hedge ratio. So it should not surprise us if we find the mean-reverting strategy to perform poorly, with a negative APR.

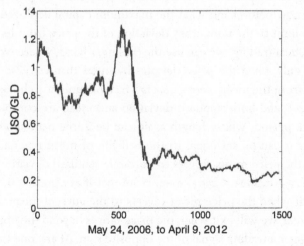

May 24, 2006, to April 9, 2012

FIGURE 3.2   Ratio = USO/GLD

(*Continued*)

Example 3.1 (*Continued*)

```
lookback=20; % Lookback is set arbitrarily
ratio=y./x;
ratio(1:lookback)=[]; % Removed to have same test set as
    % price spread and log price spread strategies
x(1:lookback)=[];
y(1:lookback)=[];


% Apply a simple linear mean reversion strategy to GLD-USO
numUnits=-(ratio-movingAvg(ratio, lookback))...
    ./movingStd(ratio, lookback); positions=repmat(numUnits, ...
    [1 2]).*[-ones(size(x, 1), 1) ones(size(x, 1), 1)];
    pnl=sum(lag(positions, 1).*([x y]-lag([x y], 1)). ...
    /lag([x y], 1), 2); ret=pnl./sum(abs(lag(positions, 1)), 2);
```

■ Bollinger Bands

The only mean-reversal strategy I have described so far is the linear strategy: simply scale the number of units invested in a stationary unit portfolio to be proportional to the deviation of the market value (price) of the unit portfolio from a moving average. This simple strategy is chosen because it is virtually parameterless, and therefore least subject to data-snooping bias. While this linear strategy is useful for demonstrating whether mean reversion trading can be profitable for a given portfolio, it is not practical because we don't know beforehand what the maximum capital deployed will be, as there is no limit to the temporary deviation of the price from its average.

For practical trading, we can use the Bollinger band, where we enter into a position only when the price deviates by more than *entryZscore* standard deviations from the mean. *entryZscore* is a free parameter to be optimized in a training set, and both standard deviation and mean are computed within a look-back period, whose length again can be a free parameter to be optimized, or it can be set equal to the half-life of mean reversion. We can exit when the price mean-reverts to *exitZscore* standard deviations from the mean, where *exitZscore* < *entryZscore*. Note that if *exitZscore* = 0, this means we will exit when the price mean-reverts to the current mean. If *exitZscore* = −*entryZscore*, we will exit when the price moves beyond the opposite band so as to trigger a trading signal of the opposite sign. At any one time, we can have either zero or one unit (long or short) invested, so it is very easy to allocate capital to this strategy or to manage its risk. If we set the look-back to a short period, and small *entryZscore* and *exitZscore* magnitude, we will get a shorter holding period and more round trip trades and generally higher profits. We illustrate the Bollinger band technique in Example 3.2 using the pair GLD-USO we discussed above.

Example 3.2: Bollinger Band Mean Reversion Strategy

We traded GLD-USO in Example 3.1 using price spread USO-hedgeRatio*GLD as the signal with a linear mean reversion strategy. Here, we simply switch to a Bollinger band strategy, using the *entryZscore* = 1 and *exitZscore* = 0, with the first part of the program identical to *PriceSpread.m*. The present source code is in *bollinger.m*. Notice that the entry signals *longsEntry* and *shortsEntry* are Tx1 logical arrays, as are the exit signals *longsExit* and *shortsExit*. We initialize the number of units of the unit portfolio on the long side, *numUnitsLong*, a Tx1 array, and then set one of its values to 1 if we have a long entry signal, and to 0 if we have a long exit signal; and vice versa for the number of units on the short side. For those days that do not have any entry or exit signals, we use the *fillMissingData* function to carry forward the previous day's units. (*fillMissingData* starts with the second row of an array, and overwrites any cell's NaN value with the corresponding cell's value in the previous row. It can be downloaded from my website.) Once *numUnitsLong* and *numUnitsShort* are computed, we can combine them to find the net number of units denoted by *numUnits*. The rest of the program is the same as in Example 3.1's *PriceSpread.m*.

```
% Bollinger band strategy
entryZscore=1;
exitZscore=0;

zScore=(yport-movingAvg(yport, lookback))./movingStd(yport, ...
  lookback);

longsEntry=zScore < -entryZscore; % a long position means we
  % should buy EWC
longsExit=zScore >= -exitZscore;

shortsEntry=zScore > entryZscore;
shortsExit=zScore <= exitZscore;

numUnitsLong=NaN(length(yport), 1);
```

(Continued)

Example 3.2 (*Continued*)

```
numUnitsShort=NaN(length(yport), 1);

numUnitsLong(1)=0;
numUnitsLong(longsEntry)=1;
numUnitsLong(longsExit)=0;
numUnitsLong =fillMissingData(numUnitsLong);

numUnitsShort(1)=0;
numUnitsShort(shortsEntry)=-1;
numUnitsShort(shortsExit)=0;
numUnitsShort =fillMissingData(numUnitsShort);

numUnits= numUnitsLong + numUnitsShort;
```

The Bollinger band strategy has an APR = 17.8 percent, and Sharpe ratio of 0.96, quite an improvement from the linear mean reversal strategy! The cumulative returns curve is shown on Figure 3.3.

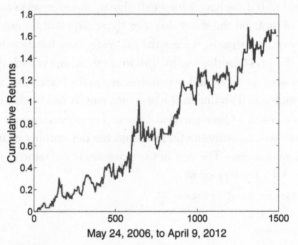

May 24, 2006, to April 9, 2012

FIGURE 3.3 Cumulative Returns of Bollinger Band Strategy on GLD-USO

■ Does Scaling-in Work?

The notion of scaling into a position with a mean-reverting strategy is familiar to many traders. (Another name for it is *averaging-in*.) As the price (of an asset, a spread, or a portfolio) deviates further and further from its mean, the potential profit to be reaped from an eventual reversal is also increasing; thus, it makes sense to increase the capital invested. This is exactly what our linear mean-reversal strategy does. Note also that this type of scaling-in strategies also scale out gradually: We do not have to wait until the price reverts to its mean before taking profits. The advantage of being able to exit whenever the price reverts by a small increment is that even if the price series is not really stationary and therefore never really reverts to its mean, we can still be profitable by constantly realizing small profits. An added benefit is that if you are trading large sizes, scaling-in and -out will reduce the market impact of the entry and exit trades. If we want to implement scaling-in using Bollinger bands, we can just have multiple entries and exits: for example, $entryZscore = 1, 2, 3, \ldots, N$ and $exitZscore = 0, 1, 2, \ldots, N - 1$. Of course, N is another parameter to be optimized using a training data set.

All of these seemed very commonsensical until the research by Schoenberg and Corwin proved that entering or exiting at two or more Bollinger bands is never optimal; that is, you can always find a single entry/exit level that will generate a higher average return in a backtest (Schoenberg and Corwin, 2010). They call this optimal single entry method "all-in."

To illustrate their point, let's say a future contract has recently dropped to a price L_1, and you expect it to revert to a higher final price $F > L_1$ (we have to assume mean reversion to compare averaging-in versus all-in), though there is a probability p that the price will go lower to $L_2 < L_1$ before rebounding to F. These possibilities are illustrated in Figure 3.4. We have just enough buying power to invest in a total of two contracts, whether at prices L_1, L_2, or F. Let's compare the three different methods of entry:

I. All-in at L_1: We invest all our capital when the price reaches L_1, not caring whether it will go lower to L_2.

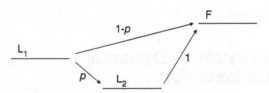

FIGURE 3.4 Two Possible Paths of Mean Reversion. Path 1 (with probability p) has price drops further from L_1 to L_2 before reverting to F. Path 2 (with probability $1 - p$) has price immediately reverts to F. (Note that mean reversion is guaranteed one way or the other in this example.)

II. All-in at L_2: We wait until the price reaches L_2 before investing all our capital. (Therefore, we invest nothing and earn zero returns if the price never reaches L_2.)

III. Average-in: We invest in one contract when the price reaches L_1, and in another contract if the price reaches L_2.

In all cases, we exit all contracts only when the price reaches F (so no average-out, even if there is average-in). What are the expected profits of each alternative? The expected profits in points are:

I. $2(F - L_1)$
II. $2p(F - L_2)$
III. $p[(F - L_1) + (F - L_2)] + (1 - p)(F - L_1) = (F - L_1) + p(F - L_2)$

Obviously, if $p = 0$, method I is the most profitable. If $p = 1$, method II is the most profitable. In fact, there is a transition probability $\hat{p} = (F - L_1) / (F - L_2)$ such that if $p < \hat{p}$, method I is more profitable than II, and vice versa if $p > \hat{p}$. It is also easy to show that if $p < \hat{p}$, method I is also more profitable than III, and if $p > \hat{p}$, method II is more profitable than III. So there is no situation where the average-in strategy is the most profitable one!

So does that mean the whole idea of scaling-in/averaging-in has been debunked? Not necessarily. Notice the implicit assumption made in my illustration: the probability of deviating to L_2 before reverting to F is constant throughout time. In real life, we may or may not find this probability to be constant. In fact, volatility is usually not constant, which means that p will not be constant either. In this circumstance, scaling-in is likely to result in a better realized Sharpe ratio if not profits. Another way to put it is that even though you will find that scaling-in is never optimal in-sample, you may well find that it outperforms the all-in method out-of-sample.

■ Kalman Filter as Dynamic Linear Regression

For a pair of truly cointegrating price series, determination of the hedge ratio is quite easy: just take as much historical data as you can find, and use ordinary least square (OLS) for a regression fit or use the Johansen test to find the eigenvectors. But as we have emphasized before, stationarity and cointegration are ideals that few real price series can achieve. So how best to estimate the current hedge ratio for a pair of real price series when it can vary with time? In all the mean-reverting strategies we have discussed so far, we just took a moving look-back period and computed the regression coefficient or Johansen eigenvector over data in that period only. This has the disadvantage that if the look-back period is short, the deletion of the earliest bar and the inclusion of the latest bar as time moves forward can have an abrupt and artificial impact on the hedge ratio. We face the same problem if we use moving averages or moving standard deviations to calculate the current mean and standard deviation of a price series. In all cases, we may be able to improve the estimate by using a weighting scheme that gives more weight to the latest data, and less weight to the earlier data, without an arbitrary cutoff point. The familiar exponential moving average (EMA) is one such weighting scheme, but it is not clear why an exponential decrease in weights is optimal either. Here, we will describe a scheme of updating the hedge ratio using the Kalman filter that avoids the problem of picking a weighting scheme arbitrarily (Montana, Triantafyllopoulos, and Tsagaris, 2009).

Kalman filter is an optimal linear algorithm that updates the expected value of a hidden variable based on the latest value of an observable variable. (For a good exposition of this topic, see Kleeman, 2007.) It is linear because it assumes that the observable variable is a linear function of the hidden variable with noise. It also assumes the hidden variable at time t is a linear function of itself at time $t - 1$ with noise, and that the noises present in these functions have Gaussian distributions (and hence can be specified with an evolving covariance matrix, assuming their means to be zero.) Because of all these linear relations, the expected value of the hidden variable at time t is also a linear function of its expected value prior to the observation at t, as well as a linear function of the value of the observed variable at t. The Kalman filter is optimal in the sense that it is the best estimator available if we assume that the noises are Gaussian, and it minimizes the mean square error of the estimated variables.

For every application of Kalman filtering, we need to first figure out what these variables and matrices are:

- Observable variable (vector)

- Hidden variable (vector)

- State transition model (matrix)

- Observation model (matrix)

This is actually the only creative part of the application because once these quantities are specified, the rest is just a robotic application of an existing algorithm. As traders, we don't need to know how to derive the relationships between these quantities—we only need to know where to find a good software package that gives us the right answer.

In our application where the focus is to find the hedge ratio and the average mean and volatility of the spread, the *observable variable* is one of the price series y, and the *hidden variable* is the hedge ratio β. The linear function that relates y and β is, of course,

$$y(t) = x(t)\,\beta(t) + \epsilon(t), \qquad \text{(``Measurement equation'')} \qquad (3.5)$$

where x is the price series of the other asset, and ϵ is a Gaussian noise with variance V_ϵ. As we typically allow the spread between x and y to have a nonzero mean, we will use a 2×1 vector β to denote both the intercept μ and the slope of the linear relation between x and y, and we will augment $x(t)$ with a column vector of ones to create an $N \times 2$ array to allow for the constant offset between x and y. x actually serves as the *observation model* in the Kalman filter lingo.

It may seem strange that we regard only $y(t)$ as an observable but not $x(t)$, but this is just a mathematical trick, as every variable in the Kalman filter equations is observable except for the hidden variable and the noises, and so we have the freedom to designate which variable is *the* "observable" (y) and which one is the "observation model" (x). Next, we make a crucial assumption that the regression coefficient (our hidden variable) at time t is the same as that at time $t-1$ plus noise

$$\beta(t) = \beta(t-1) + \omega(t-1), \qquad \text{(``State transition'')} \qquad (3.6)$$

where ω is also a Gaussian noise but with covariance V_ω. In other words, the *state transition model* here is just the identity matrix.

Given the specification of the four important quantities in italics, Kalman filtering can now iteratively generate the expected value of the hidden variable β given an observation at t. One noteworthy benefit of using the Kalman filter to find β is that not only do we obtain a dynamic hedge ratio between the two assets, we also simultaneously obtain what we used to call "the moving average" of the spread. This is because, as we mentioned, β includes both the slope and the intercept between y and x. The best current estimate of the intercept is used in place of the moving average of the spread. But, as your telemarketer often reminds you, that's not all! As a by-product, it also generates an estimate of the standard deviation of the forecast error of the observable variable, which we can use in place of the moving standard deviation of a Bollinger band.

Despite the linearity of Kalman filtering, the matrix relations relating various quantities may seem quite complex, so I relegate them to Box 3.1 here for the patient reader to peruse.

Actually, besides the iterative equations, we also need to specify the (co) variances V_ϵ and V_ω of the measurement and state transition equations. These specifications will be included in Box 3.1 as well.

BOX 3.1

The Iterative Equations of the Kalman Filter

We denote the expected value of β at t given observation at $t - 1$ by $\hat{\beta}(t|t - 1)$, the expected value of β given observation at t by $\hat{\beta}(t|t)$, and the expected value of $y(t)$ given the observation at $t - 1$ by $\hat{y}(t|t - 1)$. Given the quantities $\hat{\beta}(t - 1|t - 1)$ and $R(t - 1|t - 1)$ at time $t - 1$, we can make the one-step predictions

$$\hat{\beta}(t|t - 1) = \hat{\beta}(t - 1|t - 1) \quad \text{("State prediction")} \quad (3.7)$$

$$R(t|t - 1) = R(t - 1|t - 1) + V_w \quad \text{("State covariance prediction")} \quad (3.8)$$

$$\hat{y}(t) = x(t)\hat{\beta}(t|t - 1) \quad \text{("Measurement prediction")} \quad (3.9)$$

$$Q(t) = x(t)'R(t|t - 1)x(t) + V_e \quad \text{("Measurement variance prediction")} \quad (3.10)$$

where $R(t|t - 1)$ is $\text{cov}(\beta(t) - \hat{\beta}(t|t - 1))$, measuring the covariance of the error of the hidden variable estimates. (It is a covariance instead of a variance because β has two independent components.) Similarly, $R(t|t)$ is $\text{cov}(\beta(t) - \hat{\beta}(t|t))$. Remembering that the hidden variable consists of both the mean of the spread as well as the hedge ratio, R is a 2×2 matrix. $e(t) = y(t) - x(t)\hat{\beta}(t|t - 1)$ is the forecast error for $y(t)$ given observation at $t - 1$, and $Q(t)$ is $\text{var}(e(t))$, measuring the variance of the forecast error.

After observing the measurement at time t, the famous Kalman filter state estimate update and covariance update equations are

$$\hat{\beta}(t|t) = \hat{\beta}(t|t - 1) + K(t) * e(t) \quad \text{("State update")} \quad (3.11)$$

$$R(t|t) = R(t|t - 1) - K(t) * x(t) * R(t|t - 1) \quad \text{("State covariance update")} \quad (3.12)$$

where $K(t)$ is called the Kalman gain and is given by

$$K(t) = R(t|t - 1) * x(t)/Q(t) \quad (3.13)$$

To start off these recursions, we assume $\hat{\beta}(1|0) = 0$, $R(0|0) = 0$. But what about V_w and V_e? There is a method to estimate these variances from data called autocovariance least squares developed by Rajamani and Rawlings (2007, 2009). There is even a free Matlab/Octave package for implementing

(Continued)

77

IMPLEMENTING MEAN REVERSION STRATEGIES

BOX 3.1 (Continued)

this method at http://jbrwww.che.wisc.edu/software/als. But for simplicity, we will follow Montana and assume $v_\omega = \frac{\delta}{1-\delta} I$, where δ is a parameter between 0 and 1, and I is a 2 × 2 identity matrix. If $\delta = 0$, this means $\beta(t) = \beta(t-1)$, which reduces the Kalman filter to ordinary least square regression with a fixed offset and slope. If $\delta = 1$, this means the estimated β will fluctuate wildly based on the latest observation. The optimal δ, just like the optimal lookback in a moving linear regression, can be obtained using training data. With the benefit of hindsight, we pick $\delta = 0.0001$. With the same hindsight, we also pick $V_e = 0.001$.

In Example 3.3, we describe the actual implementation of using the Kalman filter to estimate a dynamic β for the EWA-EWC pair we discussed in Example 2.7.

Example 3.3: Kalman Filter Mean Reversion Strategy

We will now implement the Kalman filter equations 3.5 through 3.13 and apply them to the EWA-EWC pair. The code can be downloaded as *KF_beta_EWA_EWC.m*. We assume the price series of EWA is stored in a Tx1 array *x*, and that of EWC is stored in a Tx1 array *y*.

```
% Augment x with ones to accommodate possible offset in the
  % regression
% between y vs x.
x=[x ones(size(x))];

delta=0.0001; % delta=0 allows no change (like traditional
  % linear regression).

yhat=NaN(size(y)); % measurement prediction
e=NaN(size(y)); % measurement prediction error
Q=NaN(size(y)); % measurement prediction error variance

% For clarity, we denote R(t|t) by P(t).
% initialize P and beta.
P=zeros(2);
beta=NaN(2, size(x, 1));
Vw=delta/(1-delta)*diag(ones(2, 1));
Ve=0.001;

% Initialize beta(:, 1) to zero
beta(:, 1)=0;
```

Example 3.3 (*Continued*)

```
for t=1:length(y)
    if (t > 1)
        beta(:, t)=beta(:, t-1); % state prediction.
          % Equation 3.7
        R=P+Vw; % state covariance prediction. Equation 3.8
    end

    yhat(t)=x(t, :)*beta(:, t); % measurement prediction.
      % Equation 3.9

    Q(t)=x(t, :)*R*x(t, :)'+Ve; % measurement variance
      % prediction. Equation 3.10


    % Observe y(t)
    e(t)=y(t)-yhat(t); % measurement prediction error

    K=R*x(t, :)'/Q(t); % Kalman gain

    beta(:, t)=beta(:, t)+K*e(t); % State update.
      % Equation 3.11
    P=R-K*x(t, :)*R; % State covariance update. Euqation 3.12

End
```

We can see from Figure 3.5 that with $\delta = 0.0001$, the Kalman-updated slope $\beta(1, t)$ of a linear fit between EWC (y) and EWA (x) oscillates around 1.

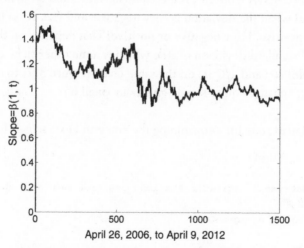

April 26, 2006, to April 9, 2012

FIGURE 3.5 Kalman Filter Estimate of the Slope between EWC (y) and EWA (x)

(*Continued*)

Example 3.3 (*Continued*)

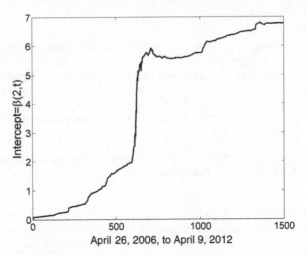

April 26, 2006, to April 9, 2012

FIGURE 3.6 Kalman Filter Estimate of the Intercept between EWC (y) and EWA (x)

We can also see from Figure 3.6 that the Kalman-updated intercept $\beta(2, t)$ increases monotonically with time.

We can utilize these and other quantities computed from the Kalman filter to create a mean-reverting strategy. The measurement prediction error $e(t)$ (previously called the forecast error for $y(t)$ given observation at $t - 1$) is none other than the deviation of the spread EWC-EWA from its predicted mean value, and we will buy this spread when the deviation is very negative, and vice versa if it is very positive. How negative or positive? That depends on the predicted standard deviation of $e(t)$, which is none other than $\sqrt{Q(t)}$. We can plot $e(t)$ and $\sqrt{Q(t)}$ on the same chart (Figure 3.7) to see that $\sqrt{Q(t)}$ changes quite slowly given our small δ.

The Matlab code for determining the entry and exit signals follows.

```
y2=[x(:, 1) y];

longsEntry=e < -sqrt(Q); % a long position means we should
    % buy EWC
longsExit=e > -sqrt(Q);

shortsEntry=e > sqrt(Q);
shortsExit=e < sqrt(Q);
```

Example 3.3 (*Continued*)

Once the entry and exit signals are determined, the rest of the code is the same as *bollinger.m*—just substitute *beta(1, :)* in place of *hedgeRatio*. It has a reasonable APR of 26.2 percent and a Sharpe ratio of 2.4. Its cumulative returns are plotted on Figure 3.8.

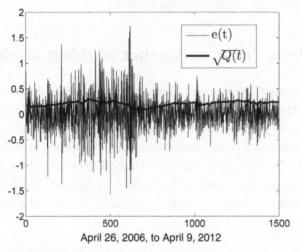

April 26, 2006, to April 9, 2012

FIGURE 3.7 Measurement Prediction Error *e(t)* and Standard Deviation of *e(t)*

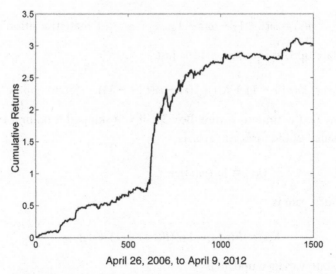

April 26, 2006, to April 9, 2012

FIGURE 3.8 Cumulative Returns of Kalman Filter Strategy on EWA-EWC

(*Continued*)

Example 3.3 (*Continued*)

Instead of coding the Kalman filter yourself as we demonstrated, you can also use many free open-source MATLAB codes available. One such package can be found at www.cs.ubc.ca/~murphyk /Software/Kalman/kalman.html. Kalman filters are also available from MATLAB's Control System Toolbox.

■ Kalman Filter as Market-Making Model

There is another noteworthy application of Kalman filter to a mean-reverting strategy. In this application we are concerned with only one mean-reverting price series; we are not concerned with finding the hedge ratio between two cointegrating price series. However, as before, we still want to find the mean price and the standard deviation of the price series for our mean reversion trading. So the mean price $m(t)$ is the hidden variable here, and the price $y(t)$ is the observable variable. The measurement equation in this case is trivial:

$$y(t) = m(t) + \epsilon(t), \qquad \text{(“Measurement equation”)} \quad (3.14)$$

with the same state transition equation

$$m(t) = m(t-1) + \omega(t-1). \qquad \text{(“State transition”)} \quad (3.15)$$

So the state update equation 3.11 is just

$$m(t \mid t) = m(t \mid t-1) + K(t)(y(t) - m(t \mid t-1)). \quad \text{(“State update”)} \quad (3.16)$$

(This may be the time to review Box 3.1 if you skipped it on first reading.) The variance of the forecast error is

$$Q(t) = Var(m(t)) + V_e. \qquad (3.17)$$

The Kalman gain is

$$K(t) = R(t \mid t-1)/(R(t \mid t-1) + V_e), \qquad (3.18)$$

and the state variance update is

$$R(t \mid t) = (1 - K(t))R(t \mid t-1). \qquad (3.19)$$

Why are these equations worth highlighting? Because this is a favorite model for market makers to update their estimate of the mean price of an asset, as Euan Sinclair pointed out (Sinclair, 2010). To make these equations more practical, practitioners make further assumptions about the measurement error V_e, which, as you may recall, measures the uncertainty of the observed transaction price. But how can there be uncertainty in the observed transaction price? It turns out that we can interpret the uncertainty in such a way that if the trade size is large (compared to some benchmark), then the uncertainty is small, and vice versa. So V_e in this case becomes a function of t as well. If we denote the trade size as T and the benchmark trade size as T_{max}, then V_e can have the form

$$V_e = R(t \mid t - 1) \left(\frac{T}{T_{max}} - 1 \right) \tag{3.20}$$

So you can see that if $T = T_{max}$, there is no uncertainty in the observed price, and the Kalman gain is 1, and hence the new estimate of the mean price $m(t)$ is exactly equal to the observed price! But what should T_{max} be? It can be some fraction of the total trading volume of the previous day, for example, where the exact fraction is to be optimized with some training data.

Note the similarity of this approach to the so-called volume-weighted average price (VWAP) approach to determine the mean price, or fair value of an asset. In the Kalman filter approach, not only are we giving more weights to trades with larger trade sizes, we are also giving more weights to more recent trade prices. So one might compare this to volume *and* time-weighted average price.

■ The Danger of Data Errors

Data errors have a particularly insidious effect on both backtesting and executing mean-reverting strategies.

If there are errors, or "outliers," in the historical data used for backtesting, then these errors usually inflate the backtest performance of mean-reverting strategies. For example, if the actual trade prices of a stock at 11:00, 11:01, and 11:02 were $100, $100, and $100, but the historical data erroneously recorded them as $100, $110, $100, then your mean-reverting strategy's backtest is likely to have shorted the stock at 11:01 ($110), and then covered the position at 11:02 ($100) and made a tidy but fictitious profit of $10. You can see that data quality is particularly important for intraday data, because they present much more numerous opportunities for such errors. That's why reputable data vendors took great care in incorporating the exchange-provided cancel-and-correct codes to correct any trades that may have been canceled due to transaction prices that are too far from "normal." (What constitutes a "normal" price is solely determined, sometimes on a case-by-case basis, by the relevant exchange.) Thomas Falkenberry (2002) has written more on data cleansing issues.

However, this type of data error will suppress the backtest performance of momentum strategies, so it is not as dangerous. In the preceding example, a momentum strategy will likely buy the stock at 11:01 ($110) in backtest, and may be stopped out at a loss at 11:02 ($100).

The same kind of errors will, of course, trigger wrong trades in live trading as well, often resulting in real-life losses. In the preceding example, if the prices were bid prices, and we have the erroneous bid at $110 at 11:02, then our execution program may have sent a short market sell order at that time, which unfortunately will be filled at $100 instead since there was actually no bid at $110.

This problem with erroneous live bid/ask quotes is particularly dangerous when trading pairs or other arbitrage strategies, because in these strategies we often depend on the *differences* of the price quotes from various instruments to trigger trading signals. The difference of a pair of quotes is usually of much smaller magnitude than the quotes themselves, so any error in the quotes results in a much bigger percentage error in the spread. For example, if we are trading a pair of stocks X and Y, and X has a true bid price of $100 and Y has a true ask price of $105, so the spread Y−X is $5, which may be too small to trigger an market order to buy X and sell Y. But if data error causes Y to display an ask price of $106, then the erroneous spread becomes $6, an increase of 20 percent over the real spread of $5, and this may be enough to trigger an erroneous order to buy X and sell Y.

I have seen this problem in live trading when I used a broker's data feed to drive an equities pair-trading strategy. That data feed quite regularly triggered losing trades that I could not explain, until I switched the data feed to a third-party provider (nothing fancier than Yahoo! real-time quotes) and the bad trades stopped. Later on, I had access to Bloomberg's live data feed, and it didn't trigger any of these bad trades either.

Bad ticks in live data will also cause momentum strategies to send wrong orders. So they are equally loss-inducing to the execution of those strategies.

- Do you want to construct a mean-reverting portfolio with a fixed number of shares during the duration of a trade? Use price series to determine the hedge ratios.

- Do you want to construct a mean-reverting portfolio with fixed market values for each constituent during the duration of a trade? Use log price series to determine the hedge ratios.

- Ratio, instead of spreads, is often a good indicator for trading currency pairs.

- Afraid that the hedge ratio, mean, and standard deviation of a spread may vary in the future? Use a moving look-back period or the Kalman filter.

- A practical implementation of a linear trading strategy is the Bollinger bands with scaling-in.

- Scaling-in may not be optimal in backtests but is often useful for live trading where volatilities and probabilities do change.

- Do you want to dynamically update the expected price of an instrument based on its latest trade (price and size)? Use the Kalman filter.

- Data errors can inflate the backtest results of mean-reverting strategies but not momentum strategies.

- Strategies based on spreads are particularly sensitive to small data errors, whether in backtest or live trading.

CHAPTER 4

Mean Reversion of Stocks and ETFs

The stock market is, in a sense, the most fertile ground for finding mean-reverting instruments and for the application of those basic mean reversion trading techniques described in the previous two chapters. In theory, we can form pairs of stocks belonging to any sector and expect them to cointegrate due to their exposure to many common economic factors. Their number is large, so diversification is easy. In practice, though, there are some serious difficulties with applying these generic techniques to trading stocks and ETFs. This chapter will examine issues specific to stocks and ETFs. I will also demonstrate that simple mean-reverting strategies actually work better for ETF pairs and triplets.

But we need not limit ourselves to those strategies described in Chapter 3 when looking for mean reversion in stocks or ETFs. We find that in the short term, most stocks exhibit mean-reverting properties under normal circumstances. (Normal circumstance means there isn't any news on the stock, a topic that is taken up in Chapter 7.) This is despite the fact that stock prices follow geometric random walks over the long term. We will build a strategy to exploit this short-term, or "seasonal," mean reversion.

Index arbitrage is another familiar mean reversion strategy. In this case, we are counting on the cointegration of stocks versus futures or stocks versus ETFs. Because little profit is left using the traditional implementation of index arbitrage, we give an example of a modified strategy.

As mentioned before, in addition to the familiar time series mean reversion to which we have devoted all our attention so far, there is the phenomenon of cross-sectional mean reversion, which is prevalent in baskets of stocks. Recall that in time series mean reversion, the prices are reverting to a mean determined by their own historical prices, while cross-sectional mean reversion means that the cumulative returns of the instruments in a basket will revert to the cumulative return of the basket. The statistical tests for time series mean reversion are largely irrelevant for cross-sectional mean reversion. This additional type of mean reversion makes creating any sort of mean-reverting strategy for stocks even easier.

Because of this ease of finding mean-reverting patterns, the stock market attracts a large number of traders, often called *statistical arbitrageurs,* to exploit such patterns. As a result, the returns in such strategies have generally decreased. We discuss a few simple tricks that can boost their otherwise declining performances.

Once again, we emphasize that the backtesting results in this book do not include transaction costs. One reason for this omission is that transaction costs can depend quite sensitively on the exact execution method used and the exact stock universe chosen for the stock models. A more specific pitfall included in the backtesting of the stock models is the use of data with survivorship bias, since survivorship bias-free data is more cumbersome and expensive to assemble. The hope is that the results are not too unrealistic, at least for results in the past year or two. If you intend to redo the backtests with survivorship bias–free databases, you should remember that the chosen stock index (typically Standard & Poor's [S&P] 500) has a changing composition throughout its history, too. To do this properly, you would need a database containing the historical daily index compositions. Remember also the issue of primary versus consolidated stock prices discussed in Chapter 1. The historical prices used here are all consolidated opens and closes. But if you implement some of these strategies using market-on-open (MOO) or limit-on-open (LOO) orders, or similarly market-on-close (MOC) or limit-on-close (LOC) orders, you will be filled at the primary exchange open or close. Usually, this means that the actual returns will be lower than those reported here.

■ The Difficulties of Trading Stock Pairs

Pair trading of stocks is the first type of algorithmic mean reversion strategy institutional traders invented, reportedly by Gerry Bamberger at Morgan Stanley (Patterson, 2010). Yet nowadays it can be surprisingly difficult to squeeze profits out of it.

If we test the daily price series of individual stocks, they almost never meet the definition of stationarity as defined in Chapter 2. The geometric random walk describes their behaviors fairly well: once they walked away, they seldom returned to their starting points. (Their intraday and seasonal mean-reverting properties are special cases to be discussed later on.)

Even if you pair them up in some sensible way (e.g., Exxon versus Chevron, or Citibank versus Bank of America), they are seldom cointegrating *out-of-sample*. I emphasize out-of-sample because it is quite easy to find cointegrating stock pairs in any chosen period of time, but they can just as easily lose cointegration in the subsequent out-of-sample period. The reason for this difficulty is that the fortunes of one company can change very quickly depending on management decisions and the competition. The fact that two companies are in the same industry sector does not guarantee that they will be subjected to the same fortune (think AAPL versus BBRY). The upshot is that it is difficult to be consistently profitable in trading a single pair of stocks using a mean-reverting strategy unless you have a fundamental understanding of each of the companies and can exit a position in time before bad news on one of them becomes public.

What if we trade a large number of pairs of stocks, so that occasional derailment of some pairs would not affect the profitability of the entire portfolio? The law of large numbers will only work in our favor if the expected return of an individual pair in the out-of-sample period is positive, but I have not found this to be the case for stock pairs. Apparently, the small profits gained by the "good" pairs have been completely overwhelmed by the large losses of the pairs that have gone "bad."

Other than these fundamental problems with stock pairs trading, there are two additional technical difficulties.

The first difficulty is short-sale constraint. It is particularly dangerous for a stock pair that involves shorting a hard-to-borrow stock, because even if your position is ultimately profitable, you may be forced to liquidate it at the most unprofitable and inopportune time. This may happen when you are short this stock and it suddenly jumps up in value due to some unexpected good news, and many lenders of this stock are eager to sell them. In this case, your borrowed stock may be recalled, and you will be forced to buy to cover this position at a big loss, while selling the long position on the other leg. This is called the *short squeeze*.

Under the same heading of short-sale constraint, the new alternative uptick rule in effect in the U.S. stock markets since 2010 also creates uncertainty in both backtesting and live executions of stock pairs strategy. Once the circuit breaker is triggered, we are essentially forbidden to send short market orders.

The second difficulty arises in the intraday trading of stock pairs. Since the profit margins in stock pairs trading have been decreasing through the years, it becomes imperative to enter and exit positions intraday to capture the best prices. Also, if traders refrain from taking overnight positions in stock pairs, they may be able to avoid the changes in fundamental corporate valuations that plague longer-term positions mentioned above. However, intraday pair trading of stocks runs into the problem that the national best bid and offer (NBBO) quote sizes for stocks (and for ETFs) have become very small. This may be due to the prevalence of using dark pools or undisplayed "iceberg" orders by institutional traders, the breaking up of large orders into very small child orders by smart execution algorithms, the advent of high-frequency traders submitting small orders that they can cancel and replace frequently, and, finally, the reluctance of market makers to display large order sizes to avoid being taken advantage of by high-frequency traders.

For example, it is not unusual for AAPL to have an NBBO size of just 100 shares! Therefore, backtesting a stock pair–trading strategy using either trade or quote prices is not very realistic unless you trade only 100 shares or if you include a substantial transaction cost. The same phenomenon leads to difficulties in live execution also. If we were to submit market orders for both sides after a trading signal was triggered by the NBBO prices, we could have suffered a substantial slippage. We are forced to send limit orders for one side (or for both sides with small fractions of an order and suffer temporary small unhedged positions) and actively manage the possible cancellations and resubmissions of this order in case they are not fully filled.

Why was pair trading stocks so profitable in the past? One general reason is that the market was much more inefficient back then, so the normal profits from the pairs that do mean-revert are large enough to cover those losses from pairs that don't. This is, of course, a common plague for any profitable strategies, but it is particularly acute for such well-known strategies as pair trading of stocks. One specific reason for the decline in profits of stock pairs trading is the decimalization of U.S. stock prices. Decimalization caused bid-ask spreads to dramatically narrow, so pair traders, who act as a type of market makers, find that their market-making profits decrease also (Serge, 2008).

Of course, the fact that pair trading of stocks is not very profitable in the highly efficient U.S. markets does not mean that they are not profitable in other countries. But for the U.S. market, we have the alternative of profitably pair trading ETFs instead.

■ Trading ETF Pairs (and Triplets)

The one advantage of trading ETF pairs instead of stock pairs is that, once found to be cointegrating, ETF pairs are less likely to fall apart in out-of-sample data. That is because the fundamental economics of a basket of stocks changes much more slowly than that of a single company. For example, since both Australia and Canada are commodity-based economies, EWA and EWC (their respective stock index ETFs) are good candidates for cointegration tests. And, indeed, we confirmed their cointegration in Chapter 3. I mentioned this pair back in 2009 on my blog (http://epchan .blogspot.com/2009/11/in-praise-of-etfs.html?showComment=125743 4002472#c1235760260813269054), and their cointegration continues as of this writing (November 2012). The pair selection process for ETFs is quite easy: we need to find ETFs that are exposed to common economic factors. Besides country ETFs, sector ETFs are another fertile ground for finding cointegrated instruments. For example, the retail fund RTH cointegrates with the consumer staples fund XLP. With the proliferation of ETFs tracking more or less the same sector, pair-trading opportunities are steadily increasing.

Another favorite ETF pairing of mine is between a commodity ETF and an ETF of companies that produce that commodity. The gold fund GLD versus the gold miners fund GDX is a good example. The rationale is that since the main asset of a gold-mining company is gold, their values should cointegrate with gold spot prices. And, indeed, they have done so—until July 14, 2008, or thereabout. If we test for cointegration of GLD versus GDX between May 23, 2006, and July 14, 2008, using the Johansen test, we find that they cointegrate with 99 percent probability, but if we test over the period July 15, 2008, to April 9, 2012, they have lost the cointegration. What happened on July 14, 2008? That's when oil (the West Texas Intermediate flavor) price peaked at around $145 per barrel, an all-time high. What has oil price got to do with the cointegration between gold price and gold miners' share prices? A lot, apparently. It turns out that when oil prices are expensive, it costs a lot more to mine gold, and therefore the profits of gold miners are reduced, leading to the underperformance of their share prices relative to gold spot prices ("The Wacky World of Gold," 2011).

To gather empirical support for this explanation, we can introduce the oil fund USO into the portfolio and see if this triplet cointegrates over the entire period from 2006 to 2012. The Johansen test shows that they do, with a 99 percent probability that there exists one cointegrating relationship. Hence, instead of just trading GLD and GDX, we can trade this portfolio of triplets instead. Even if you find trading a triplet too cumbersome, you should at least have a rule in place to cease trading GLD versus GDX whenever oil price exceeds a certain threshold.

This example has particular significance. When scientists first come upon an unexplained phenomenon, they form a hunch about its cause, and then they find ways to test this hunch empirically. We should adopt the same scientific process in approaching trading. When a trading strategy stops working, we should form a hypothesis of the reason, and then test empirically whether that hypothesis is supported by data. The outcome of this process is often a modified strategy that regains profitability.

One might think that the oil fund USO versus the energy sector fund XLE is another example of a commodity versus commodity producer pair, but there is a problem with this pairing. While GLD owns gold, and thus reflects the gold spot price, USO doesn't actually own oil. It invests in oil futures contracts. As we will discuss in Chapter 5, futures price of a commodity differs from its spot price. Even if XLE cointegrates with the spot price of oil, it may not necessarily cointegrate with USO. Of course, this problem plagues any commodity futures fund versus commodity producer fund. Mean reversion trading of such pairs would be much less risky if the commodity fund holds the actual commodity rather than the futures.

The mechanics of trading ETF pairs is the same as trading stock pairs. The old uptick rule exempted ETFs, but the new alternative uptick rule covers all securities traded on U.S. stock exchanges. However, the NBBO sizes for ETFs are certainly much larger than that for stocks. For example, on a typical day, the NBBO sizes for EWC can be around 5,000 shares.

■ Intraday Mean Reversion: Buy-on-Gap Model

Stock prices follow geometric random walks, as many financial scholars have tirelessly reminded us (Malkiel, 2008). But this is true only if we test their price series for mean reversion strictly at regular intervals (such as using their daily closes). Our job as traders is to find special conditions, or special periods, such that mean reversion occurs with regularity, while at the same time avoiding data-snooping bias. As the following strategy will show, there may indeed be seasonal mean reversion occurring at the intraday time frame even for stocks.

The rules for the strategy are:

1. Select all stocks near the market open whose returns from their previous day's lows to today's opens are lower than one standard deviation. The standard deviation is computed using the daily close-to-close returns of the last 90 days. These are the stocks that "gapped down."
2. Narrow down this list of stocks by requiring their open prices to be higher than the 20-day moving average of the closing prices.
3. Buy the 10 stocks within this list that have the lowest returns from their previous day's lows. If the list has fewer than 10 stocks, then buy the entire list.
4. Liquidate all positions at the market close.

The rationale for this strategy is that on days when the stock index futures are down before the open, certain stocks suffer disproportionately due to panic selling at the open. But once this panic selling is over, the stock will gradually appreciate over the course of the day.

Rule 2 is often very useful in mean-reverting strategies: it is basically a momentum filter superimposed on a mean-reverting strategy, a technique that we will reprise often. Usually, those stocks that dropped "just a little" have a better chance of reversal than those that dropped "a lot" because the latter are often the ones that have negative news such as poor earnings announcements. Drops caused by negative news are less likely to revert. We can actually develop momentum strategies based on such breaking news (more on this in Chapter 7). Furthermore, the fact that a stock is higher than a long-term moving average attracts selling pressure from larger players such as long-only funds, whose trading horizons tend to be longer. This demand for liquidity at the open may exaggerate the downward pressure on the price, but price moves due to liquidity demands are more likely to revert when such demands vanish than price moves due to a shift in the fundamental economics of the stock. Therefore, this strategy can succeed in a news-heavy environment where traditional interday stock pairs trading will likely fail.

The MATLAB code to backtest this strategy is displayed in Example 4.1.

Example 4.1: Buy-on-Gap Model on SPX Stocks

This code, which backtests the Buy-on-Gap model, can be downloaded as *bog.m*. It requires as input three $T \times N$ arrays, *op*, *lo*, and *cl*, where T is the number of days, N is the number of stocks in the universe, and *op* contains the daily open prices, *lo* contains the daily lows, and *cl* the daily closes. The stock universe we used to backtest is the S&P 500, but one that has survivorship bias.

```
topN=10; % Max number of positions
entryZscore=1;
lookback=20; % for MA

stdretC2C90d=backshift(1, smartMovingStd(calculateReturns ...
   (cl, 1), 90));
buyPrice=backshift(1, lo).*(1-entryZscore*stdretC2C90d);

retGap=op-backshift(1, lo))./backshift(1, lo);

pnl=zeros(length(tday), 1);

positionTable=zeros(size(cl));

ma=backshift(1, smartMovingAvg(cl, lookback));

for t=2:size(cl, 1)
        hasData=find(isfinite(retGap(t, :)) & op(t, :) ...
           < buyPrice(t, :) & op(t, :) > ma(t, :));

           [foo idxSort]=sort(retGap(t, hasData), 'ascend');
           positionTable(t, hasData(idxSort(1:min(topN, ...
              length(idxSort)))))=1;
end

retO2C=(cl-op)./op;
pnl=smartsum(positionTable.*(retO2C), 2);
ret=pnl/topN;
ret(isnan(ret))=0;
```

This strategy has an annual percentage rate (APR) of 8.7 percent and a Sharpe ratio of 1.5 from May 11, 2006, to April 24, 2012. The cumulative returns curve is depicted in Figure 4.1.

I have traded a version of it quite profitably in my personal account as well as in a fund that I comanaged. Unfortunately, that version

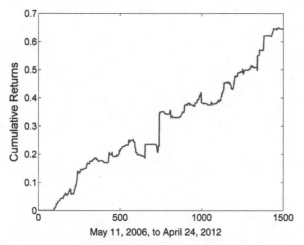

0.7
0.6
0.5
0.4
0.3
0.2
0.1
0

Cumulative Returns

0   500   1000   1500

May 11, 2006, to April 24, 2012

FIGURE 4.1 Cumulative Returns of Buy-on-Gap Model

does not include rule 2, and it suffered from diminishing returns from 2009 onward. The long-only nature of the strategy also presents some risk management challenges. Finally, the number of stocks traded each day is quite small, which means that the strategy does not have a large capacity.

The astute reader may wonder how we can use open prices to determine the trading signals for entry at the open and be filled at the official open prices. The short answer is, of course: We can't! We can, however, use the preopen prices (for example, at ARCA) to determine the trading signals. The signals thus determined will not exactly match the ones determined by the actual open prices, but the hope is that the difference will not be so large as to wipe out the returns. We can call this difference *signal noise*. Also, note the pitfall of backtesting this strategy using consolidated prices versus primary exchange prices, as explained in Chapter 1.

What about the mirror image of this strategy? Can we short stocks that gap up a standard deviation but are still lower than their 20-day moving average? Yes, we can. The APR is 46 percent and the Sharpe ratio is 1.27 over the same period. Despite the seemingly higher return than the long-only strategy, the short-only one does have steeper drawdown (see Figure 4.2), and it suffered from the same short-sale constraint pitfall discussed before.

This strategy is actually quite well known among traders, and there are many variations on the same theme. For example, you can obviously trade both the long-only and short-only versions simultaneously. Or you can trade a hedged version that is long stocks but short stock index futures. You can

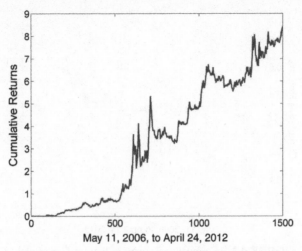

FIGURE 4.2   Cumulative Returns of Short-on-Gap Model

buy a larger number of stocks, but restricting the number of stocks within the same sector. You can extend the buying period beyond the market open. You can impose intraday profit caps. But the important message is: Price series that do not exhibit mean reversion when sampled with daily bars can exhibit strong mean reversion during specific periods. This is seasonality at work at a short time scale.

■ Arbitrage between an ETF and Its Component Stocks

Many readers would be familiar with the strategy of "index arbitrage," which trades on the difference in value between a portfolio of stocks constituting an index and the futures on that index. If the stocks are weighted in the same way used to construct the index, then the market value of the portfolio will cointegrate very tightly with the index futures. Maybe too tightly—unfortunately, this is such a well-known strategy that the difference in market values has become extremely small (Reverre, 2001). All but the most sophisticated traders can profit from this strategy, and it most certainly needs to be traded intraday, perhaps at high frequency (see Box 4.1). In order to increase this difference, we can select only a subset of the stocks in the index to form the portfolio. The same concept can be applied to the arbitrage between a portfolio of stocks constituting an ETF and the ETF itself. In this case, we choose just a proper subset of the constituent stocks to form the portfolio. One selection method is to just pick all the stocks that cointegrate individually with the ETF. We will demonstrate the method by using the most famous ETF of all: SPY.

We will pick one year of data (in our example, January 1, 2007, to December 31, 2007) as a training set and look for all the stocks that cointegrate with SPY with at least 90 percent probability using the Johansen test. Then we form a portfolio of these stocks with equal capital on each stock, and confirm using the Johansen test again that this long-only portfolio still cointegrates with SPY. This step is necessary because an arbitrary assignment of equal capital weight to each stock does not necessarily produce a portfolio price series that cointegrates with that of SPY, even if each of the constituent stocks is cointegrating with SPY. We are using log price in this second test because we expect to rebalance this portfolio every day so that the capital on each stock is constant. (See the discussions in Chapter 3.) After confirming cointegration, we can then backtest the linear mean reversion strategy described in Chapter 2. The MATLAB source codes are displayed in Example 4.2.

Example 4.2: Arbitrage between SPY and Its Component Stocks

This code can be downloaded as *indexArb.m*. It requires as input a TxN array *cl*, where *T* is the number of days, *N* is the number of stocks in the universe, and *cl* the daily closes. The stock universe we used to backtest is the same as that used in Example 4.1, and the symbols it contains are in a cell array *stocks*. All these arrays are packaged in a structure *stks*. In addition, we need a Tx1 array *cl* for the daily closes of SPY. These are packaged in a structure *etf*. Of course, we must ensure that dates for *stks* and *etf* match. The common trading dates are contained in a Tx1 array *tday*. We will run the Johansen test on only the first part of this data: January 1, 2007, to December 31, 2007. This is designated as the training set.

```
trainDataIdx=find(tday>=20070101 & tday<=20071231);
testDataIdx=find(tday > 20071231);

isCoint=false(size(stks.stocks));
for s=1:length(stks.stocks)
        % Combine the two time series into a matrix y2 for
        % input into Johansen test
        y2=[stks.cl(trainDataIdx, s), etf.cl(trainDataIdx)];
        badData=any(isnan(y2), 2);
        y2(badData, :)=[]; % remove any missing data

        if (size(y2, 1) > 250)
                results=johansen(y2, 0, 1); % johansen test
                    % with non-zero offset but zero drift, and with
                    % the lag k=1.
                if (results.lr1(1) > results.cvt(1, 1))
                        isCoint(s)=true;
                end
        end
end

length(find(isCoint))
```

Based on the Johansen test between each stock in SPX with SPY over the training set, we find that there are 98 stocks that cointegrate (each separately) with SPY. Now we can form a long-only portfolio with all stocks that cointegrate with SPY, with equal capital allocation. We must then test the cointegration of this portfolio with SPY.

Example 4.2 (*Continued*)

```
yN=stks.cl(trainDataIdx, isCoint);

logMktVal_long=sum(log(yN), 2); % The net market value of
   the long-only portfolio is same as the "spread"

% Confirm that the portfolio cointegrates with SPY
ytest=[logMktVal_long, log(etf.cl(trainDataIdx))];
results=johansen(ytest, 0, 1); % johansen test with non-zero
   offset but zero drift, and with the lag k=1.
prt(results);


% Output:
% Johansen MLE estimates
% NULL:           Trace Statistic  Crit 90%  Crit 95%  Crit 99%
% r <= 0  variable 1     15.869      13.429    15.494    19.935
% r <= 1  variable 2      6.197       2.705     3.841     6.635
%
% NULL:           Eigen Statistic  Crit 90%  Crit 95%  Crit 99%
% r <= 0  variable 1      9.671      12.297    14.264    18.520
% r <= 1  variable 2      6.197       2.705     3.841     6.635


results.evec
%
% ans =
%
%      1.0939        -0.2799
%   -105.5600        56.0933
```

The Johansen test indicates that the long-only portfolio does cointegrate with SPY with better than 95 percent probability. So we can form a long-short stationary portfolio comprising both the stocks and SPY, using the Johansen eigenvector to determine the weights of SPY versus that of the stock portfolio. (There are, in fact, two cointegrating relations, but we will pick the one with the largest eigenvalue—the first column of the eigenmatrix—to form this stationary portfolio.) As the Johansen test was performed on the log prices, the hedge ratios (represented by the *weights* array) on the stocks or SPY represent dollar capital allocation, not number of shares, as explained in Chapter 3. (The weight on each individual stock is, of course, the same, due to our assumption of equal capital allocation, but it differs from the weight on SPY.)

(*Continued*)

Example 4.2 (*Continued*)

We then apply the linear mean reversion strategy on this portfolio over the test period January 2, 2008, to April 9, 2012, much in the same way as Example 2.8, except that in the current program we have fixed the look-back used for calculating the moving average and standard deviations of the portfolio market value to be 5, with the benefit of hindsight.

```
% Apply linear mean-reversion model on test set
yNplus=[stks.cl(testDataIdx, isCoint), etf.cl(testDataIdx)]; ...
    % Array of stock and ETF prices
weights=[repmat(results.evec(1, 1), size(stks.cl(testDataIdx,
    isCoint))), ...
       repmat(results.evec(2, 1), size(etf.cl(testDataIdx)))]; ...
         % capital allocation among the stocks and SPY.

logMktVal=smartsum(weights.*log(yNplus), 2); % Log market
    % value of long-short portfolio

lookback=5;
numUnits=-(logMktVal-movingAvg(logMktVal, lookback)) ...
    ./movingStd(logMktVal, lookback);
    positions=repmat(numUnits, [1 size(weights, 2)]).*weights;
       % positions is the dollar capital in each stock or SPY.
pnl=smartsum(lag(positions, 1).*(log(yNplus)- ...
    lag(log(yNplus), 1)), 2);
    ret=pnl./smartsum(abs(lag(positions, 1)), 2);
    ret(isnan(ret))=0;
```

The APR of this strategy is 4.5 percent, and the Sharpe ratio is 1.3. As you can see from the cumulative returns chart (Figure 4.3), the performance decreases as time goes on, partly because we have not retrained the model periodically to select new constituent stocks with new hedge ratios. In a more complete backtest, we can add this dynamic updating of the hedge ratios.

The same methodology can, of course, be applied to any ETFs, indices, or subindices you like. Furthermore, we can use a future instead of an ETF if such a future exists that tracks that index or subindex, although in this case one has to be careful that the prices of the future used in backtest are contemporaneous with the closing prices for the stocks. (This was pointed out as a potential pitfall in Chapter 1.)

Example 4.2 (*Continued*)

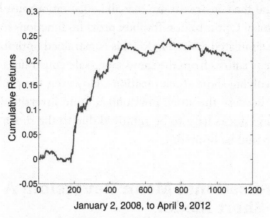

January 2, 2008, to April 9, 2012

FIGURE 4.3 Cumulative Returns of Arbitrage between SPY and Its Component Stocks

You may wonder why we didn't just directly run a Johansen cointegration test on all 500 stocks in SPX plus SPY, and let the algorithm automatically find an eigenvector of cointegrating instruments that include the SPY. (Not all cointegrating relations from the stocks+SPY universe necessarily include SPY, but we need only pick one that does.) The problem with this approach is twofold:

1. The Johansen test implementation that I know of can accept a maximum of 12 symbols only (LeSage, 1998).
2. The eigenvectors will usually involve both long and short *stock* positions. This means that we can't have a long-only portfolio of stocks that is hedged with a short SPY position or vice versa. This is a problem because if we have short positions in the stock portfolio and a short SPY position simultaneously, we would be double short on some stocks even when we are long the stock portfolio, increasing our specific risks.

There is an alternative method of constructing a long-only portfolio of stocks. We can still use Johansen test to individually test each stock in SPX for cointegration with SPY. After this subset of stocks is found, we include them in a stock portfolio and then use a constrained optimization method (e.g., genetic algorithm or simulated annealing) to minimize the average absolute difference between this stock portfolio price series and the SPY price series. The variables that we want to optimize in this case are the hedge ratios of the stocks, and the constraints are that all hedge ratios must be positive. The MATLAB Global Optimization Toolbox provides functions for either genetic algorithm or simulated annealing for this constrained optimization task.

This strategy suffers from the same short-sale constraint that plagued any strategies involving short stock positions. However, the problem is not too serious here because the stock portfolio is quite diversified with about 98 stocks. If a few stocks have to be removed due to the short-sale constraint, the impact should be limited.

■ Cross-Sectional Mean Reversion: A Linear Long-Short Model

In mean reversion trading based on cointegration, we form a portfolio with a fixed set of instruments and with either a fixed number of shares or a fixed dollar capital for each instrument. This fixed number may be determined by fiat (as in Example 4.2), linear regression, the Johansen test, or constrained optimization. But there is no reason why the portfolio has to consist of the same fixed set of instruments or the same weightings over this set of instruments every day. For many portfolio stock-trading strategies, the edge comes precisely from the intelligent daily selection or reweighting of stocks.

In this type of so-called "cross-sectional" mean reversion strategy, the individual stock (and this type of strategy most commonly involves stocks, not futures or currencies) price does not necessarily revert to its own historical mean. Rather, the focus is on their short-term relative returns, and we rely on the serial anti-correlation of these relative returns to generate profits. In most cases, the relative returns are computed as a stock's return minus the average returns of all the stocks in a particular universe. So we expect the underperformance of a stock to be followed by overperformance, and vice versa. Since we are measuring only relative return, it is quite possible that we will short a stock even though its previous (absolute) return is negative, as long as it is not as negative as the average return across all stocks in the universe.

One interesting feature of cross-sectional strategies is that, in contrast to "time series" strategies, we should not expect profits from every individual stock, as some of them may serve as "hedges" on some days. Rather, profits can be obtained only in the aggregate across all the stocks.

I described in my previous book just such a strategy proposed by Khandani and Lo (Example 3.7 of Chan, 2009; original paper is Khandani and Lo, 2007). With this strategy, we invest in every stock from some favorite index such as S&P 500, S&P 1500, or Russell 2000, but with different capital allocation per stock. Near the market close of each day, we will determine the long or short capital w_i allocated to the ith stock as

$$w_i = -(r_i - \langle r_j \rangle)/ \sum_k |r_k - \langle r_j \rangle| \qquad (4.1)$$

where r_i is the daily return of the ith stock, and $\langle r_j \rangle$ is the average daily return of all the stocks in the index. In other words, if a stock has a very positive return relative to its peers, we will short lots of it, and if it has a very negative return relative to its peers, we will buy lots of it. Note that we always invest the same total gross capital of $1 to the portfolio every day because of the normalization factor in the denominator. The MATLAB code fragment for this is displayed in Example 4.3.

Example 4.3: Linear Long-Short Model on Stocks

The implementation of Equation 4.1 in MATLAB is very compact. We assume an input $T \times N$ array cl of daily closing prices, where as usual T is the number of trading days and N is the number of stocks in the SPX. This code can be downloaded as *andrewlo_2007_2012.m*.

```
ret=(cl-lag(cl, 1))./lag(cl, 1); % daily returns

marketRet=smartmean(ret, 2); % equal weighted market index
    % return

weights=-(ret-repmat(marketRet, [1 size(ret, 2)]));
weights=weights./repmat(smartsum(abs(weights), 2), ...
    [1 size(weights, 2)]);

dailyret=smartsum(backshift(1, weights).*ret, 2); % Capital
    % is always one
```

It has an APR of 13.7 percent and Sharpe ratio of 1.3 from January 2, 2007, to December 30, 2011, even if we backtest on the SPX. (Usually, backtesting on a smaller cap universe will generate even higher returns.) The cumulative returns are plotted in Figure 4.4.

(Continued)

Example 4.3 (*Continued*)

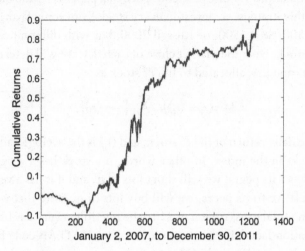

January 2, 2007, to December 30, 2011

FIGURE 4.4   Cumulative Returns of Linear Long-Short Model

The notable feature of this strategy is that it is completely linear, has no parameters, and is almost perfectly dollar neutral. What strategy can be simpler than this? And remarkably, it achieved an APR of 30 percent in 2008, the year of Lehman Brothers' bankruptcy, and an APR of 11 percent in 2011, a year filled with high anxiety about the U.S. federal debt rating downgrade and the Greek default. (Its performance since the beginning of 2008 is a true out-of-sample test, as the strategy was published in 2007.)

In my previous book, I also suggested that we may enhance the returns of this strategy by using the return from the previous close to today's open to determine the weights for entry at the open. All the positions will be liquidated at the market close, thus turning it into an intraday strategy. The modified MATLAB code fragment is displayed in Example 4.4.

There are possibly other variables (also called "factors") that are better at predicting cross-sectional mean reversion of stock prices than the relative returns that we have used in Examples 4.3 and 4.4. One popular variable that traders use to rank stocks is the price-earnings (P/E) ratio, where the earnings may be that of the last quarter, or they may be projected earnings estimated by the analysts or the companies themselves. The reasoning is that

In addition to the inputs required in Example 4.3, we need also the $T \times N$ array *op*, which contains the daily open prices of the stocks.

```
ret=(op-backshift(1, cl))./backshift(1, cl); % daily returns

marketRet=smartmean(ret, 2); % equal weighted market index
  % return

weights=-(ret-repmat(marketRet, [1 size(ret, 2)]));
weights=weights./repmat(smartsum(abs(weights), 2), ...
  [1 size(weights, 2)]);
dailyret=smartsum(weights.*(cl-op)./op, 2) ...
  ./smartsum(abs(weights), 2);
```

The APR and Sharpe ratio over the same period are 73 percent and 4.7, respectively. Despite such seemly stellar performance, the open-to-close version suffers from a few drawbacks that the close-to-close version does not have.

First, the transaction costs (not included in our backtests) will be doubled, because we are trading twice a day instead of just once a day. Second, since this strategy also has to use "open" prices to determine the trading signals for entry at the open, it is subject to the same trading signal noise that I mentioned in the Buy-on-Gap Model in Example 4.1.

Actually, even for the close-to-close strategy, we also can't use the exact closing price to determine the weights and then enter at exactly those prices. But in that case, the prices just a few seconds before the close are typically much closer to the actual official (primary exchange) closing prices because these preclose prices are printed when the primary market is open and has high liquidity.

stock prices will drift toward a new equilibrium value if there are earning announcements or estimates changes. So a stock that experiences a positive change in earnings estimates will likely enjoy a positive return, and we should not expect the price to mean-revert if this return is in line with the percent change in its earnings estimates. We can therefore avoid shorting such a stock if we use P/E ratio to rank the stocks.

- Are you tempted to trade pairs of stocks because of the enormous number of choices? Beware of changes in companies' fundamentals that can render out-of-sample performance quite poor despite stellar backtest results.

- Trading a portfolio of cointegrating ETFs can be better than pair-trading stocks.

- Are you pair trading ETFs that hold futures? Beware of the role of roll returns in determining total returns of futures.

- Seasonal or intraday mean reversion is hard to detect with usual stationarity or cointegration tests, but can be very profitable.

- Imposing momentum filter on mean-reversal strategies typically improves their consistency.

- Do you think that index arbitrage between stocks and futures is no longer profitable? Try selecting only a subset of the stocks in the index.

- Cross-sectional mean reversion strategies can be implemented very easily with a linear long-short strategy.

- The variable used for ranking stocks in a cross-sectional mean reversion strategy is typically relative return, but it can be other fundamental factors such as P/E ratio.

CHAPTER 5

Mean Reversion of Currencies and Futures

Conventional wisdom tells us that currencies and futures are the domain of momentum traders, and conventional wisdom is right about this. Indeed, most CTAs (Commodities Trading Advisors) are momentum based. It is also true that most currency or future pairs would not cointegrate, and most portfolios of currencies or futures do not exhibit cross-sectional mean reversion. So opportunities for mean reversion strategies in currencies and futures are limited, but not nonexistent. This chapter will guide the reader toward those situations where mean reversion is the exception rather than the rule, such as the trading of futures calendar spreads. In particular, we will discuss a trading strategy for one unique futures intermarket spread: the volatility future versus the stock index future.

In the course of exploring mean reversion in futures, we will also discuss a simple mathematical model of futures prices that will illuminate concepts such as spot versus roll returns and backwardation versus contango. Understanding this model will also help suggest new futures trading strategies without resorting to ad hoc technical indicators.

Trading currencies has certain nuances that are foreign to stock traders. Care must be taken when testing for cointegration of currencies or when computing the returns of a portfolio of currencies by making sure that a point move in one currency pair has the same dollar value as a point move in another currency pair; otherwise, the results will not make sense. Furthermore, rollover interests might sometimes play an important role in determining total returns. These nuances will be covered in this chapter.

■ Trading Currency Cross-Rates

The basic idea in forming a stationary portfolio of foreign currencies is very similar to the trading of stock index ETF pairs from different countries: we need to find countries that have similar economic fundamentals. Since we found, for example, that EWA (Australian stock index ETF) and EWC (Canadian stock index ETF) cointegrate, we might expect to find AUD (Australian dollar) to cointegrate with CAD (Canadian dollar) as well. In addition, because both Australia and South Africa have major mining revenues, we might expect AUD to cointegrate with ZAR (South African rand). In fact, traders have called these and other currencies such as the Norwegian krone *commodity currencies*.

Trading currency pairs has a number of advantages compared to trading their corresponding stock index ETF pairs. Usually, liquidity in currencies is higher (especially for best bid/ask sizes), thus lowering transaction costs. The leverage that can be employed for currencies is also much higher, though this can be a double-edged sword of course. There are no short-sale constraints for currencies. Finally, currency trading can be done around the clock, at least five days a week from 5:00 P.M. ET on Sunday to 5:00 P.M. ET on Friday. (ET can be either EDT or EST; i.e., it is either GMT-4 or GMT-5.) This means that we have a lot more trading opportunities in currencies, and we can also employ stop losses in a meaningful way. (If a market is closed for a long period, stop losses are useless as the market can gap up or down when it reopens.)

Despite the conceptual similarity with trading ETF pairs, the mechanics of currency trading is quite different. Let's start with some basic terminology. If we are trading the cross-rate AUD.ZAR, then AUD is called the *base* currency, and ZAR is the *quote* currency. (My personal mnemonic for this: B is ahead of Q alphabetically, so the order is B.Q.) If AUD.ZAR is quoted at 9.58, it takes 9.58 South African rand to buy 1 Australian dollar. Buying 100,000 AUD.ZAR means buying 100,000 Australian dollars, while selling the equivalent amount ($100,000 \times 9.58 = 958,000$ at the preceding quote) of South African rand. However, few brokers actually offer AUD.

ZAR as a cross-rate. So usually we have to buy X units of B.ZAR and sell X units of B.AUD to effectively buy X Australian dollar worth of AUD.ZAR, where B is some other base currency. We usually choose a very liquid base currency such as USD or EUR for this operation. We can denote such a synthetic pair as USD.ZAR/USD.AUD, since the quote of AUD.ZAR will be exactly equal to this ratio of quotes. When we actually trade this synthetic pair live, the realized profit and loss (P&L) will be denominated in both ZAR and AUD. In general, when we compute the returns of a strategy trading B.Q, we are assuming that the profits are denominated in our local currency (USD for U.S. investors), which may be *neither* B nor Q. So in order for our actual realized P&L to conform to our backtest P&L, we need to regularly convert B and Q into our local currency. For example, if our local currency is USD, and we have realized profits of X units of AUD and Y units of ZAR after a round trip trade, we need to buy X units of ZAR.USD and Ẏ units of ZAR.AUD. If we don't do this regularly, a large accumulated P&L in AUD and ZAR may cause significant deviation from our backtest results.

Even when a cross-rate such as AUD.CAD is ready-made for trading, we may sometimes find it advantageous to weigh the two currencies differently by trading AUD.USD versus USD.CAD separately. The code in Example 5.1 illustrates such a strategy. In this strategy we use the Johansen test to find out the best hedge ratio of capital, or capital weights, between AUD.USD versus CAD.USD. Why not use the conventional quote USD.CAD instead of CAD.USD? That's because in order to interpret the eigenvector from the Johansen test as capital weights, the two price series must have the same quote currency. Otherwise, the point moves of the two presumptive cointegrating instruments would not have the same value, rendering the Johansen test meaningless. Using CAD.USD in our backtest program doesn't make live trading any more difficult: Whenever the program sends an order to "Buy 1 unit of CAD.USD," we should just "Sell $1/y$ of USD.CAD," provided y is the current quote for USD.CAD.

In Example 5.1, we focus on trading two currencies that can ultimately be reduced to a pair with a common quote currency USD: B_1.USD − B_2.USD. So the returns of a portfolio with n_1 units of B_1.USD and n_2 units of B_2.USD is

$$r(t+1) = \frac{n_1 y_{1,U}(t) r_1(t+1) + n_2 y_{2,U}(t) r_2(t+1)}{|n_1| y_{1,U}(t) + |n_2| y_{2,U}(t)} \quad (5.1)$$

as displayed in the last line of the MATLAB code in the example. Here r_i is the return of B_i. USD:

$$r_i(t+1) = (y_{i,U}(t+1) - y_{i,U}(t))/y_{i,U}(t) \qquad (5.2)$$

where $y_{i,U}(t)$ and $y_{i,U}(t+1)$ are the quotes for B_i. USD at t and $t+1$ respectively. This is because one unit of B_i. USD is worth $y_{i,U}$ in U.S. dollars.

However, if a portfolio has n_1' units of USD.Q_1 and n_2' units of USD.Q_2 instead, then the return can be written more simply as

$$r(t+1) = \frac{n_1' r_1(t+1) + n_2' r_2(t+1)}{|n_1'| + |n_2'|} \qquad (5.3)$$

where

$$r_i(t+1) = (y_{U,i}(t+1) - y_{U,i}(t))/y_{U,i}(t) \qquad (5.4)$$

and $y_{U,i}(t)$ and $y_{U,i}(t+1)$ are the quotes for USD.Q_i at t and $t+1$, respectively. This is because one unit of USD.Q_i is worth exactly one U.S. dollar.

Let me immediately say that Equations 5.2 and 5.4 are not strictly correct, as we have ignored the *rollover interests*, which we will discuss in the next section. But the impact of rollover interests is usually not large for short-term strategies like the one I describe in Example 5.1, so we have omitted them here for simplicity.

Example 5.1: Pair Trading USD.AUD versus USD.CAD Using the Johansen Eigenvector

This is a classic linear mean-reverting strategy similar to the one in Example 3.1 (*PriceSpread.m*). Previously, we used a look-back of 20 days to compute the hedge ratio, while here we use a fixed training set of 250 days (which gives better results in hindsight), though we are still using a look-back of 20 days for computing the moving average and standard deviation. However, our current strategy is very different from a typical forex strategy such as the one in Example 2.5. Here, the hedge ratio between the two currencies is not one, so we cannot trade it as one cross-rate AUD.CAD. Instead

Example 5.1 (*Continued*)

of running the Johansen test on USD.AUD versus USD.CAD, we actually should run it on AUD.USD and CAD.USD, so that the dollar value of a point move in each instrument is the same. Intuitively, this also makes sense, since in a mean-reverting strategy we want to buy CAD if CAD.USD is much lower than AUD.USD.

We assume the input to be two $T \times 1$ arrays *usdcad* and *usdaud*, both daily price series. The $T \times 1$ array *yport* is the market value of a unit portfolio of AUD.USD and CAD.USD expressed in USD, while *numUnits* is the number of units of this unit portfolio our strategy asks us to own. The $T \times 2$ array *positions* denote the market values in USD of AUD.USD and CAD.USD that we should own. Naturally, the P&L (in USD again) is just the sum of the market value of each instrument times their returns, and the daily return of the portfolio is the P&L divided by the total gross market value of the portfolio at the end of the previous day.

The code can be downloaded as *AUDCAD_unequal.m*.

```
cad=1./usdcad.cl;
aud=audusd.cl;

y=[ aud cad ];
trainlen=250;
lookback=20;
hedgeRatio=NaN(size(y));
numUnits=NaN(size(y, 1), 1);
for t=trainlen+1:size(y, 1)
  res=johansen(log(y(t-trainlen:t-1, :)), 0, 1);
  hedgeRatio(t, :)=res.evec(:, 1)';
  yport=sum(y(t-lookback+1:t, :).* ...
    repmat(hedgeRatio(t, :), [lookback 1]), 2);
  ma=mean(yport);
  mstd=std(yport);
  zScore=(yport(end)-ma)/mstd;
  numUnits(t)=-(yport(end)-ma)/mstd;
end

positions=repmat(numUnits, [1 size(y, 2)]).*hedgeRatio.*y;
pnl=sum(lag(positions, 1).*(y-lag(y, 1))./lag(y, 1), 2);
ret=pnl./sum(abs(lag(positions, 1)), 2);
```

(*Continued*)

Example 5.1 (*Continued*)

Taking care to exclude the first 250 days of rolling training data when computing the strategy performance, the APR is 11 percent and the Sharpe ratio is 1.6, for the period December 18, 2009, to April 26, 2012. The cumulative returns curve is plotted in Figure 5.1.

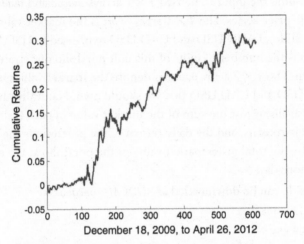

FIGURE 5.1 Cumulative Returns of USD.AUD versus USD.CAD Strategy

You may sometimes find profitable opportunities trading two pairs of entirely different cross-rates against each other: $B_1.Q_1$ versus $B_2.Q_2$. If the strategy calls for a portfolio of n_1 units of $B_1.Q_1$ and n_2 units of $B_2.Q_2$, the daily return (in the presumed local currency of USD) of the portfolio is given by the same Equation 5.1. The r_i there will be the return of $B_i.Q_i$, so Equation 5.2 is replaced by

$$r_i(t+1) = \{\log(y_{i,Qi}(t+1)) - \log(y_{i,Qi}(t))\} \qquad (5.5)$$

where $y_{i,Qi}(t)$ is the quote for $B_i.Q_i$. The same equations, 5.1 through 5.5, are valid if we had used EUR or any other currency instead of USD as the local currency for computing returns.

As you can see, the key difficulty in backtesting currency arbitrage strategies is not the complexity of the strategies, but the right way to prepare the data series for cointegration tests, and the right formula to measure returns!

■ Rollover Interests in Currency Trading

A feature of trading currency cross-rate is the differential interest rate earned or paid if the cross-rate position is held overnight. Note that "overnight" in currency trading means holding a position untill or beyond 5:00 P.M. ET. If we are long a pair B.Q overnight, the interest differential is $i_B - i_Q$, where i_B and i_Q are the daily interest rates of currency B and Q, respectively. If $i_Q >$ i_B, then this interest differential, also called a rollover interest, is actually a debit interest (i.e., your account will be debited). Actually, for reasons that have to do with the T + 2 day settlement system, if a position was held past the 5 P.M. ET close on day T, and day T + 3 is a weekend or holiday for either currency of the cross-rate, the rollover interest accrued on that position will be multiplied by one plus the number of days the market remains closed. So if a position was held past 5 P.M. ET on Wednesday, the rollover interest is three times the daily rate since the market is closed on Saturday and Sunday. A further exception to this rule applies when we are trading USD.CAD or USD.MXN, where the settlement occurs on day T + 1, so we only multiply the rollover interest by one plus the number of nontrading days if day T + 2 is a weekend or holiday. (Thus, only if a position was held past 5:00 P.M. ET on *Thursday* will the rollover interest be three times the daily rate.) All these considerations impinge on the accuracy of a backtest of strategies that hold overnight positions.

When we calculate the Sharpe ratio for any strategy, we need to calculate the excess return, because the Sharpe ratio is the ratio of the average excess return divided by the standard deviation of the excess returns, suitably annualized. The excess return is the return of the positions that the strategy holds minus the financing cost of those positions. So if we have only intraday positions, the financing cost is zero. If we are trading a long-short dollar neutral equity portfolio, we can assume the financing cost is close to zero, even though the credit interest is usually slightly less than the absolute value of the debit interest. For futures positions, the financing cost is also zero, because futures positions are just contracts, not assets that require cash to finance. (We do not count the margin cash requirement, since that cash generates interest in the account.) In the case of currency cross-rates, we can again set the financing cost to be zero, as long as we are careful to add the rollover interest to the percent change of the cross-rate. That is, we need to modify Equation 5.5 so that the excess return r_{t+1} from holding a cross-rate position $POS_{B.Q}$ from day t to day $t+1$ is

$$r(t+1) = \{\log(y_{B.Q}(t+1)) - \log(y_{B.Q}(t)) + \log(1 + i_B(t)) - \log(1 + i_Q(t))\}$$

(5.6)

where $y(t)$ and $y(t+1)$ are the quotes for BQ at t and $t+1$, respectively (Dueker, 2006).

In Example 5.2, we see how we can take into account rollover interests in backtesting the linear mean-reverting strategy on AUD.CAD.

Example 5.2: Pair Trading AUD.CAD with Rollover Interests

We continue to use the linear mean-reverting strategy in this example, but in contrast to Example 5.1 and in the interest of simplicity, we trade the ready-made pair AUD.CAD, not USD.CAD versus AUD. USD separately. We will take into account the overnight rollover interest rates because this strategy holds beyond 5 P.M. ET. We assume the daily closing prices of AUD.CAD are contained in a $T \times 1$ array *dailyCl* and the corresponding trading dates in the $T \times 1$ array *tday*. The historical interest rates are taken from the Reserve Bank of Australia website's money market rate, www.rba.gov.au/statistics/tables/#interest_rates, and the Bank of Canada web site's overnight money market financing rates, www.bankofcanada.ca/wp-content/uploads/2010/09/selected_historical_page33.pdf. The daily AUD and CAD interest rates are assumed to be two $T \times 1$ arrays *aud_dailyRates* and *cad_dailyRates* respectively, matching the dates in *tday*.

The source code can be downloaded as *AUDCAD_daily.m*

```
lookback=20;

% Triple rollover interest on Wednesdays for AUD
isWednesday=weekday(datenum(num2str(tday), 'yyyymmdd'))==4;
aud_dailyRates(isWednesday)=3*aud_dailyRates(isWednesday);

cad_dailyRates=zeros(size(tday));
% Triple rollover interest on Thursdays for CAD
```

Example 5.2 (*Continued*)

```
isThursday=weekday(datenum(num2str(tday), 'yyyymmdd'))==5;
cad_dailyRates(isThursday)=3*cad_dailyRates(isThursday);

ma=movingAvg(dailyCl, lookback);
z=(dailyCl-ma);

ret=lag(-sign(z), 1).*(log(dailyCl)- ...
   lag(log(dailyCl)+log(1+aud_dailyRates)- ...
   log(1+cad_dailyRates), 1));
```

This simple mean reversion strategy yields an APR of 6.2 percent, with a Sharpe ratio of 0.54, which are much weaker results than those in Example 5.1, which, as you may recall, use a nonunity hedge ratio. It is also worth noting that even if we had neglected to take into account the rollover interest in this case, the APR would increase just slightly to 6.7 percent and the Sharpe ratio to 0.58, even though the annualized average rollover interest would amount to almost 5 percent.

■ Trading Futures Calendar Spread

Futures contracts with different expiration dates (or "maturities") have different prices, and they have slightly different returns. Pairing up futures contracts with different maturities creates what are known as *calendar spreads*. Since both legs of a calendar spread track the price of the underlying asset, one would think that calendar spreads potentially offer good opportunities for mean reversion trading. But in reality they do not generally mean-revert. To understand why, we need to understand more about what drives the returns of futures in general.

Roll Returns, Backwardation, and Contango

The fact that futures contracts with different maturities have different prices implies that a futures position will have nonzero return even if the underlying spot price remains unchanged, since eventually all their prices have to converge toward that constant spot price. This return is called the *roll return* or *roll yield*. Despite its name, a futures position suffers this return whether we actually "roll forward" to the next contract. It is an intrinsic

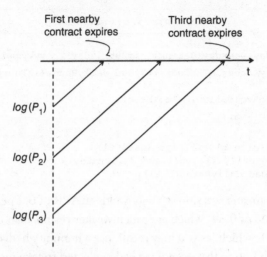

FIGURE 5.2 Log Prices of Futures with Different Maturities in Backwardation as a Function of Time

part of its total return, which can be decomposed into a spot return and a roll return.

If the contracts are in backwardation, meaning the near (close to expiring) contracts have higher prices than the far contracts, then the roll returns will be positive; otherwise if the contracts are in contango, then the roll returns will be negative. To see this, imagine that the spot price is unchanged throughout time, represented by the horizontal line in Figure 5.2.

We can also pretend that the log futures prices with different maturities conform to the same linear function of time with the same slope but with different offsets, intersecting the spot price at expirations. The question is: Should the slope be positive or negative? Graphically, if the nearer futures have a higher price than the farther futures and have to intersect the horizontal line earlier, they must be upward sloping and have positive roll return, as shown in Figure 5.2. At any given time, the price of the first nearby contract P_1 is higher than that of the second nearby contract P_2, and so on. The opposite is true if they are in contango, as illustrated in Figure 5.3. (We display log prices instead of raw prices so that a contract with a constant compounded total return will appear as a straight line.)

Note that this graphical argument merely serves as a mnemonic, not a proof, as, of course, real log futures prices are not linear functions of time, they may even intersect (two contracts of different maturities having the

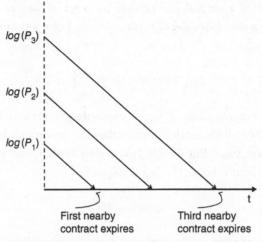

$\log(P_3)$

$\log(P_2)$

$\log(P_1)$

t

First nearby
contract expires

Third nearby
contract expires

FIGURE 5.3 Log Prices of Futures with Different
Maturities in Contango as a Function of Time

same price) before they expire, and finally the spot price at expiration is
unlikely to be constant throughout time. Nevertheless, Figures 5.2 and 5.3
illustrate the typical situation. A mnemonic to help us remember whether
backwardation means near contracts have higher prices than far contracts is
presented in Box 5.1.

BOX 5.1

Mnemonic for Backwardation versus Contango

I can never remember whether backwardation means near contracts have
higher or lower price. If you are like me, you can employ the mnemonic below.

This mnemonic originated with John Maynard Keynes (Hull, 1997). He and
John Hicks argued that for *normal* commodities, those who actually own
the physical commodities (the "hedgers," such as farmers or oil producers)
tend to hedge their positions by shorting futures, expecting to lose money
on their hedges. Meanwhile, the speculators are the ones who have a net
long position, and need to be compensated for taking this risk. So they will
buy only futures with positive roll return, or equivalently futures that have
lower prices than the expected future spot price; that is, the ones in "*normal*
backwardation." So we should remember that "backwardation" is always
associated with "normal," and "normal" means the futures price is always
lower than the spot price.

Of course, this argument is not completely correct, since we will see that
crude oil, a perfectly "normal" commodity, is in contango over various periods.
But this story gives us a good mnemonic.

To calculate the spot and roll returns for a set of futures contracts, it is helpful to have a simple model of futures prices. For many commodities, we can write

$$F(t, T) = S(t)exp(\gamma(t - T))$$ (5.7)

where t is the current time, T is the expiration time, and $S(t)$ is the spot price (Hull, 1997). This model implies that the (compounded) roll return γ is constant over time. But we can take a step further, and assume that the (compounded) spot return α is also constant:

$$S(t) = c\,e^{\alpha t}$$ (5.8)

Essentially, we want to mathematically describe those lines in Figures 5.2 and 5.3, with the slight modification that they terminate not on a horizontal line, but one that has a nonzero slope. So the model we adopt for the price of a future that matures at time T is

$$F(t, T) = c\,e^{\alpha t}exp(\gamma(t - T))$$ (5.9)

where c, α, and γ are constants. The total return of a contract is given by

$$\partial(\log F(t, T))/\partial t = \alpha + \gamma$$ (5.10)

since T is fixed for a specific contract. Finally, the roll return of the futures is given by

$$-\partial(\log F(t, T))/\partial T = \gamma$$ (5.11)

Hence, we have mathematically captured the notion that *total return = spot return + roll return*.

Based on this model, we can use linear regression to estimate the spot and roll returns of a futures series, as is demonstrated in Example 5.3.

Roll returns can be a curse on many seemingly attractive strategies based on knowledge or intuition informed by the underlying spot price. For example, an ETF of commodity producers (such as XLE) usually cointegrates with the spot price of that commodity. But because of the presence of roll return, this ETF may not cointegrate with the futures price of that commodity. Not understanding this subtlety cost me more than $100,000 in trading loss, and ruined my first year (2006) as an independent trader.

Example 5.3: Estimating Spot and Roll Returns Using the Constant Returns Model

If we assume that spot and roll returns are truly constant throughout time, as we did in Equation 5.9, we can use linear regression to estimate their values. It is easy to find the spot return this way, as we just need to regress the log of the spot prices against time. But to find the roll return requires us to pick a fixed point in time, and regress the prices of the various contracts against their time to maturity. In practice, the regression coefficient will depend on that fixed time, and also on the exact set of contracts available at that time. So despite the assumption of constant roll returns, we will still end up with a slowly varying estimated γ.

We will apply this procedure to a few different futures in different categories: the Brazilian Real future BR, the corn future C, the WTI crude oil future CL, the copper future HG, and the two-year U.S. Treasury Note future TU.

In the following program, we assume that the spot price is contained in an $\tau \times 1$ array *spot*, and the futures closing price data are stored in a $\tau \times M$ array *cl*, where τ is the number of trading days, and M is the number of contracts. Certainly not all contracts exist at all times, so we will denote the prices for those days when some contracts are nonexistent as NaN.

We will first find the average annualized (compounded) spot return with a simple regression below. (The program can be downloaded as *estimateFuturesReturns.m*.)

```
T=[1:length(spot)]';
T(isBadData)=[];
res=ols(log(spot), [T ones(size(T, 1), 1)]);

fprintf(1, 'Average annualized spot return=%f\n', ...
  252*smartmean(res.beta(1)));
```

Next, we will fit the forward curve (the future price as a function of maturity date) in order to obtain the values for the roll return γ; that is, we will pick one day at a time and fit the prices of futures of five nearest maturities to their time-to-maturity T (measured in months), as long as there are five consecutive contracts for the fitting. (The forward curve might well change from contango to

(Continued)

Example 5.3 (*Continued*)

backwardation or vice versa beyond the nearest five contracts.) We store the values of γ in a τ × 1 array *gamma*.

```
Gamma=NaN(size(tday));
for t=1:length(tday)
  FT=cl(t, :)';
  idx=find(isfinite(FT));
  idxDiff=fwdshift(1, idx)-idx; % ensure consecutive months
    % futures
  if (length(idx) >= 5 && all(idxDiff(1:4)==1))
    FT=FT(idx(1:5));
    T=[1:length(FT)]';

    res=ols(log(FT), [T ones(size(T, 1), 1)]);
    gamma(t)=-12*res.beta(1);
  end
end
```

To verify that Equation 5.7 is sensible, we scatter-plot the log futures values of CL against the time to maturity at one fixed point in time in Figure 5.4 and check that they do fall on a straight line quite neatly. (We restrict ourselves to only five nearest contracts in this scatter plot. Prices of contracts farther out in maturities may not fall onto the same straight line so neatly, indicating a breakdown in Equation 5.7)

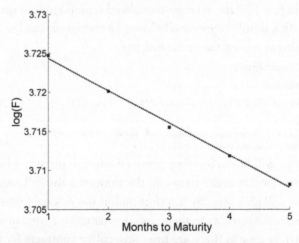

FIGURE 5.4 Scatter Plot of Log Futures Values against Time-to-Maturity for CL 2007 January to May Contracts. The log prices fall neatly on a straight line.

Example 5.3 (*Continued*)

The annualized values for γ over the period November 22, 2004, to August 13, 2012, for CL are plotted in Figure 5.5.

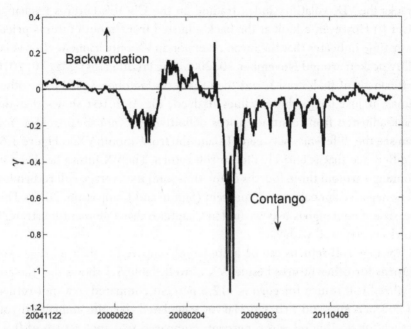

FIGURE 5.5   Values of the Roll Return γ for CL. Positive values indicate backwardation and negative values indicate contango.

I listed the average annualized values for the spot returns α and the roll returns γ for the five futures in Table 5.1. You can see that for BR, C, and TU, the magnitude of the roll returns is much larger than that of the spot returns!

TABLE 5.1	Annualized Average Spot and Roll Returns for Various Futures	
Symbol	α	γ
BR (CME)	−2.7%	10.8%
C (CBOT)	2.8%	−12.8%
CL (NYMEX)	7.3%	−7.1%
HG (CME)	5.0%	7.7%
TU (CBOT)	−0.0%	3.2%

Another example: Every student of finance knows that volatility is mean reverting; more precisely, we know that the VIX index is mean reverting. In fact, an augmented Dickey-Fuller (ADF) test will show that it is stationary with 99 percent certainty. You might think, then, that trading VX futures would be a great mean-reverting strategy. (VX is the future that tracks the VIX volatility index trading on the CBOE's Futures Exchange [CFE].) However, a look at the back-adjusted front-month futures prices over time indicates that the mean reversion in VX only happens after volatility peaked around November 20, 2008 (the credit crisis), May 20, 2010 (aftermath of flash crash), and then again on October 3, 2011. At other times, it just inexorably declines. Indeed, the ADF test shows that the back-adjusted front contract prices definitively do not mean-revert. You can see the difference between VIX and the front-month VX in Figure 5.6, a difference that is entirely due to roll return. The VX future has been in contango around three fourths of the time, and the average roll return is a very negative annualized −50 percent (Simon and Campasano, 2012). This persistent contango is why we find in Chapter 6 that a momentum strategy works pretty well with VX.

Average roll returns can be quite large compared to their average spot returns for other futures besides VX as well. Table 5.1 shows that the annualized roll return for corn is −12.8 percent compared to a spot return of 2.8 percent, and Erb and Harvey calculated that the annualized roll return for heating oil is 4.6 percent, compared to a spot return of 0.93 percent, over the period December 1982 to May 2004 (Erb and Harvey, 2006).

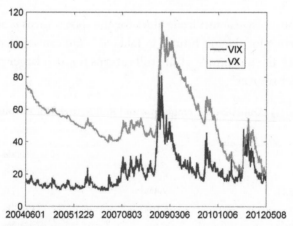

FIGURE 5.6 VIX Index versus Back-Adjusted VX Front Contract Prices

Do Calendar Spreads Mean-Revert?

A calendar spread is a portfolio that consists of a long position in one futures contract, and a short position in another futures contract with the same underlying but a different expiration month. Based on our previous experience with spreads in general, calendar spreads would seem to be great candidates for mean reversion: Aren't both legs tracking the exact same underlying asset? But here again, roll returns derail our intuition. The futures price model expressed in Equation 5.7 will make this clear.

As with any spread trading, we can choose to define the spread as the differences of log prices of the two legs in order to generate trading signals (see Chapter 3), assuming that we maintain the market value of the two legs to be the same at every period. The log market value of a spread portfolio with a long far contract and a short near contract is simply $\gamma(T_1 - T_2)$ with $T_2 > T_1$, according to Equation 5.7. (Again, this simple formula may not hold if $T_2 - T_1$ is large.) The important point is that the calendar spread trading signal does not depend at all on the spot price, only on the roll return!

As we learned in Chapter 2, return series (as opposed to price series) almost always mean-revert. Here we are considering not the total return of a future, but the roll return component only, so things may be different. (Though the model expressed in Equation 5.7 presupposes that the spot and roll returns are both constant, we may nevertheless attempt to apply it to situations where the roll return varies slowly.) We run the ADF test for 12-month log calendar spread of CL, and discovered that it is indeed stationary with 99 percent probability, and a half-life of 36 days. Furthermore, if we apply our usual linear mean-reverting strategy to the log calendar spread for CL, we do get an APR of 8.3 percent and a Sharpe ratio of 1.3 from January 2, 2008, to August 13, 2012. The details of the backtest are described in Example 5.4.

| Example 5.4: Mean Reversion Trading of Calendar Spreads |

As we discussed in the main text, the log market value of a calendar spread portfolio with a long far contract and a short near contract is simply $\gamma(T_1 - T_2)$, with $T_2 > T_1$. Since T_1 and T_2 are fixed for a particular calendar spread, we can use the (hopefully) mean-reverting γ to generate trading signals. In the program

(Continued)

Example 5.4 (*Continued*)

calendarSpdsMeanReversion.m below, we assume that the price of the CL contracts is stored in a $\tau \times M$ array *cl*, where τ is the number of trading days, and M is the number of contracts. We compute γ in the same way as in Example 5.3, and store the resulting values γ in a $\tau \times 1$ array *gamma*. As a first step, we find the half-life of γ.

```
isGoodData=find(isfinite(gamma));
gammalag=lag(gamma(isGoodData), 1);
deltaGamma=gamma(isGoodData)-gammalag;
deltaGamma(1)=[];
gammalag(1)=[];
regress_results=ols(deltaGamma, [gammalag ...
  ones(size(gammalag))]);
halflife=-log(2)/regress_results.beta(1);
```

The half-life is found to be about 36 days. To apply our linear mean reversion strategy, we need to compute the Z-Score, with the lookback set equal to the half-life, as demonstrated in Example 2.5.

```
lookback=round(halflife);
ma=movingAvg(gamma, lookback);
mstd=movingStd(gamma, lookback);
zScore=(gamma-ma)./mstd;
```

Here comes the most difficult part. We need to pick a pair of contracts, far and near, on each historical day, based on three criteria:

1. The holding period for a pair of contracts is 3 months (61 trading days).
2. We roll forward to the next pair of contracts 10 days before the current near contract's expiration.
3. The expiration dates of the near and far contracts are 1 year apart.

Once we have picked those contracts, we assume initially that we will hold a long position in the far contract, and a short position in the near one, subject to revisions later.

```
isExpireDate=false(size(cl));
positions=zeros(size(cl));
```

Example 5.4 (*Continued*)

```
isExpireDate=isfinite(cl) & ~isfinite(fwdshift(1, cl));
holddays=3*21;
numDaysStart=holddays+10;
numDaysEnd=10;
spreadMonth=12; % No. months between far and near contracts.
for c=1:length(contracts)-spreadMonth
  expireIdx=find(isExpireDate(:, c));
  expireIdx=expireIdx(end); % There may be some missing
    % data earlier on
  if (c==1)
    startIdx=max(1, expireIdx-numDaysStart);
    endIdx=expireIdx-numDaysEnd;
  else % ensure next front month contract doesn't start
    until current one ends
    myStartIdx=endIdx+1;
    myEndIdx=expireIdx-numDaysEnd;
    if (myEndIdx-myStartIdx >= holddays)
      startIdx=myStartIdx;
      endIdx=myEndIdx;
    else
      startIdx=NaN;
    end
  end

  if (~isempty(expireIdx) & endIdx > startIdx)
    positions(startIdx:endIdx, c)=-1;
    positions(startIdx:endIdx, c+spreadMonth)=1;
  end
end
```

Finally, we apply the linear mean reversion strategy to determine the true positions and calculate the unlevered daily returns of the portfolio. (The daily return is the daily P&L divided by 2 because we have two contracts.)

```
positions(isnan(zScore), :)=0;
positions(zScore > 0, :)=-positions(zScore > 0, :);
ret=smartsum(lag(positions).*(cl-lag(cl, 1))./lag(cl, 1), ...
  2)/2;
ret(isnan(ret))=0;
```

Example 5.4 (*Continued*)

This results in an attractive unlevered APR of 8.3 percent and a Sharpe ratio of 1.3 from January 2, 2008, to August 13, 2012. The cumulative returns curve is shown in Figure 5.7.

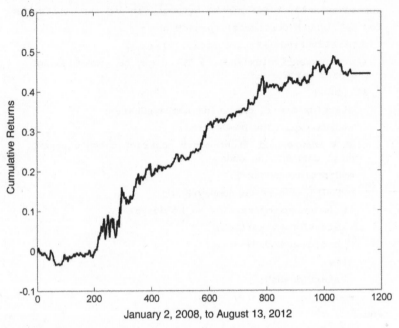

January 2, 2008, to August 13, 2012

FIGURE 5.7 Cumulative Returns of the Linear Mean Reversion Strategy Applied on CL 12-Month Calendar Spread

Students of commodities markets know that seasonality is often a prominent feature. So you may find that for a particular market, only calendar spreads of certain months (and certain months *apart*) mean-revert. However, we won't pursue these market-dependent details here.

We can try this same linear mean reversion strategy on the VX calendar spreads. It turns out that Equation 5.7 works only for a future whose underlying is a *traded* asset, and VIX is not one. (If you scatter-plot the log VX futures prices as a function of time-to-maturity as we did in Figure 5.4 for CL, you will find that they do not fall on a straight line.) Various researchers have suggested alternative formulae suitable for the VX future (see, for example, Dupoyet, Daigler, and Chen, 2011), but I have found that none can explain the mean-reverting property of VX calendar spreads in the face

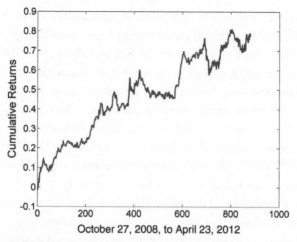

FIGURE 5.8 Cumulative Returns of Linear Mean Reversion Strategy on VX Calendar Spread

of the non-mean reversion of the VX future itself. So we can rely on only our empirical observation that an ADF test on the ratio *back/front* of VX also shows that it is stationary with a 99 percent probability. If we apply our usual linear mean-reverting strategy using ratio as the signal (and with a 15-day look-back for the moving average and standard deviations), VX yields an APR of 17.7 percent and a Sharpe ratio of 1.5 from October 27, 2008, to April 23, 2012 (see Figure 5.8 for a plot of its cumulative returns), though it performed much more poorly prior to October 2008. In the next section, I will present graphic evidence that there is a regime change in the behavior of VIX and its futures around the time of the financial crisis of 2008, so perhaps this abrupt change in the strategy performance is related to that as well.

■ Futures Intermarket Spreads

As I stated in the introduction of this chapter, it is not easy to find futures intermarket spreads (i.e., pairs of futures from different underlyings) that are mean reverting. Nevertheless, let's systematically round up some of the usual suspects.

The most obvious candidate for pair trading futures is intermarket spreads between markets that are closely related. For example, the energy complexes (WTI crude oil CL, Brent crude oil BZ, unleaded gasoline RB, and heating oil HO, all traded on the New York Mercantile Exchange [NYMEX]) should offer rich potential opportunities.

Before we run a Johansen test on these four contracts, we can first examine a well-known portfolio called the *crack spread* consisting of long three contracts of CL, short two contracts of RB, and short one contract of HO. This is called the crack spread because we can obtain gasoline and heating oil by cracking the long hydrocarbon chains of crude oil molecules, and the 3:2:1 hedge ratios come about because three barrels of CL produces approximately two barrels of RB and one barrel of heating oil, though this is not universally true for all refiners. One advantage of trading the crack spread is that NYMEX offers a ready-made basket for it, with a much lower margin requirement than if we trade them separately.

However, running an ADF test on the crack spread from May 20, 2002, to May 4, 2012, shows that this spread is not mean reverting. The chart of this spread (Figure 5.9) reveals a dramatic increase in value around March 9, 2007, to July 3, 2008, and then a sharp drop after that, and running the linear mean reversion strategy on it shows negative returns for that period. (Note that we must back-adjust the continuous contracts using prices rather than returns in this test; otherwise, this price spread will show a discontinuous jump at rollovers, as explained in Chapter 1.)

Another spread that would seem to be a good candidate is CL and BZ in a 1:1 ratio. After all, their underlyings are both crude oils. But another quick ADF test will show that it is far from stationary. BZ has relentlessly outperformed CL due to a variety of factors. The likely culprits include the increasing oil production in the United States (Friedman, 2012), the pipeline bottleneck at Cushing, Oklahoma (Philips, 2012), and geopolitical concerns

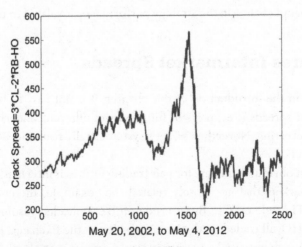

FIGURE 5.9 The Crack Spread

such as the embargo against Iranian oil in 2012, which affected Europe and therefore BZ more than the United States.

If you want to backtest intermarket spreads yourself, don't forget to make sure that their prices are synchronous, as I cautioned in Chapter 1. In particular, before BZ started trading at the NYMEX on September 5, 2001, it was traded at the Intercontinental Petroleum Exchange in London, which obviously has a different closing time than NYMEX on which CL has always been traded. So backtesting the BZ-CL spread before September 5, 2001, using closing prices would be wrong. Also, we often need to multiply the futures prices by a factor to convert points into USD.

Our search for mean-reverting intermarket futures spreads has not been fruitful so far. But I will now discuss one unusual spread that will change that.

Volatility Futures versus Equity Index Futures

Many traders have observed that volatility is anti-correlated with the stock equity market index: When the market goes down, volatility shoots up, and to a lesser extent, vice versa. One way to visualize this inverse relationship is to plot ES, the E-mini S&P 500 futures front-month prices, against VX, the VIX futures front-month prices. This can be accomplished by the "scatter" function in MATLAB, and the result is displayed in Figure 5.10.

The first obvious feature of this plot is that, indeed, the stock index has an inverse relationship with volatility. But, more interestingly, there appeared to be two main regimes, 2004 to May 2008 and August 2008 to 2012. The second regime has a notably lower volatility for a given stock index level. In plain

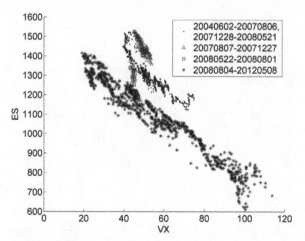

FIGURE 5.10   A Study of Volatility Regimes: ES versus VX

English, the market is less volatile nowadays. However, the range of volatilities is greater now, meaning that we have days with more extreme volatilities than before. (There are other, shorter periods that may represent transitional states, but we will ignore them in our analysis.) It would be a mistake to run a linear regression or apply the Johansen test to a mixture of both regimes, so we focus on the second one, which extends to the time of this writing.

We choose to compute the regression coefficients only for the first 500 days of the post–August 2008 data as the training set because later we would like to use the various statistics from this regression to build our trading model. Before we actually run the prices through the linear regression program, we have to remember that the futures prices of VX and ES are in different units: one point move in VX is $1,000, while one point move in ES is $50. So we need to multiply the prices of VX by 1,000 and the prices of ES by 50 in order for the hedge ratio to properly reflect the ratio in the number of contracts.

The linear relationship is shown in Equation 5.11.

$$ES \times 50 = -0.3906 \times VX \times 1,000 + \$77,150 \qquad (5.11)$$

where ES and VX are their respective futures (settlement) prices. The standard deviation of the residues is $2,047. This means that a portfolio that is long 0.3906 contracts of VX and long one contract of ES should be stationary, as a plot (Figure 5.11) of this portfolio's market value would convince us.

We can construct a Bollinger band–like mean-reverting strategy by shorting this portfolio whenever its value deviates from one standard deviation

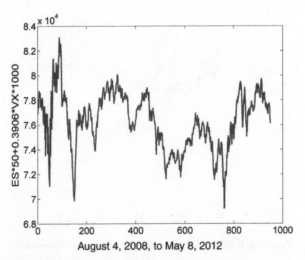

FIGURE 5.11 Stationary Portfolio of ES and VX

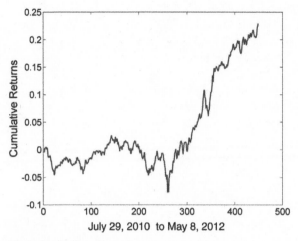

July 29, 2010 to May 8, 2012

FIGURE 5.12 Cumulative Returns of VX-ES Mean
Reversion Strategy

of the residuals determined in the training set. The APR on the test set July
29, 2010, to May 8, 2012, is 12.3 percent, with a Sharpe ratio of 1.4. It was
particularly profitable starting around the time of the Standard and Poor's
downgrade of the U.S. credit rating. The cumulative returns curve is shown
in Figure 5.12.

There is a different VX versus ES strategy that we can employ, which does
not rely on the mean-reverting properties of the spread VX-ES. Because that
is a momentum strategy, I will discuss it in the next chapter.

KEY POINTS

- "Commodity" currencies as a group offer many opportunities for
  cointegration.
- In computing the returns of a portfolio with two currency cross-rates, did
  you pay attention to whether they have the same quote currency, the same
  base currency, or neither? The formulae for computing returns are not the
  same for all cases.
- Futures returns consist of two components: spot returns and roll returns.
- Backwardation means roll returns are positive, and far contracts are
  cheaper than near contracts. Contango means roll returns are negative, and
  far contracts are more expensive than near contracts.
- Because of roll returns, mean reversion of the spot price may not induce
  mean reversion of the futures price.
- Mean reversion of futures calendar spreads of traded assets depends on
  mean reversion of roll returns.

CHAPTER 6

Interday Momentum Strategies

There are four main causes of momentum:

1. For futures, the persistence of roll returns, especially of their signs.
2. The slow diffusion, analysis, and acceptance of new information.
3. The forced sales or purchases of assets of various type of funds.
4. Market manipulation by high-frequency traders.

We will be discussing trading strategies that take advantage of each cause of momentum in this and the next chapter. In particular, roll returns of futures, which featured prominently in the last chapter, will again take center stage. Myriad futures strategies can be constructed out of the persistence of the sign of roll returns.

Researchers sometimes classify momentum in asset prices into two types: time series momentum and cross-sectional momentum, just as we classified mean reversion into two corresponding types in Chapter 2 (Moskowitz, Yao, and Pedersen, 2010). Time series momentum is very simple and intuitive: past returns of a price series are positively correlated with future returns. Cross-sectional momentum refers to the relative performance of a price series in relation to other price series: a price series with returns that outperformed other price series will likely keep doing so in the future and vice versa. We will examine examples of both types in momentum in futures and stocks.

The strategies I describe in this chapter tend to hold positions for multiple days, which is why I call them "interday" momentum strategies. I will consider the intraday, higher-frequency momentum strategies in the next chapter. The reason for this distinction is that many interday momentum strategies suffer from a recently discovered weakness, while intraday momentum strategies are less affected by it. I will highlight this weakness in this chapter, and also discuss the very different properties of momentum strategies versus their mean-reverting counterparts, as well as their pros and cons.

■ Tests for Time Series Momentum

Before we delve into the different causes of momentum, we should first see how we can measure momentum, or more specifically, time series momentum. Time series momentum of a price series means that past returns are positively correlated with future returns. It follows that we can just calculate the correlation coefficient of the returns together with its p-value (which represents the probability for the null hypothesis of no correlation). One feature of computing the correlation coefficient is that we have to pick a specific time lag for the returns. Sometimes, the most positive correlations are between returns of different lags. For example, 1-day returns might show negative correlations, while the correlation between past 20-day return with the future 40-day return might be very positive. We should find the optimal pair of past and future periods that gives the highest positive correlation and use that as our look-back and holding period for our momentum strategy.

Alternatively, we can also test for the correlations between the signs of past and future returns. This is appropriate when all we want to know is that an up move will be followed by another up move, and we don't care whether the magnitudes of the moves are similar.

If we are interested instead in finding out whether there is long-term trending behavior in the time series without regard to specific time frames, we can calculate the Hurst exponent together with the Variance Ratio test to rule out the null hypothesis of random walk. These tests were described in Chapter 2 for the detection of mean reversion, but they can just as well be used as momentum tests.

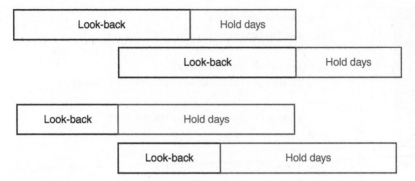

FIGURE 6.1 Nonoverlapping Periods for Correlation Calculations

I will illustrate the use of these tests below using the two-year Treasury note future TU trading on the Chicago Mercantile Exchange (CME) as an example. The correlation coefficient and its p-value can be computed using the MATLAB function *corrcoef*, while the Hurst exponent and Variance Ratio test are, as before, given by *genhurst* and *vratiotest*.

In computing the correlations of pairs of returns resulting from different look-back and holding periods, we must take care not to use overlapping data. If look-back is greater than the holding period, we have to shift forward by the holding period to generate a new returns pair. If the holding period is greater than the look-back, we have to shift forward by the look-back period. This is illustrated in Figure 6.1.

The top two bars in Figure 6.1 are for the case where look-back is greater than the holding period. The top bar represents the data set that forms the first returns pair, and the second bar from the top represents the data set that forms the second independent returns pair. The bottom two bars are for the case where the look-back is smaller than the holding. The code is listed below (and available for download as *TU_mom.m*).

BOX 6.1

Finding Correlations between Returns of Different Time Frames

```
% Correlation tests
for lookback=[1 5 10 25 60 120 250]
    for holddays=[1 5 10 25 60 120 250]
        ret_lag=(cl-backshift(lookback, cl)) ...
            ./backshift(lookback, cl);
        ret_fut=(fwdshift(holddays, cl)-cl)./cl;
        badDates=any([isnan(ret_lag) isnan(ret_fut)], 2);
```

(Continued)

BOX 6.1 (*Continued*)

```
            ret_lag(badDates)=[];
            ret_fut(badDates)=[];

            if (lookback >= holddays)
                indepSet=[1:lookback:length(ret_lag)];
            else
                indepSet=[1:holddays:length(ret_lag)];
            end

            ret_lag=ret_lag(indepSet);
            ret_fut=ret_fut(indepSet);

            [cc, pval]=corrcoef(ret_lag, ret_fut);
            fprintf(1, 'lookback=%3i holddays=%3i cc=%7.4f ...
                pval=%6.4f\n', lookback, holddays, cc(1, 2), ...
                pval(1, 2));
    end
end
```

If we shift the data forward by one day, we will get a slightly different set of returns for computing our correlations. For simplicity, I have only tested correlation of one among many possible sets of returns, but because of the large overlap of data between two different sets of returns, the results are unlikely to be greatly different. Some of the more significant results are tabulated in Table 6.1.

We see that there is a compromise between the correlation coefficient and the p-value. The following (look-back, holding days) pairs offer some of the best compromises: (60, 10), (60, 25), (250, 10), (250, 25), (250, 60), (250, 120). Of course, from a trading point of view, we prefer as short a holding period as possible as those tend to generate the best Sharpe ratios.

I have also tested the correlations between the signs of past and future returns instead, and the results are not very different from Table 6.1. I found the best pair candidates in that case are (60, 10), (250, 10), and (250, 25).

In contrast, we found that the Hurst exponent is 0.44, while the Variance Ratio test failed to reject the hypothesis that this is a random walk.

How are these two conflicting results reconciled? As we show in the correlation tests, this time series (as with many other financial time series) exhibits momentum and mean reversion at different time frames. The Variance Ratio test is unable to test the specific time frames where the correlations might be stronger than average.

TABLE 6.1	Correlations between TU Returns of Different Time Frames		
Look-back	Holding days	Correlation coefficient	*p*-value
25	1	−0.0140	0.5353
25	5	0.0319	0.5276
25	10	0.1219	0.0880
25	25	0.1955	0.0863
25	60	0.2333	0.0411
25	120	0.1482	0.2045
25	250	0.2620	0.0297
60	1	0.0313	0.1686
60	5	0.0799	0.1168
60	10	0.1718	0.0169
60	25	0.2592	0.0228
60	60	0.2162	0.2346
60	120	−0.0331	0.8598
60	250	0.3137	0.0974
120	1	0.0222	0.3355
120	5	0.0565	0.2750
120	10	0.0955	0.1934
120	25	0.1456	0.2126
120	60	−0.0192	0.9182
120	120	0.2081	0.4567
120	250	0.4072	0.1484
250	1	0.0411	0.0857
250	5	0.1068	0.0462
250	10	0.1784	0.0185
250	25	0.2719	0.0238
250	60	0.4245	0.0217
250	120	0.5112	0.0617
250	250	0.4873	0.3269

■ Time Series Strategies

For a certain future, if we find that the correlation coefficient between a past return of a certain look-back and a future return of a certain holding period is high, and the *p*-value is small, we can proceed to see if a profitable momentum strategy can be found using this set of optimal time periods. Since Table 6.1 shows us that for TU, the 250-25-days pairs of returns have a correlation coefficient of 0.27 with a *p*-value of 0.02, we will pick this look-back and holding period. We take our cue for a simple time series momentum strategy from a paper by Moskowitz, Yao, and Pedersen: simply buy (sell) the future if it has a positive (negative) 12-month return, and hold the position for 1 month (Moskowitz, Yao, and Pedersen, 2012). We will modify one detail of the original strategy: Instead of making a trading decision every month, we will make it every day, each day investing only one twenty-fifth of the total capital.

Example 6.1:TU Momentum Strategy

This code assumes the closing prices are contained in a $T \times 1$ array cl. This code is contained in *TU_mom.m*.

```
lookback=250;
holddays=25;

longs=cl > backshift(lookback, cl)  ;
shorts=cl < backshift(lookback, cl) ;

pos=zeros(length(cl), 1);

for h=0:holddays-1
    long_lag=backshift(h, longs);
    long_lag(isnan(long_lag))=false;
    long_lag=logical(long_lag);

    short_lag=backshift(h, shorts);
    short_lag(isnan(short_lag))=false;
    short_lag=logical(short_lag);

    pos(long_lag)=pos(long_lag)+1;
    pos(short_lag)=pos(short_lag)-1;
end

ret=(backshift(1, pos).*(cl-lag(cl))./lag(cl))/holddays;
```

From June 1, 2004, to May 11, 2012, the Sharpe ratio is a respectable 1. The annual percentage rate (APR) of 1.7 percent may seem low, but our return is calculated based on the notional value of the contract, which is

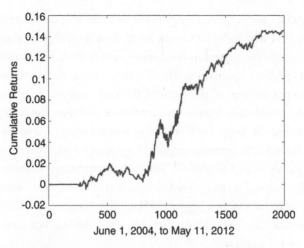

FIGURE 6.2 Equity Curve of TU Momentum Strategy

about $200,000. Margin requirement for this contract is only about $400. So you can certainly employ a reasonable amount of leverage to boost return, though one must also contend with the maximum drawdown of 2.5 percent. The equity curve also looks quite attractive (see Figure 6.2).

This simple strategy can be applied to all kinds of futures contracts, with different optimal look-back periods and the holding days. The results for three futures we considered are listed in Table 6.2.

Why do many futures returns exhibit serial correlations? And why do these serial correlations occur only at a fairly long time scale? The explanation lies in the roll return component of the total return of futures we discussed in Chapter 5. Typically, the sign of roll returns does not vary very often. In other words, the futures stay in contango or backwardation over long periods of time. The spot returns, however, can vary very rapidly in both sign and magnitude. So if we hold a future over a long period of time, and if the average roll returns dominate the average total returns, we will find serial correlation of total returns. This explanation certainly makes sense for BR, HG, and TU, since from Table 5.1 we can see that they all have

TABLE 6.2 Time Series Momentum Strategies for Various Futures

Symbol	Look-back	Holding days	APR	Sharpe ratio	Max drawdown
BR (CME)	100	10	17.7%	1.09	−14.8%
HG (CME)	40	40	18.0%	1.05	−24.0%
TU (CBOT)	250	25	1.7%	1.04	−2.5%

roll returns that are bigger in magnitude than their spot returns. (I haven't found the reason why it doesn't work for C, despite its having the largest roll return magnitude compared to its average spot return, but maybe you can!)

If we accept the explanation that the time series momentum of futures is due to the persistence of the signs of the roll returns, then we can devise a cleaner and potentially better momentum signal than the lagged total return. We can use the lagged roll return as a signal instead, and go long when this return is higher than some threshold, go short when this return is lower than the negative of that threshold, and exit any existing position otherwise. Applying this revised strategy on TU with a threshold of an annualized roll return of 3 percent yields a higher APR of 2.5 percent and Sharpe ratio of 2.1 from January 2, 2009, to August 13, 2012, with a reduced maximum drawdown of 1.1 percent.

There are many other possible entry signals besides the simple "sign of return" indicator. For example, we can buy when the price reaches a new N-day high, when the price exceeds the N-day moving average or exponential moving average, when the price exceeds the upper Bollinger band, or when the number of up days exceeds the number of down days in a moving period.

There is also a classic momentum strategy called the Alexander Filter, which tells us to buy when the daily return moves up at least x percent, and then sell and go short if the price moves down at least x percent from a subsequent high (Fama and Blume, 1966).

Sometimes, the combination of mean-reverting and momentum rules may work better than each strategy by itself. One example strategy on CL is this: buy at the market close if the price is lower than that of 30 days ago and is higher than that of 40 days ago; vice versa for shorts. If neither the buy nor the sell condition is satisfied, flatten any existing position. The APR is 12 percent, with a Sharpe ratio of 1.1. Adding a mean-reverting filter to the momentum strategy in Example 6.1 will add IBX (MEFF), KT (NYMEX), SXF (DE), US (CBOT), CD (CME), NG (NYMEX), and W (CME) to Table 6.2, and it will also improve the returns and Sharpe ratios of the existing contracts in that table.

In fact, if you don't want to construct your own time series momentum strategy, there is a ready-made index that is composed of 24 futures: the Standard & Poor's (S&P) Diversified Trends Indicator (DTI). The essential strategy behind this index is that we will long a future if it is above its exponential moving average, and short it if it is below, with monthly rebalancing. (For details, you can visit www.standardandpoors.com.) There is a mutual fund (RYMFX) as well as an exchange-traded fund (WDTI) that tracks this index. Michael Dever computed that the Sharpe ratio of this index was 1.3 with a maximum drawdown of −16.6 percent from January 1988 to December 2010 (Dever, 2011). (This may be compared to the S&P 500 index SPX, which has a Sharpe ratio of 0.61 and a maximum drawdown of −50.96 percent over the same period, according to the author.) However, in common with many other momentum strategies, its performance is poor since the 2008 financial crisis, a point that will be taken up later.

Since there aren't many trades in the relatively limited amount of test data that we used due to the substantial holding periods, there is a risk of data-snooping bias in these results. The real test for the strategy is, as always, in true out-of-sample testing.

■ Extracting Roll Returns through Future versus ETF Arbitrage

If futures' total returns = spot returns + roll returns, then an obvious way to extract roll return is buy the underlying asset and short the futures, if the roll return is negative (i.e., under contango); and vice versa if the roll return is positive (i.e., under backwardation). This will work as long as the sign of the roll return does not change quickly, as it usually doesn't. This arbitrage strategy is also likely to result in a shorter holding period and a lower risk than the buy-and-hold strategy discussed in the previous section, since in that strategy we needed to hold the future for a long time before the noisy spot return can be averaged out.

However, the logistics of buying and especially shorting the underlying asset is not simple, unless an exchange-traded fund (ETF) exists that holds the asset. Such ETFs can be found for many precious metals. For example, GLD actually owns physical gold, and thus tracks the gold spot price very closely. Gold futures have a negative roll return of −4.9 percent annualized from December 1982 to May 2004. A backtest shows that holding a long position in GLD and a short position in GC yields an annualized return of 1.9 percent and a maximum drawdown of 0.8 percent from August 3, 2007, to August 2, 2010. This might seem attractive, given that one can apply a leverage of 5 or 6 and get a decent return with reasonable risk, but in reality it is not. Remember that in contrast to owning futures, owning GLD actually incurs financing cost, which is not very different from 1.9 percent over the backtest period! So the excess return of this strategy is close to zero.

(The astute reader might notice another caveat of our quick backtest of GC versus GLD: the settlement or closing prices of GC are recorded at

1:30 P.M. ET, while those of GLD are recorded at 4:00 P.M. ET. This asynchronicity is a pitfall that I mentioned in Chapter 1. However, it doesn't matter to us in this case because the trading signals are generated based on GC closing prices alone.)

If we try to look outside of precious metals ETFs to find such arbitrage opportunities, we will be stumped. There are no ETFs that hold other physical commodities as opposed to commodities futures, due to the substantial storage costs of those commodities. However, there is a less exact form of arbitrage that allows us to extract the roll returns. ETFs containing commodities producing companies often cointegrate with the spot price of those commodities, since these commodities form a substantial part of their assets. So we can use these ETFs as proxy for the spot price and use them to extract the roll returns of the corresponding futures.

One good example is the arbitrage between the energy sector ETF XLE and the WTI crude oil futures CL. Since XLE and CL have different closing times, it is easier to study the arbitrage between XLE and the ETF USO instead, which contains nothing but front month contracts of CL. The strategy is simple:

- Short USO and long XLE whenever CL is in contango.

- Long USO and short XLE whenever CL is in backwardation.

The APR is a very respectable 16 percent from April 26, 2006, to April 9, 2012, with a Sharpe ratio of about 1. I have plotted the cumulative returns curve in Figure 6.3.

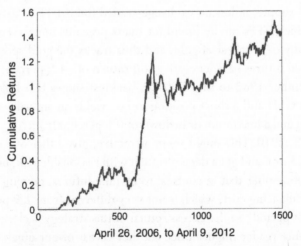

FIGURE 6.3 Cumulative Returns of XLE-USO Arbitrage

What about a future whose underlying is not a traded commodity? VX is an example of such a future: It is very expensive to maintain a basket of options that replicate the underlying VIX index, and no ETF sponsors have been foolish enough to do that. But, again, we do not need to find an instrument that tracks the spot price exactly—we just need to find one that has a high correlation (or anti-correlation) with the spot return. In the case of VIX, the familiar ETF SPY fits the bill. Because the S&P E-mini future ES has insignificant roll return (about 1 percent annualized), it has almost the same returns as the underlying asset. Because it is certainly easier to trade futures than an ETF, we will investigate the performance of our earlier arbitrage strategy using ES instead.

Volatility Futures versus Equity Index Futures: Redux

VX is a natural choice if we want to extract roll returns: its roll returns can be as low as −50 percent annualized. At the same time, it is highly anti-correlated with ES, with a correlation coefficient of daily returns reaching −75 percent. In Chapter 5, we used the cointegration between VX and ES to develop a profitable mean-reverting strategy. Here, we will make use of the large roll return magnitude of VX, the small roll return magnitude of ES, and the anticorrelation of VX and ES to develop a momentum strategy.

This strategy was proposed by Simon and Campasano (2012):

1. If the price of the front contract of VX is higher than that of VIX by 0.1 point (contango) times the number of trading days untill settlement, short 0.3906 front contracts of VX and short 1 front contract of ES. Hold for one day.
2. If the price of the front contract of VX is lower than that of VIX by 0.1 point (backwardation) times the number of trading days untill settlement, buy 0.3906 front contracts of VX and buy 1 front contract of ES. Hold for one day.

Recall that if the front contract price is higher than the spot price, the roll return is negative (see Figure 5.3). So the difference in price between VIX and VX divided by the time to maturity is the roll return, and we buy VX if the roll return is positive. Why didn't we use the procedure in Example 5.3 where we use the slope of the futures log forward curve to compute the roll return here? That is because Equation 5.7 doesn't work for VX, and therefore the VX forward prices do not fall on a straight line, as explained in Chapter 5.

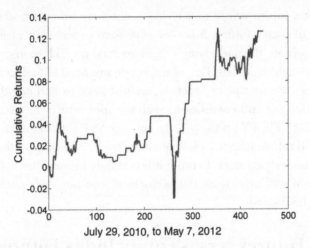

July 29, 2010, to May 7, 2012

FIGURE 6.4 Cumulative Returns of VX-ES Roll Returns Strategy

Notice that the hedge ratio of this strategy is slightly different from that reported by Simon and Campasano: It is based on the regression fit between the VX versus ES prices in Equation 5.11, not between their returns as in the original paper. The settlement is the day after the contracts expire. The APR for July 29, 2010, to May 7, 2012 (this period was not used for hedge ratio determination) is 6.9 percent, with a Sharpe ratio of 1. The cumulative return chart is displayed in Figure 6.4. You can find the MATLAB code for this strategy in *VX_ES_rollreturn.m* on my website.

■ Cross-Sectional Strategies

There is a third way to extract the often large roll returns in futures besides buying and holding or arbitraging against the underlying asset (or against an instrument correlated with the underlying asset). This third way is a cross-sectional strategy: We can just buy a portfolio of futures in backwardation, and simultaneously short a portfolio of futures in contango. The hope is that the returns of the spot prices cancel each other out (a not unreasonable expectation if we believe commodities' spot prices are positively correlated with economic growth or some other macroeconomic indices), and we are left with the favorable roll returns. Daniel and Moskowitz described just such a simple "cross-sectional" momentum strategy that is almost a mirror image of the linear long-short mean-reverting stock model proposed by Khandani and Lo described in Chapter 3, albeit one with a much longer look-back and holding period (Daniel and Moskowitz, 2011).

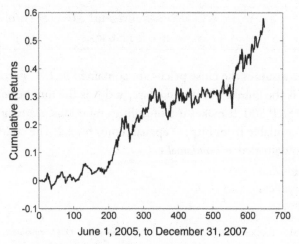

June 1, 2005, to December 31, 2007

FIGURE 6.5 Cumulative Returns of Cross-Sectional
Futures Momentum Strategy

A simplified version of the strategy is to rank the 12-month return (or 252
trading days in our program below) of a group of 52 physical commodities
every day, and buy and hold the future with the highest return for 1 month (or
25 trading days) while short and hold the future with the lowest return for the
same period. I tested this strategy from June 1, 2005, to December 31, 2007,
and the APR is an excellent 18 percent with a Sharpe ratio of 1.37. The cumulative returns are plotted in Figure 6.5. Unfortunately, this model performed
very negatively from January 2, 2008, to December 31, 2009, with an APR of
−33 percent, though its performance recovered afterwards. The financial crisis
of 2008–2009 ruined this momentum strategy, just like it did many others,
including the S&P DTI indicator mentioned before.

Daniel and Moskowitz have also found that this same strategy worked for
the universe of world stock indices, currencies, international stocks, and
U.S. stocks—in other words, practically everything under the sun. Obviously, cross-sectional momentum in currencies and stocks can no longer be
explained by the persistence of the sign of roll returns. We might attribute
that to the serial correlation in world economic or interest rate growth in
the currency case, and the slow diffusion, analysis, and acceptance of new
information in the stock case.

Applying this strategy to U.S. stocks, we can buy and hold stocks within
the top decile of 12-month lagged returns for a month, and vice versa for
the bottom decile. I illustrate the strategy in Example 6.2.

Example 6.2: Cross-Sectional Momentum Strategy for Stocks

This code assumes the close prices are contained in $T \times N$ array *cl*, where T is the number of trading days, and N is the number of the stocks in S&P 500. It makes use of utilities functions *smartsum* and *backshift*, available from http://epchan.com/book2. The code itself can be downloaded as *kentdaniel.m*.

```
lookback=252;
holddays=25;
topN=50;

ret=(cl- backshift(lookback,cl))./backshift(lookback,cl);
  % daily returns
longs=false(size(ret));
shorts=false(size(ret));

positions=zeros(size(ret));
for t=lookback+1:length(tday)
    [foo idx]=sort(ret(t, :), 'ascend');
    nodata=find(isnan(ret(t, :)));
    idx=setdiff(idx, nodata, 'stable');
    longs(t, idx(end-topN+1:end))=true;
    shorts(t, idx(1:topN))=true;
end

for h=0:holddays-1
    long_lag=backshift(h, longs);
    long_lag(isnan(long_lag))=false;
    long_lag=logical(long_lag);

    short_lag=backshift(h, shorts);
    short_lag(isnan(short_lag))=false;
    short_lag=logical(short_lag);

    positions(long_lag)=positions(long_lag)+1;
    positions(short_lag)=positions(short_lag)-1;
end

dailyret=smartsum(backshift(1, positions).*(cl-lag(cl)) ...
  ./ lag(cl), 2)/(2*topN)/holddays;

dailyret(isnan(dailyret))=0;
```

Example 6.2 (*Continued*)

The APR from May 15, 2007, to December 31, 2007, is 37 percent with a Sharpe ratio of 4.1. The cumulative returns are shown in Figure 6.6. (Daniel and Moskowitz found an annualized average return of 16.7 percent and a Sharpe ratio of 0.83 from 1947 to 2007.) However, the APR from January 2, 2008, to December 31, 2009, is a miserable −30 percent. The financial crisis of 2008–2009 also ruined this momentum strategy. The return after 2009 did stabilize, though it hasn't returned to its former high level yet.

Just as in the case of the cross-sectional mean reversion strategy discussed in Chapter 4, instead of ranking stocks by their lagged returns, we can rank them by many other variables, or "factors," as they are usually called. While we wrote *total return = spot return + roll return* for futures, we can write *total return = market return + factor returns* for stocks. A cross-sectional portfolio of stocks, whether mean reverting or momentum based, will eliminate the market return component, and its returns will be driven solely by the factors. These factors may be fundamental, such as earnings growth or book-to-price ratio, or some linear combination thereof. Or they may be statistical factors that are derived from, for example, Principal Component Analysis (PCA) as described in *Quantitative Trading* (Chan, 2009). All these factors

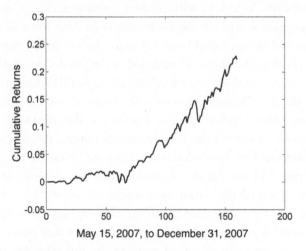

FIGURE 6.6 Cumulative Returns of Cross-Sectional Stock Momentum Strategy

with the possible exception of PCA tend to change slowly, so using them to rank stocks will result in as long holding periods as the cross-sectional models I discussed in this section.

While we are on the subject of factors, it bears mentioning that a factor model can be applied to a cross-sectional portfolio of futures as well. In this case, we can find macroeconomic factors such as gross domestic product (GDP) growth or inflation rate and correlate them with the returns of each futures instrument, or we can again employ PCA.

In recent years, with the advance of computer natural language processing and understanding capability, there is one other factor that has come into use. This is the so-called news sentiment score, our next topic.

News Sentiment as a Fundamental Factor

With the advent of machine-readable, or "elementized," newsfeeds, it is now possible to programmatically capture all the news items on a company, not just those that fit neatly into one of the narrow categories such as earnings announcements or merger and acquisition (M&A) activities. Furthermore, natural language processing algorithms are now advanced enough to analyze the textual information contained in these news items, and assign a "sentiment score" to each news article that is indicative of its price impact on a stock, and an aggregation of these sentiment scores from multiple news articles from a certain period was found to be predictive of its future return. For example, Hafez and Xie, using RavenPack's Sentiment Index, found that buying a portfolio of stocks with positive sentiment change and shorting one with negative sentiment change results in an APR from 52 percent to 156 percent and Sharpe ratios from 3.9 to 5.3 before transaction costs, depending on how many stocks are included in the portfolios (Hafez and Xie, 2012). The success of these cross-sectional strategies also demonstrates very neatly that the slow diffusion of news is the cause of stock momentum.

There are other vendors besides RavenPack that provide news sentiments on stocks. Examples include Recorded Future, thestocksonar.com, and Thomson Reuters News Analytics. They differ on the scope of their news coverage and also on the algorithm they use to generate the sentiment score. If you believe your own sentiment algorithm is better than theirs, you can subscribe directly to an elementized news feed instead and apply your algorithm to it. I mentioned before that Newsware offers a low-cost version of this type of news feeds, but offerings with lower latency and better coverage are provided by Bloomberg Event-Driven

Trading, Dow Jones Elementized News Feeds, and Thomson Reuters Machine Readable News.

Beyond such very reasonable use of news sentiment as a factor for cross-sectional momentum trading, there has also been research that suggested the general "mood" of society as revealed in the content of Twitter feeds is predictive of the market index itself (Bollen, Mao, and Zeng, 2010). In fact, a multimillion-dollar hedge fund was launched to implement this outlandish idea (Bryant, 2010), though the validity of the research itself was under attack (*Buy the Hype*, 2012).

Mutual Funds Asset Fire Sale and Forced Purchases

Researchers Coval and Stafford (2007) found that mutual funds experiencing large redemptions are likely to reduce or eliminate their existing stock positions. This is no surprise since mutual funds are typically close to fully invested, with very little cash reserves. More interestingly, funds experiencing large capital inflows tend to increase their existing stock positions rather than using the additional capital to invest in other stocks, perhaps because new investment ideas do not come by easily. Stocks disproportionately held by poorly performing mutual funds facing redemptions therefore experience negative returns. Furthermore, this asset "fire sale" by poorly performing mutual funds is contagious. Since the fire sale depresses the stock prices, they suppress the performance of other funds holding those stocks, too, causing further redemptions at those funds. The same situation occurs in reverse for stocks disproportionately held by superbly performing mutual funds with large capital inflows. Hence, momentum in both directions for the commonly held stocks can be ignited.

(This ignition of price momentum due to order flow is actually a rather general phenomenon, and it happens at even the shortest time scale. We find more details on that in the context of high-frequency trading in Chapter 7.)

A factor can be constructed to measure the selling (buying) pressure on a stock based on the net percentage of funds holding them that experienced redemptions (inflows). More precisely,

$$PRESSURE(i, t)$$
$$= \frac{\sum_j (Buy(j,i,t)\mid flow(j,t) > 5\%) - \sum_j (Sell(j,i,t)\mid flow(j,t) < -5\%)}{\sum_j Own(j,i,t-1)}$$

$$(6.1)$$

where *PRESSURE(i, t)* is the factor for stock *i* at the end of quarter *t*, *Buy(j, i, t)* = 1 if fund *j* increased its holding in stock *i* during the quarter *t* and if the fund experienced inflows greater than 5 percent of its net asset value (NAV) ("*flow(j, t)* > 5%"), and zero otherwise. *Sell(j, i, t)* is similarly defined for decreases in holdings, and $\sum_j Own(j, i, t - 1)$ is the total number of mutual funds holding stock *i* the beginning of quarter *t*.

Note that the *PRESSURE* variable does not take into account the size (NAV) of the fund, as *Buy* is a binary variable. One wonders whether weighing *Buy* by NAV will give better results.

Coval and Stafford found that a market-neutral portfolio formed based on shorting stocks with highest selling pressure (bottom decile of *PRESSURE* ranking) and buying stocks with the highest (top decile of *PRESSURE* ranking) buying pressure generates annualized returns of about 17 percent before transaction costs. (Since data on stock holdings are available generally on a quarterly basis only, our portfolio is updated quarterly as well.)

Furthermore, capital flows into and out of mutual funds can be predicted with good accuracy based on their past performance and capital flows, a reflection of the herdlike behavior of retail investors. Based on this prediction, we can also predict the future value of the pressure factor noted above. In other words, we can front-run the mutual funds in our selling (buying) of the stocks they currently own. This front-running strategy generates another 17 percent annualized return before transaction costs.

Finally, since these stocks experience such selling and buying pressures due to liquidity-driven reasons, and suffer suppression or elevation of their prices through no fault or merit on their own, their stock prices often mean-revert after the mutual fund selling or buying pressure is over. Indeed, buying stocks that experienced the most selling pressure in the $t - 4$ up to the $t - 1$ quarters, and vice versa, generates another 7 percent annualized returns.

Combining all three strategies (momentum, front running, and mean reverting) generates a total return of about 41 percent before transaction costs. However, the slippage component of the transaction costs is likely to be significant because we may experience delays in getting mutual fund holdings information at the end of a quarter. In addition, the implementation of this strategy is not for the faint-of-heart: clean and accurate mutual holdings and returns data have to be purchased from the Center for Research in Security Prices (CRSP) at a cost of about $10,000 per year of data.

Mutual funds are not the only type of funds that can induce momentum in stocks due to forced asset sales and purchases. In Chapter 7, we will discover that index funds and levered ETFs ignite similar momentum as well. In fact, forced asset sales and purchases by hedge funds can also lead to momentum in stocks, and that caused the August 2007 quant funds meltdown, as I explain in Chapter 8.

■ Pros and Cons of Momentum Strategies

Momentum strategies, especially interday momentum strategies, often have diametrically opposite reward and risk characteristics in comparison to mean reverting strategies. We will compare their pros and cons in this section.

Let's start with the cons. In my own trading experience, I have often found that it is harder to create profitable momentum strategies, and those that are profitable tend to have lower Sharpe ratios than mean-reversal strategies. There are two reasons for this.

First, as we have seen so far, many established momentum strategies have long look-back and holding periods. So clearly the number of independent trading signals is few and far in between. (We may rebalance a momentum portfolio every day, but that doesn't make the trading signals more independent.) Fewer trading signals naturally lead to lower Sharpe ratio. Example: The linear mean reversion model for S&P 500 stocks described in Chapter 4 relies on the short-term cross-sectional mean reversion properties of stocks, and the holding period is less than a day. It has a high Sharpe ratio of 4.7. For the same universe of stocks, the opposite cross-sectional momentum strategy described earlier in this chapter has a holding period of 25 days, and though it performed similarly well pre-2008, the performance collapsed during the financial crisis years.

Secondly, research by Daniel and Moskowitz on "momentum crashes" indicates that momentum strategies for futures or stocks tend to perform miserably for several years after a financial crisis (Daniel and Moskowitz, 2011). We can see that easily from a plot of the S&P DTI index (Figure 6.7). As of this writing, it has suffered a drawdown of −25.9 percent since December 5, 2008. Similarly, cross-sectional momentum in stocks also vanished during the aftermath of the stock market crash in 2008–2009, and is replaced by strong mean reversion. We still don't know how long this mean reversion regime will last: After the stock market crash of 1929, a representative momentum strategy did not return to its high watermark for more than 30 years! The cause of this crash is mainly due to the strong rebound of short positions following a market crisis.

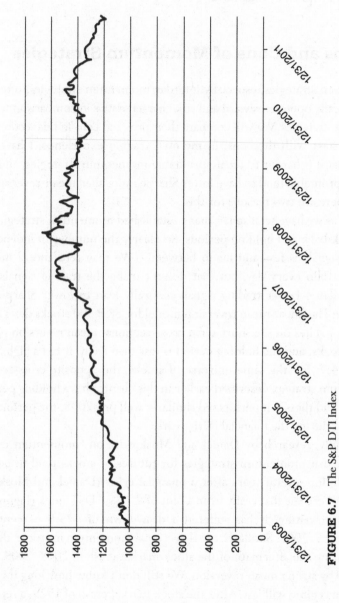

FIGURE 6.7 The S&P DTI Index

Third, and this relates mostly to the shorter-term news-driven momentum that we will talk about in the next chapter, the duration over which momentum remains in force gets progressively shorter as more traders catch on to it. For example, price momentum driven by earnings announcements used to last several days. Now it lasts barely until the market closes. This is quite understandable if we view price momentum as generated by the slow diffusion of information. As more traders learn about the information faster and earlier, the diffusion—and thus, momentum—also ends sooner. This of course creates a problem for the momentum trader, since we may have to constantly shorten our holding period, yet there is no predictable schedule for doing so.

Lest you think that we should just give up on momentum strategies, let's look at the list of pros for momentum strategies. Such lists usually start with the ease of risk management. To see why, we observe that there are two common types of exit strategies for momentum strategies: time-based and stop loss. All the momentum strategies I have discussed so far involve only time-based exits. We specify a holding period, and we exit a position when we reached that holding period. But we can also impose a stop loss as the exit condition, or maybe as an additional exit condition. Stop losses are perfectly consistent with momentum strategies. If momentum has changed direction, we should enter into the opposite position. Since the original position would have been losing, and now we have exited it, this new entry signal effectively served as a stop loss. In contrast, stop losses are not consistent with mean-reverting strategies, because they contradict mean reversion strategies' entry signals. (This point will be taken up again in Chapter 8.) Because of either a time-based exit or a stop loss, the loss of a momentum position is always limited. In contrast, we can incur an enormous drawdown with just one position due to a mean-reverting strategy. (This is not to say that the cumulative loss of successive losing positions due to a momentum strategy won't bankrupt us!)

Not only do momentum strategies survive risks well, they can thrive in them (though we have seen how poorly they did in the *aftermath* of risky events). For mean-reverting strategies, their upside is limited by their natural profit cap (set as the "mean" to which the prices revert), but their downside can be unlimited. For momentum strategies, their upside is unlimited (unless one arbitrarily imposes a profit cap, which is ill-advised), while their downside is limited. The more often "black swan" events occur, the more likely that a momentum strategy will benefit from them. The thicker the tails of the returns distribution curve, or the higher its kurtosis, the better that market is for momentum strategies. (Remember the simulation in Example 1.1? We simulated a returns series with the same kurtosis as the futures series for TU but with no serial autocorrelations. We found that it can still generate the same returns as our TU momentum strategy in 12 percent of the random realizations!)

Finally, as most futures and currencies exhibit momentum, momentum strategies allow us to truly diversify our risks across different asset classes and countries. Adding momentum strategies to a portfolio of mean-reverting strategies allows us to achieve higher Sharpe ratios and smaller drawdowns than either type of strategy alone.

KEY POINTS

- Time-series momentum refers to the positive correlation of a price series' past and future returns.
- Cross-sectional momentum refers to the positive correlation of a price series' past and future *relative* returns, in relation to that of other price series in a portfolio.
- Futures exhibit time series momentum mainly because of the persistence of the sign of roll returns.
- If you are able to find an instrument (e.g., an ETF or another future) that cointegrates or correlates with the spot price or return of a commodity, you can extract the roll return of the commodity future by shorting that instrument during backwardation, or buying that instrument during contango.
- Portfolios of futures or stocks often exhibit cross-sectional momentum: a simple ranking algorithm based on returns would work.
- Profitable strategies on news sentiment momentum show that the slow diffusion of news is a cause for stock price momentum.
- The contagion of forced asset sales and purchases among mutual funds contributes to stock price momentum.
- Momentum models thrive on "black swan" events and the positive kurtosis of the returns distribution curve.

CHAPTER 7

Intraday Momentum Strategies

In the preceding chapter we saw that most instruments, be they stocks or futures, exhibit cross-sectional momentum, and often time-series momentum as well. Unfortunately, the time horizon of this momentum behavior tends to be long—typically a month or longer. Long holding periods present two problems: They result in lower Sharpe ratios and backtest statistical significance because of the infrequent independent trading signals, and they suffer from underperformance in the aftermath of financial crises. In this chapter, we describe short-term, intraday momentum strategies that do not suffer these drawbacks.

We previously enumerated four main causes of momentum. We will see that all but one of them also operate at the intraday time frame. (The only exception is the persistence of roll return, since its magnitude and volatility are too small to be relevant intraday.)

There is an additional cause of momentum that is mainly applicable to the short time frame: the triggering of stops. Such triggers often lead to the so-called breakout strategies. We'll see one example that involves an entry at the market open, and another one that involves intraday entry at various support or resistance levels.

Intraday momentum can be triggered by specific events beyond just price actions. These events include corporate news such as earnings announcements or analyst recommendation changes, as well as macro-economic news. That these events generate time series momentum has long been known, but I present some new research on the effects of each specific category of events.

Intraday momentum can also be triggered by the actions of large funds. I examine how the daily rebalancing of leveraged ETFs leads to short-term momentum.

Finally, at the shortest possible time scale, the imbalance of the bid and ask sizes, the changes in order flow, or the aforementioned nonuniform distribution of stop orders can all induce momentum in prices. Some of the common high-frequency trading tactics that take advantage of such momentum will be presented in this chapter.

■ Opening Gap Strategy

In Chapter 4, we discussed a mean-reverting buy-on-gap strategy for stocks. The opposite momentum strategy will sometimes work on futures and currencies: buying when the instrument gaps up, and shorting when it gaps down.

After being tested on a number of futures, this strategy proved to work best on the Dow Jones STOXX 50 index futures (FSTX) trading on Eurex, which generates an annual percentage rate (APR) of 13 percent and a Sharpe ratio of 1.4 from July 16, 2004, to May 17, 2012. Example 7.1 shows the gap momentum code (available for download as *gapFutures_FSTX.m*).

Example 7.1: Opening Gap Strategy for FSTX

This code assumes the open, high, low, and close prices are contained in $T \times 1$ arrays *op, hi, lo, cl*. It makes use of utilities function *smartMovingStd* and *backshift* available from epchan.com/book2.

```
entryZscore=0.1;

stdretC2C90d=backshift(1, smartMovingStd(calculateReturns ...
  (cl, 1), 90));

longs=op  > backshift(1, hi).*(1+entryZscore*stdretC2C90d);
shorts=op < backshift(1, lo).*(1-entryZscore*stdretC2C90d);

positions=zeros(size(cl));

positions(longs)=1;
positions(shorts)=-1;

ret=positions.*(op-cl)./op;
```

The equity curve is depicted in Figure 7.1.

July 16, 2004, to May 17, 2012

FIGURE 7.1 Equity Curve of FSTX Opening Gap Strategy

The same strategy works on some currencies, too. However, the daily "open" and "close" need to be defined differently. If we define the close to be 5:00 P.M. ET, and the open to be 5:00 A.M. ET (corresponding to the London open), then applying this strategy to GBPUSD yields an APR of 7.2 percent and a Sharpe ratio of 1.3 from July 23, 2007, to February 20, 2012. Naturally, you can experiment with different definitions of opening and closing times for different currencies. Most currency markets are closed from 5:00 P.M. on Friday to 5:00 P.M. on Sunday, so that's a natural "gap" for these strategies.

What's special about the overnight or weekend gap that sometimes triggers momentum? The extended period without any trading means that the opening price is often quite different from the closing price. Hence, stop orders set at different prices may get triggered all at once at the open. The execution of these stop orders often leads to momentum because a cascading effect may trigger stop orders placed further away from the open price as well. Alternatively, there may be significant events that occurred overnight. As discussed in the next section, many types of news events generate momentum.

■ News-Driven Momentum Strategy

If, as many people believe, momentum is driven by the slow diffusion of news, surely we can benefit from the first few days, hours, or even seconds after a newsworthy event. This is the rationale behind traditional post–earnings announcement drift (PEAD) models, as well as other models based on various corporate or macroeconomic news.

Post–Earnings Announcement Drift

There is no surprise that an earnings announcement will move stock price. It is, however, surprising that this move will persist for some time after the announcement, and in the same direction, allowing momentum traders to benefit. Even more surprising is that though this fact has been known and studied since 1968 (Bernard and Thomas, 1989), the effect still has not been arbitraged away, though the duration of the drift may have shortened. What I will show in this section is that as recently as 2011 this strategy is still profitable if we enter at the market open after the earnings announcement was made after the previous close, buying the stock if the return is very positive and shorting if the return is very negative, and liquidate the position at the same day's close. Notice that this strategy does not require the trader to interpret whether the earnings announcement is "good" or "bad." It does not even require the trader to know whether the earnings are above or below analysts' expectations. We let the market tell us whether it thinks the earnings are good or bad.

Before we backtest this strategy, it is necessary to have historical data of the times of earnings annoucements. You can use the function *parseEarnings CalendarFromEarningsDotcom.m* displayed in the box to retrieve one year or so of such data from earnings.com given a certain stock universe specified by the stock symbols array *allsyms*. The important feature of this program is that it carefully selects only earnings announcements occurring after the previous trading day's market close and before today's market open. Earnings announcements occurring at other times should not be triggers for our entry trades as they occur at today's market open.

BOX 7.1

Function for Retrieving Earnings Calendar from earnings.com

This function takes an input 1xN stock symbols cell array *allsyms* and creates a 1 × N logical array *earnann*, which tells us whether (with values *true* or *false*) the corresponding stock has an earnings announcement after the previous day's 4:00 P.M. ET (U.S. market closing time) and before today's 9:30 A.M. ET (U.S. market opening time). The inputs *prevDate* and *todayDate* should be in yyyymmdd format.

```
function [earnann] = ...
    parseEarningsCalendarFromEarningsDotCom(prevDate, ...
    todayDate, allsyms)
```

BOX 7.1 (*Continued*)

```
% [earnann]==parseEaringsCalendarFromEarningsDotCom
% (prevDate,todayDate, allsyms)

earnann=zeros(size(allsyms));

prevEarningsFile=urlread(['http://www.earnings.com/earning...
  .asp?date=', num2str(prevDate), '&client=cb']);
todayEarningsFile=urlread(['http://www.earnings.com ...
  /earning.asp?date=', num2str(todayDate), '&client=cb']);

prevd=day(datenum(num2str(prevDate), 'yyyymmdd'));
todayd=day(datenum(num2str(todayDate), 'yyyymmdd'));

prevmmm=datestr(datenum(num2str(prevDate), 'yyyymmdd'), ...
  'mmm');
todaymmm=datestr(datenum(num2str(todayDate), 'yyyymmdd'), ...
  'mmm');

patternSym='<a\s+href="company.asp\?ticker=([%\*\w\._ ...
  /-]+)&coid';

% prevDate
patternPrevDateTime=['<td align="center"><nobr>', ...
  num2str(prevd), '-', num2str(prevmmm), '([ :\dABPMCO]*) ...
  </nobr>'];

symA=regexp(prevEarningsFile, patternSym , 'tokens');
timeA=regexp(prevEarningsFile, patternPrevDateTime, ...
  'tokens');

symsA=[symA{:}];
timeA=[timeA{:}];

assert(length(symsA)==length(timeA));

isAMC=~cellfun('isempty', regexp(timeA, 'AMC'));

patternPM='[ ]+\d:\d\d[ ]+PM'; % e.g. ' 6:00 PM'

isAMC2=~cellfun('isempty', regexp(timeA, patternPM));

symsA=symsA(isAMC | isAMC2);

[foo, idxA, idxALL]=intersect(symsA, allsyms);
earnann(idxALL)=1;

% today
patternTodayDateTime=['<td align="center"><nobr>', ...
  num2str(todayd), '-', num2str(todaymmm), ...
  '([ :\dABPMCO]*)</nobr>'];
```

(*Continued*)

BOX 7.1 (Continued)

```
symA=regexp(todayEarningsFile, patternSym , 'tokens');
timeA=regexp(todayEarningsFile, patternTodayDateTime, ...
  'tokens');

symsA=[symA{:}];
timeA=[timeA{:}];

symsA=symsA(1:length(timeA));

assert(length(symsA)==length(timeA));

isBMO=~cellfun('isempty', regexp(timeA, 'BMO'));

patternAM='[ ]+\d:\d\d[ ]+AM'; % e.g. ' 8:00 AM'

isBMO2=~cellfun('isempty', regexp(timeA, patternAM));

symsA=symsA(isBMO | isBMO2);

[foo, idxA, idxALL]=intersect(symsA, allsyms);
earnann(idxALL)=1;
end
```

We need to call this program for each day in the backtest for the PEAD strategy. We can then concatenate the resulting $1 \times N$ earnann arrays into one big historical $T \times N$ earnann array for the T days in the backtest.

Assuming that we have compiled the historical earnings announcement logical array, whether using our function above or through other means, the actual backtest program for the PEAD strategy is very simple, as shown in Example 7.2. We just need to compute the 90-day moving standard deviation of previous-close-to-next day's-open return as the benchmark for deciding whether the announcement is "surprising" enough to generate the post announcement drift.

Example 7.2: Backtest of Post-Earnings Annoucement Drift Strategy

We assume the historical open and close prices are stored in the $T \times N$ arrays *op* and *cl*. The input $T \times N$ logical array *earnann* indicates whether there is an earnings announcement for a stock on a given day prior to that day's market open but after the previous trading day's market close. The utility functions backshift, smartMovingStd and

Example 7.2 (*Continued*)

smartsum are available for download from epchan.com/book2. The backtest program itself is named *pead.m*.

```
lookback=90;

retC2O=(op-backshift(1, cl))./backshift(1, cl);
stdC2O=smartMovingStd(retC2O, lookback);

positions=zeros(size(cl));

longs=retC2O >= 0.5*stdC2O & earnann;
shorts=retC2O <= -0.5*stdC2O & earnann;

positions(longs)=1;
positions(shorts)=-1;

ret=smartsum(positions.*(cl-op)./op, 2)/30;
```

For a universe of S&P 500 stocks, the APR from January 3, 2011, to April 24, 2012, is 6.7 percent, while the Sharpe ratio is a very respectable 1.5. The cumulative returns curve is displayed in Figure 7.2. Note that we have used 30 as the denominator in calculating returns, since there is a maximum of 30 positions in one day during that backtest period. Of course, there is a certain degree of look-ahead bias in using this number, since we don't know exactly what the maximum will be. But given that the maximum number of

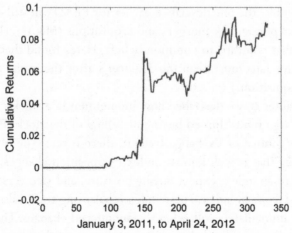

January 3, 2011, to April 24, 2012

FIGURE 7.2 Cumulative Returns Curve of PEAD Strategy

announcements per day is quite predictable, this is not a very grievous bias. Since this is an intraday strategy, it is possible to lever it up by at least four times, giving an annualized average return of close to 27 percent.

You might wonder whether holding these positions overnight will generate additional profits. The answer is no: the overnight returns are negative on average. On the contrary, many published results from 10 or 20 years ago have shown that PEAD lasted more than a day. This may be an example where the duration of momentum is shortened due to increased awareness of the existence of such momentum. It remains to be tested whether an even shorter holding period may generate better returns.

Drift Due to Other Events

Besides earnings announcements, there are other corporate events that may exhibit post-announcement drift: An incomplete list includes earnings guidance, analyst ratings and recommendation changes, same store sales, and airline load factors. (A reasonable daily provider of such data is the Dow Jones newswire delivered by Newsware because it has the code specific to the type of event attached to each story and is machine readable.) In theory, any announcements that prompt a reevaluation of the fair market value of a company should induce a change in its share price toward a new equilibrium price. (For a recent comprehensive study of all these events and their impact on the stock's post-event returns, see Hafez, 2011.) Among these events, mergers and acquisitions, of course, draw the attention of specialized hedge funds that possess in-depth fundamental knowledge of the acquirer and acquiree corporations. Yet a purely technical model like the one described earlier for PEAD can still extract an APR of about 3 percent for mergers and acquisitions (M&As). (It is interesting to note that contrary to common beliefs, Hafez found that the acquiree's stock price falls more than the acquirer's after the initial announcement of the acquisition.)

In Chapter 6, we described how momentum in a stock's price is generated by large funds' forced buying or selling of the stock. For index funds (whether mutual or exchange traded), there is one type of forced buying and selling that is well known: index composition changes. When a stock is added to an index, expect buying pressure, and vice versa when a stock is deleted from an index. These index rebalancing trades also generate momentum immediately following the announced changes. Though some researchers have reported that such momentum used to last many days, my own testing with more recent data suggests that the drift horizon has also been reduced to intraday (Shankar and Miller, 2006).

While we are on the subject of momentum due to scheduled announcements, what about the impact of macroeconomic events such as Federal Open Market Committee's rate decisions or the release of the latest consumer price index? I have tested their effects on EURUSD, but unfortunately have found no significant momentum. However, Clare and Courtenay reported that U.K. macroeconomic data releases as well as Bank of England interest rate announcements induced momentum in GBPUSD for up to at least 10 minutes after the announcements (Clare and Courtnenay, 2001). These results were based on data up to 1999, so we should expect that the duration of this momentum to be shorter in recent years, if the momentum continues to exist at all.

■ Leveraged ETF Strategy

Imagine that you have a portfolio of stocks that is supposed to track the MSCI US REIT index (RMZ), except that you want to keep the leverage of the portfolio at 3, especially at the market close. As I demonstrate in Example 8.1, this constant leverage requirement has some counterintuitive and important consequences. Suppose the RMZ dropped precipitously one day. That would imply that you would need to substantially reduce the positions in your portfolio by selling stocks across the board in order to keep the leverage constant. Conversely, if the RMZ rose that day, you would need to increase the positions by buying stocks.

Now suppose you are actually the sponsor of an ETF, and that portfolio of yours is none other than a 3X leveraged ETF such as DRN (a real estate ETF), and its equity is over a hundred million dollars. If you think that this rebalancing procedure (selling the component stocks when the portfolio's return is negative, and vice versa) near the market close would generate momentum in the market value of the portfolio, you would be right.

(A large change in the market index generates momentum in the same direction for both leveraged long or short ETFs. If the change is positive, a short ETF would experience a decrease in equity, and its sponsor would need to reduce its short positions. Therefore, it would also need to buy stocks, just as the long ETF would.)

We can test this hypothesis by constructing a very simple momentum strategy: buy DRN if the return from previous day's close to 15 minutes before market close is greater than 2 percent, and sell if the return is smaller than −2 percent. Exit the position at the market close. Note that this momentum strategy is based on the momentum of the underlying stocks, so it should be affecting the near-market-close returns of the unlevered ETFs such as SPY as well. We use the leveraged ETFs as trading instruments simply to magnify the effect. The APR of trading DRN is 15 percent with a Sharpe ratio of 1.8 from October 12, 2011, to October 25, 2012.

Naturally, the return of this strategy should increase as the aggregate assets of all leveraged ETFs increase. It was reported that the total AUM of leveraged ETFs (including both long and short funds) at the end of January 2009 is $19 billion (Cheng and Madhavan, 2009). These authors also estimated that a 1 percent move of SPX will necessitate a buying or selling of stocks constituting about 17 percent of the market-on-close volume. This is obviously going to have significant market impact, which is momentum inducing. (A more updated analysis was published by Rodier, Haryanto, Shum, and Hejazi, 2012.)

There is of course another event that will affect the equity of an ETF, leveraged or not: the flow of investors' cash. A large inflow into long leveraged ETFs will cause positive momentum on the underlying stocks' prices, while a large inflow into short leveraged ("inverse") ETFs will cause negative momentum. So it is theoretically possible that on the same day when the market index had a large positive return many investors sold the long leveraged ETFs (perhaps as part of a mean-reverting strategy). This would have neutralized the momentum. But our backtests show that this did not happen often.

■ High-Frequency Strategies

Most high-frequency momentum strategies involve extracting information from the order book, and the basic idea is simple: If the bid size is much bigger than the ask size, expect the price to tick up and vice versa. This idea is backed by academic research. For example, an approximately linear relationship between the imbalance of bid versus ask sizes and short-term price changes in the Nasdaq market was found (Maslov and Mills, 2001). As expected, the effect is stronger for lower volume stocks. The effect is not limited to just the national best bid offer (NBBO) prices: an imbalance of the entire order book also induces price changes for a stock on the Stockholm stock market (Hellström and Simonsen, 2006).

There are a number of high-frequency momentum strategies based on this phenomenon. Many of those were described in books about market microstructure or high-frequency trading (Arnuk and Saluzzi, 2012; Durbin, 2010; Harris, 2003; and Sinclair, 2010). (In my descriptions that follow, I focus on making an initial long trade, but, of course, there is a symmetrical opportunity on the short side.)

In markets that fill orders on a pro-rata basis such as the Eurodollar futures trading on CME, the simplest way to benefit from this expectation is just to "join the bid" immediately, so that whenever there is a fill on the bid side, we will get allocated part of that fill. To ensure that the bid and ask prices are more likely to move higher rather than lower after we are filled, we join the bid only when the original bid size is much larger than the ask size. This is called the *ratio trade*, because we expect the proportion of the original order to be filled is equal to the ratio between our own order size and the aggregate order size at the bid price. Once the buying pressure causes the bid price to move up one or more ticks, then we can sell at a profit, or we can simply place a sell order at the best ask (if the bid-ask spread is larger than the round trip commission per share). If the bid price doesn't move up or our sell limit order doesn't get filled, we can probably still sell at the original best bid price because of the large bid size, with the loss of commissions only.

In markets where the bid-ask spread is bigger than two ticks, there is another simple trade to benefit from the expectation of an uptick. Simply place the buy order at the best bid plus one tick. If this is filled, then we place a sell order at the best ask minus one tick and hope that it is filled. But if it is not, we can probably still sell it at the original best bid, with the loss of commissions plus one tick. This is called *ticking* or *quote matching*. For this trade to be profitable, we need to make sure that the round trip commission per share is less than the bid-ask spread minus two ticks. This strategy is illustrated in Figure 7.3.

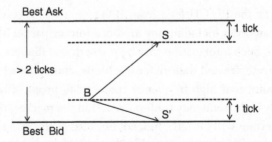

FIGURE 7.3 Ticking Strategy. The original spread must be greater than two ticks. After the buy order is filled at B, we will try to sell it at S for a profit of at least one tick. But if the sell order cannot be filled, then we will sell it at S′ at a loss of one tick.

(Ticking is not a foolproof strategy, of course. The original best bid before it was front-run may be cancelled if the trader knows that he has been front-run, leaving us with a lower bid price to unload our inventory. Or the whole situation could be set up as a trap for us: the trader who placed the original best bid actually wanted to sell us stocks at a price better than her own bid. So once we bought her stocks plus one tick, she would immediately cancel the bid.)

Even when there is no preexisting buying pressure or bid-ask size imbalance, we can create the illusion of one (often called *momentum ignition*). This works for markets with time priority for orders instead of using pro-rata fills. Let's assume we start with very similar best bid and ask sizes. We will place a large buy limit order at the best bid to create the impression of buying pressure, and simultaneously place a small sell limit order at the best ask. This would trick traders to buy at the ask price since they anticipate an uptick, filling our small sell order. At this point, we immediately cancel the large buy order. The best bid and ask sizes are now roughly equal again. Many of those traders who bought earlier expecting a large buying pressure may now sell back their holdings at a loss, and we can then buy them at the original best bid. This is called *flipping*.

There is a danger to creating the illusion of buying pressure—somebody just might call our bluff and actually fill our large buy order. In this case, we might have to sell it at a loss. Conversely, if we suspect a large buy order is due to flippers, then we can sell to the flippers and drive down the bid price. We hope that the flippers will capitulate and sell their new inventory, driving the ask price down as well, so that we can then cover our short position below the original bid price. How do we know that the large buy order is due to flippers in the first place? We may have to record how often a large bid gets canceled instead of getting filled. If you subscribe to the private data feeds from the exchanges such as ITCH from Nasdaq, EDGX Book Feed from Direct Edge, or the PITCH feed from BATS, you will receive the detailed life history of an order including any modifications or partial fills (Arnuk and Saluzzi, 2012). Such information may help you detect flippers as well.

All these strategies and their defenses, bluffs, and counterbluffs illustrate the general point that high-frequency traders can profit only from slower traders. If only high-frequency traders are left in the market, the net average profit for everyone will be zero. Indeed, because of the prevalence of these types of high-frequency strategies that "front-run" large bid or ask orders, many traditional market makers no longer quote large sizes. This has led to a general decrease of the NBBO sizes across many markets. For example, even in highly liquid stocks such as AAPL, the NBBO sizes are often just a few hundred shares. And even for the most liquid ETFs such as SPY on ARCA, the NBBO sizes are often fewer than 10,000 shares. Only after these small orders are filled will the market maker go back to requote at the same prices to avoid being taken advantage of by the high-frequency traders. (Of course, there are other reasons for avoiding displaying large quotes: market makers do not like to keep large inventories that can result from having their large quotes filled.) Similarly, large institutional orders that were formerly executed as block trades are now broken up into tiny child orders to be scattered around the different market venues and executed throughout the day.

Stop hunting is another favorite high-frequency momentum strategy. Research in the currencies markets indicated that once support (resistance) levels are breached, prices will go further down (up) for a while (Osler, 2000, 2001). These support and resistance levels can be those reported daily by banks or brokerages, or they can just be round numbers in the proximity of the current price levels. This short-term price momentum occurs because of the large number of stop orders placed at or near the support and resistance levels.

To understand this further, let's just look at the support levels, as the situation with resistance levels is symmetrical. Once the price drops enough to breach a support level, those sell stop orders are triggered and thereby drive the prices down further. Given this knowledge, high-frequency traders can, of course, create artificial selling pressure by submitting large sell orders when the price is close enough to a support level, hoping to drive the next tick down. Once the stop orders are triggered and a downward momentum is in force, these high-frequency traders can cover their short positions for a quick profit.

If we have access to the *order flow* information of a market, then we have a highly valuable information stream that goes beyond the usual bid/ask/last price stream. As Lyons discussed in the context of currencies trading, "order flow" is signed transaction volume (Lyons, 2001). If a trader buys 100 units from a dealer/market maker/order book, the order flow is 100, and it is −100 if the trader sells 100 units instead. What "buying" from an order book means is that a trader buys at the ask price, or, equivalently, the trader submits a market order to buy. Empirical research indicates that order flow information is a good predictor of price movements. This is because market makers can distill important fundamental information from order flow information, and set the bid-ask prices accordingly. For example, if a major hedge fund just learns about a major piece of breaking news, their algorithms will submit large market orders of the same sign in a split second. A market maker monitoring the order flow will deduce, quite correctly, that such large one-directional demands indicate the presence of informed traders, and they will immediately adjust their bid-ask prices to protect themselves. The urgency of using market orders indicates that the information is new and not widely known.

Since most of us are not large market makers or operators of an exchange, how can we access such order flow information? For stocks and futures markets, we can monitor and record every tick (i.e., changes in best bid, ask, and transaction price and size), and thus determine whether a transaction took place at the bid (negative order flow) or at the ask (positive order flow). For the currencies market, this is difficult because most dealers do not report transaction prices. We may have to resort to trading currency futures for this strategy. Once the order flow per transaction is computed, we can easily compute the cumulative or average order flow over some look-back period and use that to predict whether the price will move up or down.

KEY POINTS

- Intraday momentum strategies do not suffer from many of the disadvantages of interday momentum strategies, but they retain some key advantages.
- "Breakout" momentum strategies involve a price exceeding a trading range.
- The opening gap strategy is a breakout strategy that works for some futures and currencies.
- Breakout momentum may be caused by the triggering of stop orders.
- Many kinds of corporate and macroeconomic news induce short-term price momentum.
- Index composition changes induce momentum in stocks that are added to or deleted from the index.
- Rebalancing of leveraged ETFs near the market close causes momentum in the underlying index in the same direction as the market return from the previous close.
- Many high-frequency momentum strategies involve imbalance between bid and ask sizes, an imbalance that is sometimes artificially created by the high-frequency traders themselves.
- Stop hunting is a high-frequency trading strategy that relies on triggering stop orders that typically populate round numbers near the current market price.
- Order flow can predict short-term price movement in the same direction.

CHAPTER 8

Risk Management

R isk management means different things to different people. To novice traders, risk management is driven by "loss aversion": we simply don't like the feeling of losing money. In fact, research has suggested that the average human being needs to have the potential for making $2 to compensate for the risk of losing $1, which may explain why a Sharpe ratio of 2 is so emotionally appealing (Kahneman, 2011). However, this dislike of risk in itself is not rational. Our goal should be the maximization of long-term equity growth, and we avoid risk only insofar as it interferes with this goal. Risk management in this chapter is based on this objective.

The key concept in risk management is the prudent use of leverage, which we can optimize via the Kelly formula or some numerical methods that maximize compounded growth rate. But sometimes reality forces us to limit the maximum drawdown of an account. One obvious way of accomplishing this is the use of stop loss, but it is often problematic. The other way is constant proportion portfolio insurance, which tries to maximize the upside of the account in addition to preventing large drawdowns. Both will be discussed here. Finally, it may be wise to avoid trading altogether during times when the risk of loss is high. We will investigate whether the use of certain leading indicators of risk is an effective loss-avoidance technique.

■ Optimal Leverage

It is easy to say that we need to be prudent when using leverage, but much harder to decide what constitutes a prudent, or optimal, leverage for a particular strategy or portfolio because, obviously, if we set leverage to zero, we will suffer no risks but will generate no returns, either.

To some portfolio managers, especially those who are managing their own money and answerable to no one but themselves, the sole goal of trading is the maximization of net worth over the long term. They pay no mind to drawdowns and volatilities of returns. So the optimal leverage to them means one that can maximize the net worth or, equivalently, the compounded growth rate.

We'll discuss here three methods of computing the optimal leverage that maximizes the compounded growth rate. Each method has its own assumptions and drawbacks, and we try to be agnostic as to which method you should adopt. But, in all cases, we have to make the assumption that the future probability distribution of returns of the *market* is the same as in the past. This is usually an incorrect assumption, but this is the best that quantitative models can do. Even more restrictive, many risk management techniques assume further that the probability distribution of returns of the *strategy* itself is the same as in the past. And finally, the most restrictive of all assumes that the probability distribution of returns of the strategy is Gaussian. As is often the case in mathematical modeling, the most restrictive assumptions give rise to the most elegant and simple solution, so I will start this survey with the Kelly formula under the Gaussian assumption.

If the maximum drawdown of an account with a certain leverage is −100 percent, this leverage cannot be optimal because the compounded growth rate will also be −100 percent. So an optimal leverage implies that we must not be ruined (equity reaching zero) at any point in history, rather self-evidently! But sometimes our risk managers (perhaps it is a spouse for independent traders) tell us that we are allowed to have a much smaller magnitude of drawdown than 1. In this case, the maximum drawdown allowed forms an additional constraint in the leverage optimization problem.

No matter how the optimal leverage is determined, the one central theme is that the leverage should be kept constant. This is necessary to optimize the growth rate whether or not we have the maximum drawdown constraint. Keeping a constant leverage may sound rather mundane, but can be counterintuitive when put into action. For example, if you have a long stock portfolio, and your profit and loss (P&L) was positive in the last trading period, the constant leverage requirement forces you to buy more stocks for

The central requirement for all ways of optimizing leverage described in this chapter is that the leverage be kept constant at all times. This can have some counterintuitive consequences.

If you started with $100K equity in your account, and your strategy's optimal leverage was determined to be 5, then you should have a portfolio with market value of $500K.

If, however, you lost $10K in one day and your equity was reduced to $90K, with a portfolio market value of $490K, then you need to liquidate a *further* $40K of your portfolio so that its updated market value became 5 × $90K = $450K. This selling into the loss may make some people uncomfortable, but it is a necessary part of many risk management schemes.

Suppose you then gained $20K the next day. What should your portfolio market value be? And what should you do to achieve that market value?

The new portfolio market value should be 5 × ($90K + $20K) = $550K. Since your current portfolio market value was just $450K + $20K = $470K, this means you need to add $80K worth of (long or short) securities to the portfolio. Hopefully, your broker will lend you the cash to buy all these extra securities!

---

this period. However, if your P&L was negative in the last period, it forces you to sell stocks into the loss. Example 8.1 illustrates this.

Many analysts believe that this "selling into losses" feature of the risk management techniques causes contagion in financial crises. (In particular, this was cited as a cause of the August 2007 meltdown of quant funds; see Khandani and Lo, 2007). This is because often many funds are holding similar positions in their portfolios. If one fund suffers losses, perhaps due to some unrelated strategies, it is prone to liquidate positions across all its portfolios due to the constant leverage requirement, causing losses for all other funds that hold those positions. The losses force all these other funds to also liquidate their positions and thus exacerbate the losses for everyone: a vicious cycle. One might think of this as a tragedy of the commons: self-preservation ("risk management") for one fund can lead to catastrophe for all.

Kelly Formula

If one assumes that the probability distribution of returns is Gaussian, the Kelly formula gives us a very simple answer for optimal leverage f:

$$f = m/s^2, \tag{8.1}$$

where m is the mean excess return, and s^2 is the variance of the excess returns.

One of the best expositions of this formula can be found in Edward Thorp's (1997) paper, and I also devoted an entire chapter in *Quantitative Trading* (Chan, 2009) to it. It can be proven that if the Gaussian assumption is a good approximation, then the Kelly leverage f will generate the highest compounded growth rate of equity, assuming that all profits are reinvested. However, even if the Gaussian assumption is really valid, we will inevitably suffer estimation errors when we try to estimate what the "true" mean and variance of the excess return are. And no matter how good one's estimation method is, there is no guarantee that the future mean and variance will be the same as the historical ones. The consequence of using an overestimated mean or an underestimated variance is dire: Either case will lead to an overestimated optimal leverage, and if this overestimated leverage is high enough, it will eventually lead to ruin: equity going to zero. However, the consequence of using an underestimated leverage is merely a submaximal compounded growth rate. Many traders justifiably prefer the later scenario, and they routinely deploy a leverage equal to half of what the Kelly formula recommends: the so-called half-Kelly leverage.

My actual experience using Kelly's optimal leverage is that it is best viewed as an upper bound rather than as the leverage that must be used. Often, the Kelly leverage given by the backtest (or a short period of walk-forward test) is so high that it far exceeds the maximum leverage allowed by our brokers. At other times, the Kelly leverage would have bankrupted us even in backtest, due to the non-Gaussian distributions of returns. In other words, the maximum drawdown in backtest is -1 using the Kelly leverage, which implies setting the leverage by numerically optimizing the growth rate using a more realistic non-Gaussian distribution might be more practical. Alternatively, we may just optimize on the empirical, historical returns. These two methods will be discussed in the next sections.

But just using Kelly optimal leverage as an upper bound can sometimes provide interesting insights. For example, I once calculated that both the Russell 1000 and 2000 indices have Kelly leverage at about 1.8. But exchange-traded fund (ETF) sponsor Direxion has been marketing triple leveraged ETFs BGU and TNA tracking these indices. By design, they have a leverage of 3. Clearly, there is a real danger that the net asset value (NAV) of these ETFs will go to zero. Equally clearly, no investors should buy and hold these ETFs, as the sponsor itself readily agrees.

There is another usage of the Kelly formula besides setting the optimal leverage: it also tells us how to optimally allocate our buying power to different portfolios or strategies. Let's denote F as a column vector of optimal leverages that we should apply to the different portfolios based on a common pool of equity. (For example, if we have \$1 equity, then $F = [3.2 \ 1.5]^T$ means the first portfolio should have a market value of \$3.2 while the second portfolio should have a market value of \$1.5. The T signifies matrix transpose.) The Kelly formula says

$$F = C^{-1}M \qquad\qquad (8.2)$$

where C is the covariance matrix of the returns of the portfolios and M is the mean excess returns of these portfolios.

There is an extensive example on how to use this formula in *Quantitative Trading*. But what should we do if our broker has set a maximum leverage F_{max} that is smaller than the total gross leverage $\sum_i^n |F_i|$? (We are concerned with the gross leverage, which is equal to the absolute sum of the long and short market values divided by our equity, not the net leverage, which is the net of the long and short market values divided by our equity.) The usual recommendation is to multiply all F_i by the factor $F_{max} / \sum_i^n |F_i|$ so that the total gross leverage is equal to F_{max}. The problem with this approach is that the compounded growth rate will no longer be optimal under this maximum leverage constraint. I have constructed Example 8.2 to demonstrate this. The upshot of that example is that when F_{max} is much smaller than $\sum_i^n |F_i|$, it is often optimal (with respect to maximizing the growth rate) to just invest most or all our buying power into the portfolio or strategy with the highest mean excess return.

Optimization of Expected Growth Rate Using Simulated Returns

If one relaxes the Gaussian assumption and substitutes another analytic form (e.g., Student's t) for the returns distribution to take into account the fat tails, we can still follow the derivations of the Kelly formula in Thorp's

When we have multiple portfolios or strategies, the Kelly formula says that we should invest in each portfolio i with leverage F_i determined by Equation 8.2. But often, the total gross leverage $\sum_i^n |F_i|$ computed this way exceeds the maximum leverage F_{max} imposed on us by our brokerage or our risk manager. With this constraint, it is often not optimal to just multiply all these F_i by the factor $F_{max}/\sum_i^n |F_i|$, as I will demonstrate here.

Suppose we have two strategies, 1 and 2. Strategy 1 has annualized mean excess return and volatility of 30 percent and 26 percent, respectively. Strategy 2 has annualized mean excess return and volatility of 60 percent and 35 percent, respectively. Suppose further that their returns distributions are Gaussian, and that there is zero correlation between the returns of 1 and 2. So the Kelly leverages for them are 4.4 and 4.9, respectively, with a total gross leverage of 9.3. The annualized compounded growth rate is (Thorp, 1997)

$$g = F^T C F / 2 = 2.1, \qquad (8.3)$$

where we have also assumed that the risk-free rate is 0. Now, let's say our brokerage tells us that we are allowed a maximum leverage of 2.

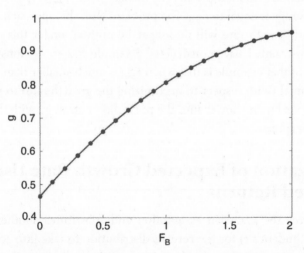

FIGURE 8.1 Constrained Growth Rate g as Function of F_2

Example 8.2 (*Continued*)

So the leverages for the strategies have to be reduced to 0.95 and 1.05, respectively. The growth rate is now reduced to

$$g = \sum_{i=1}^{2} \left(F_i M_i - F_i^2 s_i^2 / 2 \right) = 0.82. \qquad (8.4)$$

(Equation 8.3 for g applies only when the leverages used are optimal.)

But do these leverages really generate the maximum g under our maximum leverage constraint? We can find out by setting F_1 to $F_{max} - F_2$, and plot g as a function of F_2 over the allowed range 0 to $F_{max} = F_2$.

It is obvious that the growth rate is optimized when $F_2 = F_{max} = 2$. The optimized g is 0.96, which is higher than the 0.82 given in Equation 8.4. This shows that when we have two or more strategies with very different independent growth rates, and when we have a maximum leverage constraint that is much lower than the Kelly leverage, it is often optimal to just apply all of our buying power on the strategy that has the highest growth rate.

---

paper and arrive at another optimal leverage, though the formula won't be as simple as Equation 8.1. (This is true as long as the distribution has a finite number of moments, unlike, for example, the Pareto Levy distribution.) For some distributions, it may not even be possible to arrive at an analytic answer. This is where Monte Carlo simulations can help.

The expected value of the compounded growth rate as a function of the leverage f is (assuming for simplicity that the risk-free rate is zero)

$$g(f) = \langle \log(1 + fR) \rangle, \qquad (8.5)$$

where $\langle \cdots \rangle$ indicates an average over some random sampling of the unlevered return-per-bar $R(t)$ of the strategy (not of the market prices) based on some probability distribution of R. (We typically use daily bars for $R(t)$, but the bar can be as long or short as we please.) If this probability distribution is Gaussian, then $g(f)$ can be analytically reduced to $g(f) = fm - f^2 m^2 / 2$, which is the same as Equation 8.4 in the single strategy case. Furthermore, the maxima of $g(f)$ can of course be analytically determined by taking the derivative of $g(f)$ with respect to f and setting it to zero. This will reproduce the Kelly formula in Equation 8.1 and will reproduce the maximum growth rate indicated by Equation 8.3 in the single strategy case. But this is not our interest here. We would like to compute Equation 8.5 using a non-Gaussian distribution of R.

Even though we do not know the true distribution of R, we can use the so-called Pearson system (see www.mathworks.com/help/toolbox/stats /br5k833-1.html or mathworld.wolfram.com/PearsonSystem.html) to model it. The Pearson system takes as input the mean, standard deviation, skewness, and kurtosis of the empirical distribution of R, and models it as one of seven probability distributions expressible analytically encompassing Gaussian, beta, gamma, Student's t, and so on. Of course, these are not the most general distributions possible. The empirical distribution might have nonzero higher moments that are not captured by the Pearson system and might, in fact, have infinite higher moments, as in the case of the Pareto Levy distribution. But to capture all the higher moments invites data-snooping bias due to the limited amount of empirical data usually available. So, for all practical purposes, we use the Pearson system for our Monte Carlo sampling.

We illustrate this Monte Carlo technique by using the mean reversion strategy described in Example 5.1. But first, we can use the daily returns in the test set to easily calculate that the Kelly leverage is 18.4. We should keep this number in mind when comparing with the Monte Carlo results. Next, we use the first four moments of these daily returns to construct a Pearson system and generate 100,000 random returns from this system. We can use the *pearsrnd* function from the MATLAB Statistics Toolbox for this. (The complete code is in *monteCarloOptimLeverage.m*.)

BOX 8.1

We assume that the strategy daily returns are contained in the Nx1 array *ret*. We will use the first four moments of *ret* to generate a Pearson system distribution, from which any number of simulated returns *ret_sim* can be generated.

```
moments={mean(ret), std(ret), skewness(ret), kurtosis(ret)};

[ret_sim, type]=pearsrnd(moments{:}, 100000, 1);
```

In the code, *ret* contains the daily returns from the backtest of the strategy, whereas *ret_sim* are 100,000 randomly generated daily returns with the same four moments as *ret*. The *pearsrnd* function also returns *type*, which indicates which type of distribution fits our data best. In this example, *type* is 4, indicating that the distribution is not one of the standard ones such as Student's *t*. (But we aren't at all concerned whether it has a name.) Now we can use *ret_sim* to compute the average of $g(f)$. In our code, $g(f)$ is an inline function with leverage *f* and a return series *R* as inputs.

BOX 8.2

An inline function for calculating the compounded growth rate based on leverage f and return per bar of R.

```
g=inline('sum(log(1+f*R))/length(R)', 'f', 'R');
```

Plotting $g(f)$ for $f = 0$ to $f = 23$ reveals that $g(f)$ does in fact have a maximum somewhere near 19 (see Figure 8.2), and a numerical optimization using the *fminbnd* function of the MATLAB Optimization Toolbox yields an optimal *f* of 19, strikingly close to the Kelly's optimal *f* of 18.4!

BOX 8.3

Finding the minimum of the negative of the growth rate based on leverage f and the simulated returns *ret_sim* (same as finding the maximum of the positive growth rate).

```
minusGsim=@(f)-g(f, ret_sim);

optimalF=fminbnd(minusGsim, 0, 24);
```

Of course, if you run this program with a different random seed and therefore different series of simulated returns, you will find a somewhat different value for the optimal *f*, but ideally it won't be too different from my value. (As a side note, the only reason we minimized $-g$ instead of maximized g is that MATLAB does not have a *fmaxbnd* function.)

There is another interesting result from running this Monte Carlo optimization. If we try *f* of 31, we shall find that the growth rate is -1; that is, ruin. This is because the most negative return per period is -0.0331, so any leverage higher than $1 / 0.0331 = 30.2$ will result in total loss during that period.

Optimization of Historical Growth Rate

Instead of optimizing the expected value of the growth rate using our analytical probability distribution of returns as we did in the previous section,

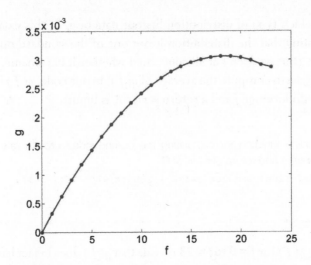

FIGURE 8.2 Expected Growth Rate g as Function of f.

one can of course just optimize the historical growth rate in the backtest with respect to the leverage. We just need one particular realized set of returns: that which actually occurred in the backtest. This method suffers the usual drawback of parameter optimization in backtest: data-snooping bias. In general, the optimal leverage for this particular historical realization of the strategy returns won't be optimal for a different realization that will occur in the future. Unlike Monte Carlo optimization, the historical returns offer insufficient data to determine an optimal leverage that works well for many realizations.

Despite these caveats, brute force optimization over the backtest returns sometimes does give a very similar answer to both the Kelly leverage and Monte Carlo optimization. Using the same strategy as in the previous section, and altering the optimization program slightly to feed in the historical returns *ret* instead of the simulated returns *ret_sim*.

BOX 8.4

Finding the minimum of the negative of the growth rate based on leverage f and the historical returns *ret*.

```
minusG=@(f)-g(f, ret);

optimalF=fminbnd(minusG, 0, 21);
```

we obtain the optimal f of 18.4, which is again the same as the Kelly optimal f.

Maximum Drawdown

For those portfolio managers who manage other people's assets, maximizing the long-term growth rate is not the only objective. Often, their clients (or employers) will insist that the absolute value of the drawdown (return calculated from the historic high watermark) should never exceed a certain maximum. That is to say, they dictate what the maximum drawdown can be. This requirement translates into an additional constraint into our leverage optimization problem.

Unfortunately, this translation is not as simple as multiplying the unconstrained optimal leverage by the ratio of the maximum drawdown allowed and the original unconstrained maximum drawdown. Using the example in the section on optimization of expected growth rate with simulated returns *ret_sim*, the maximum drawdown is a frightening −0.999. This is with an unconstrained optimal f of 19.2. Suppose our risk manager allows a maximum drawdown of only half this amount. Using half the optimal f of 9.6 still generates a maximum drawdown of −0.963. By trial and error, we find that we have to lower the leverage by a factor of 7, to 2.7 or so, in order to reduce the magnitude of the maximum drawdown to about 0.5. (Again, all these numbers depend on the exact series of simulated returns, and so are not exactly reproducible.)

BOX 8.5

Using my function *calculateMaxDD* (available on http://epchan.com/book2) to compute maximum drawdowns with different leverages on the same simulated returns series *ret_sim*.

```
maxDD=calculateMaxDD(cumprod(1+optimalF/7*ret_sim)-1);
```

Of course, setting the leverage equal to this upper bound will only prevent the simulated drawdown from exceeding the maximum allowed, but it will not prevent our future drawdown from doing so. The only way to guarantee that the future drawdown will not exceed this maximum is to either use constant proportion insurance or to impose a stop loss. We will discuss these techniques in the next two sections.

It is worth noting that this method of estimating the maximum drawdown is based on a simulated series of strategy returns, not the historical strategy returns generated in a backtest. We can, of course, use the historical strategy returns to calculate the maximum drawdown and use that to determine the optimal leverage instead. In this case, we will find that we just need to decrease the unconstrained optimal f by a factor of 1.5 (to 13) in order to reduce the maximum drawdown to below -0.49.

Which method should we use? The advantage of using simulated returns is that they have much better statistical significance. They are akin to the value-at-risk (VaR) methodology used by major banks or hedge funds to determine the likelihood that they will lose a certain amount of money over a certain period. The disadvantage is the maximum drawdown that occurs in the simulation may be so rare that it really won't happen more than once in a million years (a favorite excuse for fund managers when they come to grief). Furthermore, the simulated returns inevitably miss some crucial serial correlations that may be present in the historical returns and that may persist into the future. These correlations may be reducing the maximum drawdown in the real world. The advantage of using the historical strategy returns is that they fully capture these correlations, and furthermore the drawdown would cover a realistic life span of a strategy, not a million years. The disadvantage is, of course, that the data are far too limited for capturing a worst-case scenario. A good compromise may be a leverage somewhere in between those generated by the two methods.

■ Constant Proportion Portfolio Insurance

The often conflicting goals of wishing to maximize compounded growth rate while limiting the maximum drawdown have been discussed already. There is one method that allows us to fulfill both wishes: constant proportion portfolio insurance (CPPI).

Suppose the optimal Kelly leverage of our strategy is determined to be f. And suppose we are allowed a maximum drawdown of $-D$. We can simply set aside D of our initial total account equity for trading, and apply a leverage of f to this subaccount to determine our portfolio market value. The other $1 - D$ of the account will be sitting in cash. We can then be assured that we won't lose all of the equity of this subaccount, or, equivalently, we won't suffer a drawdown of more than $-D$ in our total account. If our trading strategy is profitable and the total account equity reaches a new high water mark, then we can reset our subaccount equity so that it is again D of the total equity, moving some cash back to the "cash" account. However, if the strategy suffers losses, we will not transfer any cash between the cash and the trading subaccount. Of course, if the losses continue and we lose all the equity in the trading subaccount, we have to abandon the strategy because it has reached our maximum allowed drawdown of $-D$. Therefore, in addition to limiting our drawdown, this scheme serves as a graceful, principled way to wind down a losing strategy. (The more common, less optimal, way to wind down a strategy is driven by the emotional breakdown of the portfolio manager.)

Notice that because of this separation of accounts, this scheme is *not* equivalent to just using a leverage of $L = fD$ in our total account equity. There is no guarantee that the maximum drawdown will not exceed $-D$ even with a lowered leverage of fD. Even if we were to further impose a stop loss of $-D$, or if the drawdown never went below $-D$, applying the leverage of fD to the full account still won't generate the exact same compounded return as CPPI, unless every period's returns are positive (i.e., maximum drawdown is zero). As long as we have a drawdown, CPPI will decrease order size much faster than the alternative, thus making it almost impossible (due to the use of Kelly leverage on the subaccount) that the account would approach the maximum drawdown $-D$.

I don't know if there is a mathematical proof that CPPI will be the same as using a leverage of fD in terms of the long-run growth rate, but we can use the same simulated returns in the previous sections to demonstrate that after 100,000 days, the growth rate of CPPI is very similar to the alternative scheme: 0.002484 versus 0.002525 per day in one simulation with $D = 0.5$. The main advantage of CPPI is apparent only when we look at the maximum drawdown. By design, the magnitude of the drawdown in CPPI is less than 0.5, while that of the alternative scheme without using stop loss is a painful 0.9 even with just half of the optimal leverage. The code for computing the growth rate using CPPI is shown in Box 8.6.

BOX 8.6

Computing Growth Rate Using CPPI

Assume the return series is *ret_sim* and the optimal leverage is *optimalF*, both from previous calculations. Also assume the maximum drawdown allowed is $-D = -0.5$.

```
g_cppi=0;
drawdown=0;
D=0.5;
for t=1:length(ret_sim)
    g_cppi=g_cppi+log(1+ ret_sim (t)*D*optimalF*(1+drawdown));
    drawdown=min(0, (1+drawdown)*(1+ ret_sim (t))-1);
end
g_cppi=g_cppi/length(ret_sim);
```

Note that this scheme should only be applied to an account with one strategy only. If it is a multistrategy account, it is quite possible that the profitable strategies are "subsidizing" the nonprofitable ones such that the drawdown is never large enough to shut down the complete slate of strategies. This is obviously not an ideal situation unless you think that the losing strategy will somehow return to health at some point.

There is one problem with using CPPI, a problem that it shares with the use of stop loss: It can't prevent a big drawdown from occurring during the overnight gap or whenever trading in a market has been suspended. The purchases of out-of-the-money options prior to an expected market close can eliminate some of this risk.

■ Stop Loss

There are two ways to use stop losses. The common usage is to use stop loss to exit an existing position whenever its unrealized P&L drops below a threshold. But after we exit this position, we are free to reenter into a new position, perhaps even one of the same sign, sometime later. In other words, we are not concerned about the cumulative P&L or the drawdown of the strategy.

The less common usage is to use stop loss to exit the strategy completely when our drawdown drops below a threshold. This usage of stop loss is awkward—it can happen only once during the lifetime of a strategy, and ideally we would never have to use it. That is the reason why CPPI is preferred over using stop loss for the same protection. The rest of this section is concerned with the first, more common usage of stop loss.

Stop loss can only prevent the unrealized P&L from exceeding our self-imposed limit if the market is always open whenever we are holding a position. For example, it is effective if we do not hold positions after the market closes or if we are trading in currencies or some futures where the electronic market is always open except for weekends and holidays. Otherwise, if the prices "gap" down or up when the market reopens, the stop loss may be executed at a price much worse than what our maximum allowable loss dictates. As we said earlier, the purchases of options will be necessary to eliminate this risk, but that may be expensive to implement and is valuable only for expected market downtime.

In some extreme circumstances, stop loss is useless even if the market is open but when all liquidity providers decide to withdraw their liquidity simultaneously. This happened during the flash crash of May 6, 2010, since modern-day market makers merely need to maintain a bid of $0.01 (the infamous "stub quote") in times of market stress (Arnuk and Saluzzi, 2012). This is why an unfortunate sell stop order on Accenture, a company with multibillion-dollar revenue, was executed at $0.01 per share that day.

But even if the market is open and there is normal liquidity, it is a matter of controversy whether we should impose stop loss for mean-reverting strategies. At first blush, stop loss seems to contradict the central assumption of mean reversion. For example, if prices drop and we enter into a long position, and prices drop some more and thus induce a loss, we should expect the prices to rise eventually if we believe in mean reversion of this price series. So it is not sensible to "stop loss" and exit this position when the price is so low. Indeed, I have never backtested any mean-reverting strategy whose APR or Sharpe ratio is increased by imposing a stop loss.

There is just one problem with this argument: What happens if the mean reversion model has permanently stopped working while we are in a position? In finance, unlike in physics, laws are not immutable. As I have been repeating, what was true of a price series before may not be true in the future. So a mean-reverting price series can undergo a regime change and become a trending price series for an extended period of time, maybe forever. In this case, a stop loss will be very effective in preventing catastrophic losses, and it will allow us time to consider the possibility that we should just shut down the strategy before incurring a 100 percent loss. Furthermore, these kinds of "turncoat" price series that regime-change from mean reversion to momentum would never show up in our catalog of profitable mean reversion strategies because our catalog would not have included mean-reverting strategies that failed in their backtests. Survivorship bias was in action when I claimed earlier that stop loss always lowers the performance of mean-reverting strategies. It is more accurate to say that stop loss always lowers the performance of mean-reverting strategies when the prices *remain mean reverting*, but it certainly improves the performance of those strategies when the prices suffer a regime change and start to trend!

Given this consideration of regime change and survivorship bias, how should we impose a stop loss on a mean-reverting strategy, since any successfully backtested mean-reverting strategy suffers survivorship bias and will always show lowered performance if we impose a stop loss? Clearly, we should impose a stop loss that is greater than the backtest maximum intraday drawdown. In this case, the stop loss would never have been triggered in the backtest period and could not have affected the backtest performance, yet it can still effectively prevent a black swan event in the future from leading to ruin.

In contrast to mean-reverting strategies, momentum strategies benefit from stop loss in a very logical and straightforward way. If a momentum strategy is losing, it means that momentum has reversed, so logically we should be exiting the position and maybe even reversing the position. Thus, a continuously updated momentum trading signal serves as a de facto stop loss. This is the reason momentum models do not present the same kind of tail risk that mean-reverting models do.

■ Risk Indicators

Many of the risk management measures we discussed above are reactive: We lower the order size when we incur a loss, or we stop trading altogether when a maximum drawdown has been reached. But it would be much more advantageous if we could proactively avoid those periods of time when the strategy is likely to incur loss. This is the role of leading risk indicators.

The obvious distinction between leading risk indicators and the more general notion of risk indicators is that leading risk indicators let us predict whether the next period will be risky for our investment, while general risk indicators are just contemporaneous with a risky period.

There is no one risk indicator that is applicable to all strategies: What is a risky period to one strategy may be a highly profitable period for another. For example, we might try using the VIX, the implied volatility index, as the leading risk indicator to predict the risk of the next-day return of the buy-on-gap stock strategy described in Chapter 4. That strategy had an annualized average return of around 8.7 percent and a Sharpe ratio of 1.5 from May 11, 2006, to April 24, 2012. But if the preceding day's VIX is over 35, a common threshold for highly risky periods, then the day's annualized average return will be 17.2 percent with a Sharpe ratio of 1.4. Clearly, this strategy benefits from the so-called risk! However, VIX > 35 is a very good leading risk indicator for the FSTX opening gap strategy depicted in Chapter 7. That strategy had an annualized average return of around 13 percent and a Sharpe ratio of 1.4 from July 16, 2004, to May 17, 2012. If the preceding day's VIX is over 35, then the day's annualized average return drops to 2.6 percent and the Sharpe ratio to 0.16. Clearly, VIX tells us to avoid trading on the following day.

Besides VIX, another commonly used leading risk indicator is the TED spread. It is the difference between the three-month London Interbank

Offered Rate (LIBOR) and the three-month T-bill interest rate, and it measures the risk of bank defaults. In the credit crisis of 2008, TED spread rose to a record 457 basis points. Since the credit market is dominated by large institutional players, presumably they are more informed than those indicators based on the stock market where the herd-like instinct of retail investors contributes to its valuation. (The TED spread is useful notwithstanding the fraudulent manipulation of LIBOR rates by the banks to make them appear lower, as discovered by Snider and Youle, 2010. What matters is the relative value of the TED spread over time, not its absolute value.)

There are other risky assets that at different times have served as risk indicators, though we would have to test them carefully to see if they are leading indicators. These assets include high yield bonds (as represented, for example, by the ETF HYG) and emerging market currencies such as the Mexican peso (MXN). During the European debt crisis of 2011, the MXN became particularly sensitive to bad news, even though the Mexican economy remained healthy throughout. Commentators attributed this sensitivity to the fact that traders are using the MXN as a proxy for all risky assets in general.

More recently, traders can also watch the ETF's ONN and OFF. ONN goes up when the market is in a "risk-on" mood; that is, when the prices of risky assets are bid up. ONN basically holds a basket of risky assets. OFF is just the mirror image of ONN. So a high value of OFF may be a good leading risk indicator. At the time of this writing, these ETFs have only about seven months of history, so there is not enough evidence to confirm that they have predictive value.

As we mentioned in the section on high-frequency trading in Chapter 7, at short time scales, those who have access to order flow information can detect a sudden and large change in order flow, which often indicates that important information has come into the possession of institutional traders. This large change in order flow is negative if the asset in question is risky, such as stocks, commodities, or risky currencies; it is positive if the asset is low risk, such as U.S. treasuries or USD, JPY, or CHF. As we learned before, order flow is a predictor of future price change (Lyons, 2001). Thus, order flow can be used as a short-term leading indicator of risk before that information becomes more widely dispersed in the market and causes the price to change more.

There are also risk indicators that are very specific to a strategy. We mentioned in Chapter 4 that oil price is a good leading risk indicator for the pair trading of GLD versus GDX. Other commodity prices such as that of gold may also be good leading risk indicators for pair trading of ETFs for countries or companies that produce them. Similarly, the Baltic Dry Index may be a good leading indicator for the ETFs or currencies of export-oriented countries.

I should conclude, though, with one problem with the backtesting of leading risk indicators. Since the occurrence of financial panic or crises is relatively rare, it is very easy to fall victim to data-snooping bias when we try to decide whether an indicator is useful. And, of course, no financial indicators can predict natural and other nonfinancial disasters. As the order flow indicator works at higher frequency, it may turn out to be the most useful of them all.

KEY POINTS

- Maximization of long-term growth rate:
  - Is your goal the maximization of your net worth over the long term? If so, consider using the half-Kelly optimal leverage.
  - Are your strategy returns fat-tailed? You may want to use Monte Carlo simulations to optimize the growth rate instead of relying on Kelly's formula.
  - Keeping data-snooping bias in mind, sometimes you can just directly optimize the leverage based on your backtest returns' compounded growth rate.
  - Do you want to ensure that your drawdown will not exceed a preset maximum, yet enjoy the highest possible growth rate? Use constant proportion portfolio insurance.
- Stop loss:
  - Stop loss will usually lower the backtest performance of mean-reverting strategies because of survivorship bias, but it can prevent black swan events.
  - Stop loss for mean-reverting strategies should be set so that they are never triggered in backtests.
  - Stop loss for momentum strategies forms a natural and logical part of such strategies.
- Risk indicators:
  - Do you want to avoid risky periods? You can consider one of these possible leading indicators of risk: VIX, TED spread, HYG, ONN/OFF, MXN.
  - Be careful of data-snooping bias when testing the efficacy of leading risk indicators.
  - Increasingly negative order flow of a risky asset can be a short-term leading risk indicator.

Even though this book contains an abundance of strategies that should be interesting and attractive to independent or even institutional traders, it has not been a recipe of strategies, or a step-by-step guide to implementing them. The strategies described in this book serve only to illustrate the general technique or concept, but they are not guaranteed to be without those very pitfalls that I detailed in Chapter 1. Even if I were to carefully scrub them of pitfalls, good strategies can still be victims of regime changes. Readers are invited and encouraged to perform out-of-sample testing on the strategies in this book to see for themselves.

187

Instead of recipes, what I hope to convey is the deeper reasons, the basic principles, why certain strategies should work and why others shouldn't. Once we grasp the basic inefficiencies of certain markets (e.g., regression to the mean, the presence of roll returns in futures, the need for end-of-day rebalancing in leveraged exchange-traded funds [ETFs]), it is actually quite easy to come up with a strategy to exploit them. This notion of understanding the inefficiency first and constructing a strategy later is why I emphasized simple and linear strategies. Why create all kinds of arbitrary rules when the inefficiency can be exploited by a simple model?

The other notion I wanted to convey is that the approach to algorithmic trading can be rather scientific. In science, we form a hypothesis, express it as a quantitative model, and then test it against new, unseen data to see if the model is predictive. If the model failed with certain data, we try to find out the reasons for the failures, perhaps add certain variables to the model, and try again. This is a very similar process to how we should approach algorithmic trading. Recall the ETF pair GLD versus GDX that stopped cointegrating in 2008 (see Chapter 4). A hypothesis was formed that had to do with the high crude oil price. When oil price was added to the input variables, the cointegration model started to work again. This scientific process is most helpful when a strategy underperforms the backtest, and we wanted to know why. Instead of blindly adding more rules, more indicators, to the model and hoping that they miraculously improve the model performance, we should look for a fundamental reason and then quantitatively test whether this fundamental reason is valid.

Despite the efforts to make the trading process scientific and rule based, there are still areas where subjective judgment is important. For example, when there is a major event looming, do you trust that your model will behave as your backtest predicted, or do you lower your leverage or even temporarily shut down the model in anticipation? Another example is offered by the application of the Kelly formula to a portfolio of strategies. Should we allocate capital among these strategies based on the equity of the whole portfolio, so that the good performance of some strategies is subsidizing the poor performance of others in the short term? Or should we apply the Kelly formula to each strategy on its own, so that we quickly deleverage those strategies that perform poorly recently? Mathematics tells us that the former solution is optimal, but that's assuming the expected returns and volatilities of the strategies are unchanging. Can one really say that such expectations are unchanged given a recent period of severe drawdown?

(On the first judgment call, my experience has been that if your model has survived the backtest during prior stressful periods, there is no reason to lower its leverage in the face of coming crisis. It is much better to start off with a more conservative leverage during good times than to have to lower it in bad ones. As Donald Rumsfeld once said, it is the "unknown unknowns" that will harm us, not the "known unknowns." Unfortunately, we can't shut down our models before the unknown unknowns strike. On the second judgment call, my experience has been that applying Kelly to each strategy independently so as to allow each one to wither and die quickly when it underperforms is more practical than applying Kelly asset allocation across all strategies.)

As these examples show, subjective judgment is often needed because the statistical properties of financial time series are not stationary, and science can really only deal with stationary statistics. (I am using *stationary* in a sense different from the stationarity of time series in Chapter 2. Here, it means the probability distribution of prices remains unchanged throughout time.) Often, when we find that our live trading experience diverges from the backtest, it is not because we committed any of the pitfalls during backtesting. It is because there has been a fundamental change in the market structure, a regime shift, due to government regulatory or macroeconomic changes. So the fund managers still have an active ongoing role even if the strategy is supposedly algorithmic and automated—their role is to make judicious high-level judgment calls based on their fundamental understanding of the markets on whether the models are still valid.

However, the fact that judgment is sometimes needed doesn't mean that developing quantitative rules is useless or algorithmic traders are less "smart" than discretionary traders. As the oft-quoted Daniel Kahneman wrote, experts are *uniformly inferior* to algorithms in every domain that has a significant degree of uncertainty or unpredictability, ranging from deciding winners of football games to predicting longevity of cancer patients. One can hope that the financial market is no exception to this rule.

BIBLIOGRAPHY

Arnuk, Sal L., and Joseph C. Saluzzi. *Broken Markets: How High Frequency Trading and Predatory Practices on Wall Street Are Destroying Investor Confidence and Your Portfolio.* Upper Saddle River, NJ: FT Press, 2012.

Beckert, Walter. Course notes on Financial Econometrics, Birkbeck University of London, 2011. Available at www.ems.bbk.ac.uk/for _students/bsc_FinEcon/fin_economEMEC007U/adf.pdf.

Bernard, Victor L., and Jacob K. Thomas. "Post-Earnings-Announcement Drift: Delayed Price Response or Risk Premium?" *Journal of Accounting Research* 27 (1989): 1–36.

Berntson, M. "Steps in Significance/Hypothesis Testing Using the Normal Distribution." Course notes for Introduction to Sociology, Grinnell College, 2002. Available at http://web.grinnell.edu/courses/sst/s02 /sst115-03/practice/hypothesisteststeps1.pdf.

Bollen, Johan, Huina Mao, and Xiao-Jun Zeng. "Twitter Mood Predicts the Stock Market," 2010. Available at http://arxiv.org/pdf/1010.3003.pdf.

Bryant, Martin. "Investment Fund Set to Use Twitter to Judge Emotion in the Market," *The Next Web*, December 16, 2010. Available at http:// thenextweb.com/uk/2010/12/16/investment-fund-set-to-use -twitter-to-judge-emotion-in-the-market/.

Buy the Hype, "The 'Twitter Hedge Fund' Has an Out-of-Sample Experience," *Buy the Hype* (blog), May 3, 2012. Available at http://sellthenews .tumblr.com/post/22334483882/derwents-performance.

Chan, Ernest. *Quantitative Trading: How to Build Your Own Algorithmic Trading Business.* Hoboken, NJ: John Wiley & Sons, 2009.

Cheng, Minder, and Ananth Madhavan. "The Dynamics of Leveraged and Inverse Exchange-Traded Funds." *Journal of Investment Management,* Winter 2009. Available at SSRN: http://ssrn.com/abstract=1393995.

Clare, Andrew, and Roger Courtenay. "What Can We Learn about Monetary Policy Transparency from Financial Market Data?" Economic Research Centre of the Deutsche Bundesbank, 2001. Available at www.olsen .ch/fileadmin/Publications/Client_Papers//200102-ClareCourtenay -WhatLearnMonetaryPolTransparencyFinMkts.pdf.

Coval, Joshua, and Erik Stafford. "Asset Fire Sales (and Purchases) in Equity Markets." *Journal of Financial Economics* 86 (2007): 479–512. Available at www.people.hbs.edu/estafford/Papers/AFS.pdf.

Daniel, Ken, and Tobias Moskowitz. "Momentum Crashes." Preprint, 2011. Available at www.columbia.edu/~kd2371/papers/unpublished /mom4.pdf.

Dever, Michael. *Jackass Investing.* Thornton, PA: Ignite LLC, 2011.

Dueker, Michael J., and Christopher J. Neely. "Can Markov Switching Models Predict Excess Foreign Exchange Returns?" Federal Reserve Bank of St. Louis Working Paper 2001-021F, 2001. Available at http://research .stlouisfed.org/wp/2001/2001-021.pdf.

Dupoyet, Brice, Robert T. Daigler, and Zhiyao Chen. "A Simplified Pricing Model for Volatility Futures." *Journal of Futures Markets* 31, no. 4 (2011): 307–339. Available at www2.fiu.edu/~dupoyetb/vix_futures.pdf.

Durbin, Michael. *All About High-Frequency Trading.* New York: McGraw-Hill, 2010.

Durden, Tyler. "Why the Market Is Slowly Dying," *Zero Hedge* (blog), April 14, 2012, www.zerohedge.com/news/why-market-slowly-dying.

Engle, R. F., and C. W. Granger. "Co-integration and Error-Correction: Representation, Estimation, and Testing." *Econometrica* 55 (1987): 251–276.

Erb, Claude B., and Campbell R. Harvey. "The Strategic and Tactical Value of Commodity Futures." *Financial Analysts Journal* 62, no. 20 (2006): 69. Available at http://ciber.fuqua.duke.edu/~charvey/Research /Published_Papers/P91_The_strategic_and.pdf.

Falkenberry, Thomas N. "High Frequency Data Filtering," 2002. Available at www.tickdata.com/pdf/Tick_Data_Filtering_White_Paper.pdf.

Fama, Eugene F., and Marshall E. Blume. "Filter Rules and Stock-Market Trading." *Journal of Business* 39, no. 1 (1966): 226–231. Available at www.e-m-h.org/FaBl66.pdf.

Friedman, Thomas. "A Good Question." *New York Times* Op-ed, February 25, 2012.

Gill, Jeff. "The Insignificance of Null Hypothesis Significance Testing." *Political Research Quarterly* 52, no. 3 (1999): 647–674. Available at www.artsci.wustl.edu/~jgill/papers/hypo.pdf.

Greenblatt, Joel. *The Little Book that Beats the Market.* Hoboken, NJ: John Wiley & Sons, 2006. Also see magicformulainvesting.com.

Hafez, Peter A. "Event Trading Using Market Response," July 22, 2011, www.ravenpack.com/research/marketresponsepaperform.htm.

Hafez, Peter A., and Junqiang Xie. "Short-Term Stock Selection Using News Based Indicators," May 15, 2012, www.ravenpack.com/research/shorttermstockselectionpaperform.htm.

Harris, Larry. *Trading and Exchanges.* New York: Oxford University Press, 2003.

Hellström, Jörgen, and Ola Simonsen. "Does the Open Limit Order Book Reveal Information About Short-run Stock Price Movements?" Umeå Economic Studies, 2006.

Hull, John C. *Options, Futures, and Other Derivatives,* 3rd ed. Upper Saddle River, NJ: Prentice-Hall, 1997.

Johnson, Barry. *Algorithmic Trading & DMA.* London: 4Myeloma Press, 2010.

Kahneman, Daniel. *Thinking, Fast and Slow.* New York: Farrar, Straus and Giroux. 2011.

Khandani, Amir, and Andrew Lo. "What Happened to the Quants in August 2007?" Preprint, 2007. Available at http://web.mit.edu/alo/www/Papers/august07.pdf.

Kleeman, Lindsay. "Understanding and Applying Kalman Filtering." Course notes on Robotic Motion Planning, Carnegie Mellon University, 2007. Available at www.cs.cmu.edu/~motionplanning/papers/sbp_papers/integrated3/kleeman_kalman_basics.pdf.

Kozola, Stuart. "Automated Trading with MATLAB-2012." Webinar, 2012. www.mathworks.com/matlabcentral/fileexchange/37932-automated-trading-with-matlab-2012.

Kuznetsov, Jev. "ActiveX vs Java API What's the Difference?" *Quantum blog,* November 25, 2010, http://matlab-trading.blogspot.ca/2010/11/activex-vs-java-api-whats-difference.html.

LeSage, James P. "Spatial Econometrics," 1998. Available at www.spatial-econometrics.com/html/wbook.pdf.

Lo, Andrew W., and A. Craig MacKinlay. *A Non-Random Walk Down Wall Street.* Princeton, NJ: Princeton University Press, 2001.

Lo, Andrew W., Harry Mamaysky, and Jiang Wang. "Foundations of Technical Analysis: Computational Algorithms, Statistical Inference, and Empirical Implementation." *Journal of Finance* 55, no. 4 (2000): 1705–1770. Available at http://ideas.repec.org/p/nbr/nberwo/7613.html.

Lyons, Richard. *The Microstructure Approach to Exchange Rates.* Cambridge, MA: MIT Press, 2001.

Malkiel, Burton. *A Random Walk Down Wall Street: The Time-Tested Strategy for Successful Investing.* New York: W. W. Norton, 2008.

Maslov, Sergei, and Mark Mills. "Price Fluctuations from the Order Book Perspective: Empirical Facts and a Simple Model." *Physica A* 299, no. 1–2 (2001): 234–246.

Montana, Giovanni, Kostas Triantafyllopoulos, and Theodoros Tsagaris. "Flexible Least Squares for Temporal Data Mining and Statistical Arbitrage." *Expert Systems with Applications* 36 (2009): 2819–2830. Available at www2.econ.iastate.edu/tesfatsi/FLSTemporalDataMining.GMontana2009.pdf.

Moskowitz, Tobias, Hua Ooi Yao, and Lasse Heje Pedersen. "Time Series Momentum." *Journal of Financial Economics* 104, no. 2 (2012): 228–250.

Osler, Carol. "Support for Resistance: Technical Analysis and Intraday Exchange Rates." *Federal Reserve Bank of New York Economic Policy Review* 6 (July 2000): 53–65.

Osler, Carol. "Currency Orders and Exchange-Rate Dynamics: An Explanation for the Predictive Success of Technical Analysis," 2001. Forthcoming, *Journal of Finance.* Available at http://newyorkfed.org/research/staff_reports/sr125.pdf.

Patterson, Scott. *The Quants.* New York: Crown Business, 2010.

Philips, Matthew. "Unlocking the Crude Oil Bottleneck at Cushing." *Bloomberg Business Week,* May 16, 2012. Available at www.businessweek.com/articles/2012-05-16/unlocking-the-crude-oil-bottleneck-at-cushing#p1.

Rajamani, Murali. "Data-Based Techniques to Improve State Estimation in Model Predictive Control." PhD thesis, University of Wisconsin-Madison, 2007.

Rajamani, Murali R., and James B. Rawlings. "Estimation of the Disturbance Structure from Data Using Semidefinite Programming and Optimal Weighting. *Automatica* 45 (2009): 142–148.

Reverre, Stephane. *The Complete Arbitrage Deskbook.* New York: McGraw-Hill, 2001.

Rodier, Arthur, Edgar Haryanto, Pauline M. Shum, and Walid Hejazi. "Intraday Share Price Volatility and Leveraged ETF Rebalancing." October 2012. Available at SSRN: http://ssrn.com/abstract=2161057.

Schoenberg, Ron, and Alan Corwin. "Does Averaging-in Work?" 2010. www.optionbots.com/DOE/does_averaging_in_work.pdf. Accessed January 10, 2010.

Serge, Andrew. "Where Have All the Stat Arb Profits Gone?" Columbia University Financial Engineering Practitioners Seminars, January 2008.

Shankar, S. Gowri, and James M. Miller. "Market Reaction to Changes in the S&P SmallCap 600 Index." *Financial Review* 41, no. 3 (2006): 339–360. Available at SSRN: http://papers.ssrn.com/sol3/papers.cfm?abstract_id=886141.

Simon, David P., and Jim Campasano. "The VIX Futures Basis: Evidence and Trading Strategies," 2012. Available at SSRN: http://papers.ssrn.com/sol3/papers.cfm?abstract_id=2094510.

Sinclair, Euan. *Option Trading: Pricing and Volatility Strategies and Techniques.* Hoboken, NJ: John Wiley & Sons, 2010.

Snider, Connan Andrew, and Thomas Youle. "Does the LIBOR Reflect Banks' Borrowing Costs?" 2010. Available at SSRN: http://papers.ssrn.com/sol3/papers.cfm?abstract_id=1569603.

Sorensen, Bent E. Course notes on Economics. University of Houston, 2005. Available at www.uh.edu/~bsorense/coint.pdf.

"The Wacky World of Gold." *The Economist,* June 2011.

Thorp, Edward. "The Kelly Criterion in Blackjack, Sports Betting, and the Stock Market," 1997. Available at www.EdwardOThorp.com.

ABOUT THE AUTHOR

Ernest Chan is the managing member of QTS Capital Management, LLC, a commodity pool operator. Ernie has worked for various investment banks (Morgan Stanley, Credit Suisse, Maple) and hedge funds (Mapleridge, Millennium Partners, MANE) since 1997. He received his PhD in physics from Cornell University and was a member of IBM's Human Language Technologies group before joining the financial industry. He was a cofounder and principal of EXP Capital Management, LLC, a Chicago-based investment firm. He is also the author of *Quantitative Trading: How to Build Your Own Algorithmic Trading Business,* published by John Wiley & Sons in 2009, and a popular financial blogger at http://epchan.blogspot.com. Find out more about Ernie at www.epchan.com.

ABOUT THE WEBSITE

All of the examples in this book are built around MATLAB codes, and they are all available for download from www.wiley.com/go /algotrading (password: chan2E). Once redirected to the website with the codes, you will be asked for another username and password—use "kelly" for both. Readers unfamiliar with MATLAB may want to study the tutorial in *Quantitative Trading*, or watch the free webinars on www.mathworks.com. Furthermore, the MATLAB Statistics Toolbox was occasionally used. (All MATLAB products are available as free trials from MathWorks.)

For more from the author on the topic of algorithmic trading and more, go to www.epchan.com or http://epchan.blogspot.com.

INDEX

201

Moving average for mean-reverting strategies, 48–49, 66
Multithreading and high-frequency trading of multiple symbols, 35
Mutual funds
  asset fire sale, 149–151
  composition changes in, 162–163

National best bid and offer (NBBO) quote sizes for stocks, 90, 166–167
Neural net trading model, 23
News-driven momentum strategies
  drift due to other events, 162–163
  overview, 157–158
  post-earnings announcement drift, 158–162
News-driven trading and special-purpose platforms, 35–36
News sentiment as fundamental factor, 148–149
Newsware, 148, 162
Nonlinear trading models, approximating, 5
Normal commodities, 117
Null hypothesis, 16

Opening gap strategy, 156–157
Optimal leverage
  Kelly formula, 172–173
  maximum drawdown, 179–180
  optimization of expected growth rate using simulated returns, 173–177
  optimization of historical growth rate, 177–178
  overview, 170–171
Order flow, ignition of price momentum due to, 149
Order flow information, access to, 167–168, 185
Ornstein-Uhlenbeck formula, 6, 46
Out-of-sample cointegrating stock pairs, 89
Out-of-sample data and data-snooping bias, 4–5, 7
Out-of-sample testing, 187
Overnight, holding position, 113
Overnight gap, 157

Pairs trading strategies
  cointegration and, 51
  currencies, 66, 108
  currencies with rollover interests, 114–115
  ETFs, 91–92

intraday, 90
  price spreads, log price spreads, and ratios for, 64–70
  stocks, 89–91, 102
Pearson system, 176
P/E (price-earnings) ratio, ranking stocks using, 104–105
Pitfalls
  of mean-reversion strategies, 60–61, 83–84, 153
  of momentum strategies, 151–154
  of strategies in general, 1, 187
Pitfalls of backtesting
  data-snooping bias, 4–7, 60, 186
  futures close compared to settlement prices, 14–16, 100
  futures continuous contracts, 12–14
  look-ahead bias, 4
  primary compared to consolidated stock prices, 9–10
  short-sale constraints, 11–12, 89–90, 102
  stock splits and dividend adjustments, 7–8
  survivorship bias, 8–9, 88
  venue dependence of currency quotes, 10–11
Post-earnings announcements, price momentum generated by, 153, 158–162
Predictive power of backtesting, 24–25
"Prefabricated" financial price series, 39–40, 50
Price-earnings (P/E) ratio, ranking stocks using, 104–105
Price spreads, trading pairs using, 64–70
Primary exchanges
  finding historical prices from, 9–10
  orders filled at, 88
Principal Component Analysis, 147–148
Profits from pair trading of stocks, 90–91, 102
Programming skill and choice of software platform, 25–29
Progress Apama, 26, 28, 29, 35
P-value, 16–17
Python scripting language, 28, 29, 35

QuantHouse, 28, 29
Quantitative Trading (Chan), 147, 172, 173
Quote currency, 108
Quote matching strategy, 165–166
Quotes aggregators, 11

INDEX